AQUILEIA

ARCHAEOLOGICAL HISTORIES

Series editors: Thomas Harrison, Duncan Garrow and Michele George

An important series charting the history of sites, buildings and towns from their construction to the present day. Each title examines not only the physical history and uses of the site but also its broader context: its role in political history, in the history of scholarship, and in the popular imagination.

AQUILEIA

A FRONTIER COLONY BETWEEN THE MEDITERRANEAN AND EUROPE

Jacopo Bonetto and Andrea Raffaele Ghiotto

BLOOMSBURY ACADEMIC

LONDON • NEW YORK • OXFORD • NEW DELHI • SYDNEY

BLOOMSBURY ACADEMIC
Bloomsbury Publishing Plc, 50 Bedford Square, London, WC1B 3DP, UK
Bloomsbury Publishing Inc, 1359 Broadway, New York, NY 10018, USA
Bloomsbury Publishing Ireland, 29 Earlsfort Terrace, Dublin 2, D02 AY28, Ireland

BLOOMSBURY, BLOOMSBURY ACADEMIC and the Diana logo are trademarks of
Bloomsbury Publishing Plc

First published in Great Britain 2026

Cover image: Aquileia archaeological area, Roman Forum. Guido/Adobe Stock

A catalogue record for this book is available from the British Library.

A catalog record for this book is available from the Library of Congress.

ISBN: HB: 978-1-3504-4092-0
        PB: 978-1-3504-4093-7
        ePDF: 978-1-3504-4094-4
        eBook: 978-1-3504-4095-1

Series: Archaeological Histories

Typeset by RefineCatch Limited, Bungay, Suffolk
Printed and bound in Great Britain

For product safety related questions contact productsafety@bloomsbury.com.

To find out more about our authors and books visit www.bloomsbury.com
and sign up for our newsletters.

CONTENTS

ILLUSTRATIONS

ABBREVIATIONS

AE	L'Année Épigraphique (1886–), Paris.
CIL	Corpus inscriptionum Latinarum (1863–), Berlin.
IG	Inscriptiones Graecae (1860–), Berlin.
ILS	Dessau, H. (1892–1916), Inscriptiones Latinae selectae, Berlin.
Inscr. Aq.	Brusin, G. B. (1991–3), Inscriptiones Aquileiae, Udine.

ACKNOWLEDGEMENTS

It is significant for us to remember that the research work we present here is the fruit of many years of work conducted in Aquileia, which has benefited from the collaboration of several people and prestigious institutions. For this, we want to extend our thanks to the representatives of the Ministry of Culture in Aquileia, such as Marta Novello, Serena Di Tonto and Paola Ventura, but also to those who promote the great Basilica of Aquileia, like Andrea Bellavite, or those engaged in the management of the Fondazione Aquileia, such as Roberto Corciulo and Cristiano Tiussi as well as Anna Del Bianco.

We extend equal gratitude to our colleagues from the Department of Cultural Heritage at the University of Padua (Guido Furlan, Caterina Previato, Simone Dilaria, Andrea Stella, Monica Salvadori and Francesca Ghedini), who work with us in Aquileia, and from the departments of other Italian universities active in the Upper Adriatic town (Marina Rubinich, Matteo Cadario, Antonio Dell'Acqua, Emanuela Murgia, Daniela Cottica, Andrea Cipolato, Patrizia Basso and Diana Dobreva), as well as to the many historians and archaeologists who work there with passion and assiduity (Monika Verzár, Gino Bandelli, Monica Chiabà, Claudio Zaccaria, Fulvia Mainardis, Ludovico Rebaudo, Maurizio Buora, Stefano Magnani, Stefan Groh, Luca Villa, Annalisa Giovannini, Luciana Mandruzzato, Dario Gaddi, Valentina Degrassi, Anna Riccato, Simone Berto, Alessandro Mortera and others). Among the monuments of Aquileia we have also met some who are no longer with us, such as Federica Fontana and Giuseppe Cuscito: our thoughts go out to them.

Thanks, then, to the Soprintendenza Archeologia, Belle Arti e Paesaggio del Friuli Venezia Giulia, which coordinates the always complex operations of protection indispensable to the safeguarding of Aquileia and its monumental testimonies. Similar gratitude is extended to the Fondazione Aquileia, which for more than fifteen years has been working in the field of enhancing the small Friulian town and supporting research activities. The collaboration with these institutions and with the National Archaeological Museum has contributed, and continues to contribute, to generating works like this one.

As far as the realization of the volume is concerned, it seems appropriate to express particular thanks to Jeremy Hayne for the accuracy of his translation from Italian to English. The help of Erica Zanon, Elena Braidotti, Annarita Lepre and Enrico Degrassi has also been precious in providing the images from the Fondazione Aquileia, the National Archaeological Museum of Aquileia and the Ikon Digital Farm respectively. Finally, we would like to thank the staff at Bloomsbury Academic Publishers for their prompt assistance, particularly Lily Mac Mahon.

Jacopo Bonetto and Andrea Raffaele Ghiotto

Padova, April 2025

INTRODUCTION

At the time of Emperor Theodosius, towards the end of the fourth century, the poet Ausonius wrote his work *Ordo urbium nobilium*, offering detailed accounts of what he considered the twenty most important cities of the Roman Empire. Among these, Aquileia occupied the ninth place and was celebrated for its walls and its port.

It was precisely in the decades that had preceded this description that the city located on the northernmost shores of the Adriatic Sea, and of the wider Mediterranean basin, had reached the apex of its political, monumental and commercial greatness, extending over an area of more than 80 hectares. At that time, Aquileia appeared as the most important urban centre in northern Italy together with Milan.

However, the importance of this city had ancient roots, because Aquileia was born many centuries earlier (in 181 BCE) as the main outpost of Rome at a time when it aimed to expand its power beyond the Alps towards the Danubian regions. The foundation of the Upper Adriatic city is narrated with emphasis by the historian Livy. It saw the settlement of colonists who transformed a small indigenous nucleus of Venetic culture into a large agrarian colony, with an early and distinct commercial and strategic vocation.

During the first century BCE, Aquileia became the reference point for the military campaigns conducted by Caesar, Augustus and Tiberius in Gaul or in the Danubian and Illyrian regions. Its particular geographic position, between Italy and the transalpine area, strengthened its identity and wealth and transformed Aquileia into a port and commercial hub of the first order, capable of relating with the Mediterranean East as well as with the caravan routes leading to the Baltic Sea, from which Aquileia drew the magical amber.

It was precisely this strategic location that also made Aquileia a crucial reference point in those centuries, when the areas outside Italy became the origin of military threats and devastating enemy raids. From the second century onwards, Aquileia thus assumed the role of a military bulwark to counter the increasingly threatening invasions that came mainly from the Danubian provinces. For three centuries, the city was the 'gateway to Italy', regulating threatening flows and deciding the fate of the empire, often the object of threats from usurping generals and peoples eager to move their settlements towards Italy.

At the height of this parabola, Aquileia was finally the scene of one of the best-known historical events of the entire period that plunged the West into crisis: the invasion of Attila, king of the Huns, who, according to an account mixing truth and legend, besieged and managed to capture the city in 452. In the imagination of many ancient men and some modern historians, this date symbolically represented the end of the ancient history of the Upper Adriatic city.

Severely tested and certainly transformed in its internal structure, the settlement nevertheless continued to live during the Middle Ages and the modern age, assuming as a patriarchal centre a renewed religious power, and for a certain period also political power, with jurisdiction over a vast geographical area extending between north-eastern Italy and the neighbouring regions.

The never-forgotten memory of ancient greatness led, from the eighteenth century onwards, to a rethinking of the glories and material testimonies of the past, which over time became an object of interest for antiquarians, epigraphists and Italian and European historians and archaeologists. Research intensified during the Austro-Hungarian government, with the consequent opening of the great Archaeological Museum of Aquileia in 1882. In the decades spanning the nineteenth and twentieth centuries, and then further following the annexation of these territories by Italy (1915), Aquileia experienced an extraordinary fervour in archaeological research, which has made it possible to reconstruct the history of the city through the study of the testimonies of its past.

Today, thanks also to the acquisition of vast state-owned areas, the ancient city and the modern town have become an extremely important centre of cultural tourist attraction, which has progressively grown since the 1990s until the recent project for the creation of a large Archaeological Park by the Fondazione Aquileia, where thousands of tourists visit the archaeological areas, museums, basilicas and cultural spaces within a framework of highly charming natural beauties.

However, Aquileia is not just a *memory of the past*, but also a place of continuous *research into the past* thanks to the work of numerous university research institutions that for many decades have made the ancient city the heart of their activities. In fact, Italian and foreign universities, with teams of professors, researchers and students, have been working for some decades to rediscover the ancient buildings, producing a continuous renewal of knowledge that is then disseminated to those who visit the Archaeological Park.

It is precisely this commitment by researchers that has given rise to this volume, commissioned by Bloomsbury, to narrate to the general public the birth, life and transformation of one of the greatest cities of ancient Italy based on the results of the archaeological investigations (Figure 0.1).

The narration starts from an environmental framework and proceeds with the long history of the city, marked by an architectural and monumental evolution that transformed the village of huts of the Iron Age into a metropolis of stone and marble. However, the troubled times experienced by the city between the end of antiquity and the beginning of the Middle Ages, as well as the events in Aquileia during the long patriarchal phase, are not overlooked. Finally, the volume also aims to present the history of the rediscovery of the antiquities of Aquileia and to describe the current layout of the Archaeological Park, with its numerous accessible areas and its prestigious museums, recently renovated.

With the information presented in this study, every lover of ancient history or curious visitor will be able to immerse themselves in the fascinating past of Aquileia and to

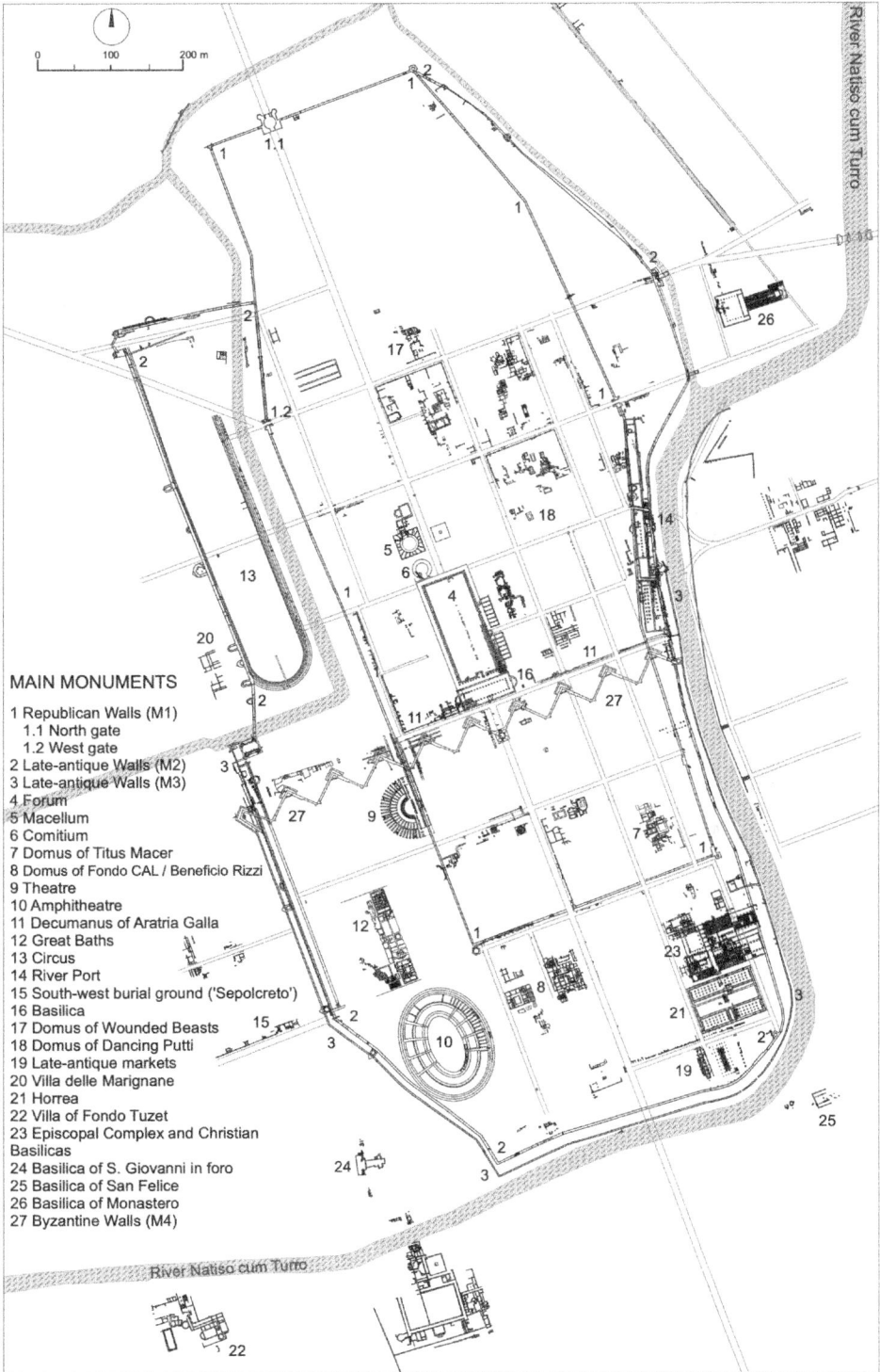

MAIN MONUMENTS

1 Republican Walls (M1)
  1.1 North gate
  1.2 West gate
2 Late-antique Walls (M2)
3 Late-antique Walls (M3)
4 Forum
5 Macellum
6 Comitium
7 Domus of Titus Macer
8 Domus of Fondo CAL / Beneficio Rizzi
9 Theatre
10 Amphitheatre
11 Decumanus of Aratria Galla
12 Great Baths
13 Circus
14 River Port
15 South-west burial ground ('Sepolcreto')
16 Basilica
17 Domus of Wounded Beasts
18 Domus of Dancing Putti
19 Late-antique markets
20 Villa delle Marignane
21 Horrea
22 Villa of Fondo Tuzet
23 Episcopal Complex and Christian Basilicas
24 Basilica of S. Giovanni in foro
25 Basilica of San Felice
26 Basilica of Monastero
27 Byzantine Walls (M4)

Figure 0.1 Aquileia. Plan of the M1, M2, M3, M4 fortification walls and the city (J. Bonetto).

understand its genesis and development, but also to plan a visit to appreciate its monuments, the wonderful works of art kept in the museum halls, or the Christian basilica with its extraordinary mosaics. Such a complex and important history has necessarily been summarized but, for readers wishing to explore specific aspects in more depth, there is a rich bibliographic collection at the end of the text. Of course, this bibliography cannot be exhaustive. However, it lists the most significant or recent publications on the various historical and archaeological topics, with useful references to other works.

The following pages are the result of shared work between the two authors. Specifically, Jacopo Bonetto is responsible for chapters 1, 2, 3, 4 and Appendix; Andrea Raffaele Ghiotto for chapters 5, 6, 7, 8 and 9. The translation from Italian into English was carried out by Jeremy Hayne.

CHAPTER 1
THE LANDSCAPE OF AQUILEIA: BETWEEN THE ADRIATIC SEA, THE LAGOON AND THE ALPS

Scholars have always highlighted the fundamental importance of the environment for understanding the history of Aquileia, from its birth to its decline.[1] This is why, in recent decades, particular attention has been paid to recreating the environment and ancient landscape, in order to offer more reliable reconstructions of the settlement's various fortunes, which were strongly conditioned by the city's geography.

The environment has been studied using an interdisciplinary methodological approach with various scholars making important and complementary contributions through archaeology (e.g. excavations, ground surveys and archival work) and geology (core drilling and sedimentological analyses).[2]

In the 1990s studies looked at both the ancient hydrographic network (project SARA),[3] in part different from the present one, and the wider geomorphologic, sedimentary and paleoclimatic context. More recently, advances in methodology have allowed us to deepen the investigations and understand new details about the natural context of specific areas of the city (Fondi Cossar, area of the Great Baths, Amphora Canal).[4]

Thanks to this research on different areas of the city and the opening up to a much broader regional prospect, it is now possible to draw a general and detailed picture of the landscape where Aquileia existed for 1,500 years.

The city is in the eastern Friulan lowlands, close to the innermost part of the Adriatic Sea (Figure 1.1). The plain is bounded to the east by the Karst mountains, whilst to the north the Alps and the pre-Alpine uplands form its natural boundaries.[5]

Geological studies have shown that the whole Friuli Venezia Giulia region and the narrower area of the plain where Aquileia was built have extensive still-active faults. These huge fractures in the deep subsoils cause small soil movements and may have led to various (even important) changes in the past, such as shifts in river courses. Estimates suggest that the land has risen by 0.1 millimetre per year.

The plain where the city is located was formed after the last great Ice Age, which ended around 19,000 years ago.[6] During this time, large amounts of sediment were deposited due to the maximum expansion of the ice fronts that occurred around 26,000 years ago. The sediments from the Alpine area varied in type, with coarse materials like gravel and sand in the uplands, and finer materials like silts and clays in the mid and lower plains. The transition between the highlands and low plains is marked by the line of resurgencies, where groundwater reaches the surface and creates rivers that flow to the sea. The lower plains, where Aquileia is located, are characterized by fine, gently sloping

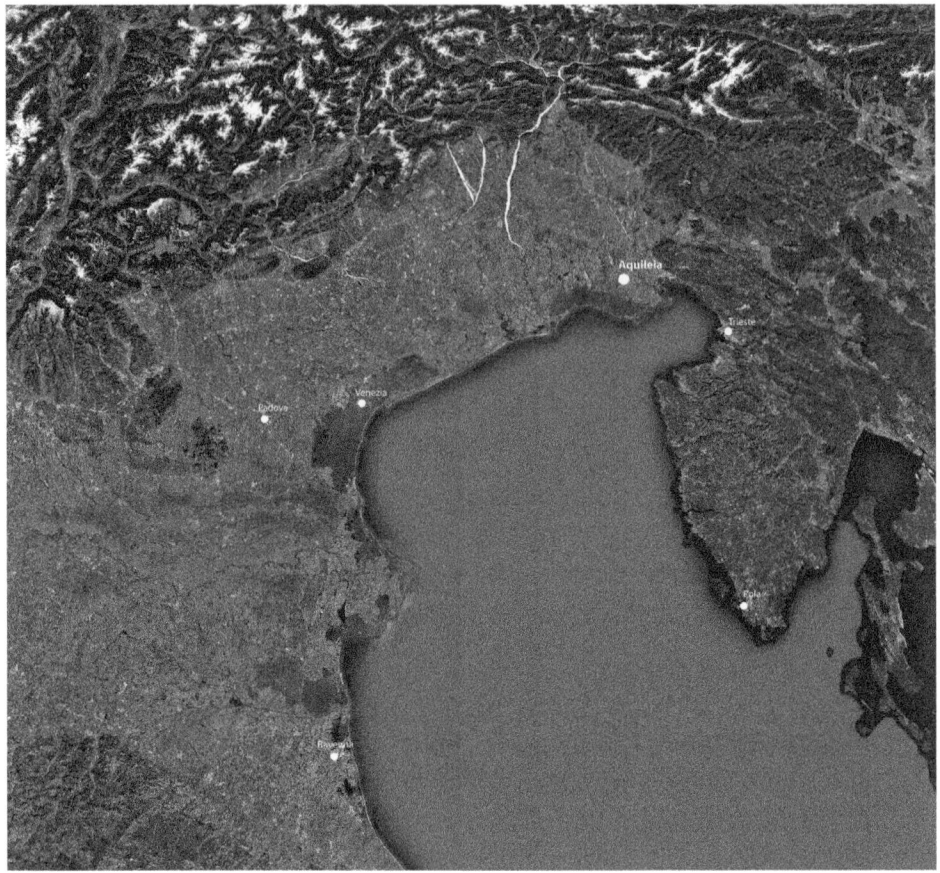

Figure 1.1 Satellite image of the Northern Adriatic Sea region and the Eastern Alps with the location of the Aquileia site.

soils crossed by single watercourses. These watercourses typically meander, creating ever-changing routes and deviations along the alluvial plain.[7]

Over time, the Torre, Natisone and Isonzo rivers changed their courses and together created the sedimentary deposits on which the first settlement of Aquileia was built.[8] In more recent times, during the Mid-Holocene (8,000–3,500 years ago), there was a rise in sea level and the formation of the Grado and Marano lagoons, which are currently dated to around 4,000 BCE. However, some scholars believe that the Grado lagoon, closest to Aquileia, was only formed in the post-ancient period, around 1,500 years ago, at the start of the medieval period.

Aquileia was therefore located at some distance from the Adriatic, separated from it by these lagoon areas.[9] They were of crucial importance both for food sources and the safe navigation they guaranteed.

The environmental setting outlined above took shape over several thousand years and resulted in extremely favourable conditions for the creation of human settlements in the area where Aquileia was later built. The environmental conditions were, in fact, the basis for making Aquileia one of the greatest metropolises of antiquity.

The significant post-glacial transformations created ideal conditions for the establishment of the city. Historically, Aquileia was built on a river hummock formed over millennia by the flooding of the Torre/Natisone river, with possible contributions from a paleo-Isonzo.[10] This ridge was slightly elevated compared to the surrounding plain. Recent soundings in the Fondi Cossar area, just north of the Christian basilica, have confirmed its presence. These soundings found sands and silts transported by the rivers at a depth of 3.4 to 3.5 metres from the ground level. These sediments cover a thick silty clay layer down to a depth of 5.7 metres, consistent with the formation of a river ridge in the alluvial plain. The soundings also located the current surface water table between 1.8 and 3.5 metres below ground level.

The elevated position of this wide ridge provided the area and the settlement that developed on it with good protection against flooding, swamping and stagnant water that threatened the lower plains (Figure 1.2). This is why the oldest and most central parts of the city were built on this hummock, which extended from north to south for many hundreds of metres (Figure 0.1). To the west of the ridge was an area known as the Marignane, which marked the city's boundary. This area was much lower and prone to swamping. The name 'Marignane' comes from the root 'Mar-', which in many Indo-European languages indicates a marshy place.

Figure 1.2 Geomorphological elevation map of the area where the city is located (F. Polisca).

The ridge where the settlement developed was bounded to the east by the river that created it, still active today and known since the Middle Ages as the Natissa.[11] Sources from the Roman period[12] expressly mention this river at the *Natiso cum Turro* and state that this watercourse was formed by the contribution of the two rivers still known today as the Natisone and Torre, which originate in the Alpine and pre-Alpine area and flow to the lower plains. According to the most recent studies the Isonzo may also have contributed to the formation of the river that lapped the settlement and the adjacent ridge.[13]

It is clear that from at least the proto-historic age the contributions from the three rivers created a large river channel, much bigger than the present-day Natissa. The ancient riverbed was likely over 40 metres wide. This is significant as it shows that the river along which Aquileia stood was navigable, at least from the city to the sea.

The convergence of several rivers on the town is evidenced by the discovery of two Roman bridges north of the town, at Monastero. However, the ancient hydrographic network must have been even more complex. Paleo-hydrographic and archaeological studies[14] reveal that the entire city was surrounded by a network of natural and artificial canals. These canals were essential for moving goods between different areas of the ancient city[15] and for managing the hydraulic control of the low plains, which had high rainfall and a fragile environmental balance. The southern and western suburban areas, located at the edge of the raised ridge, were particularly prone to swamping, flooding and marine ingress. The watercourses, both natural and specially dug, in these areas helped drain and dispose of excess water, ensuring the land and buildings remained in good condition.

The complex hydrographic network that covered the city was reinforced by a hydraulic infrastructure that was unique in importance and size. To the west of the city, a canal called the 'Amphora Canal' still exists today, leading from the ancient city towards the Grado lagoon (Figure 1.3).[16] This waterway will be described in the chapter on the territory but should be briefly mentioned here because of its importance in shaping the landscape around the town. Its perfectly straight course between the western limits of the city and the present-day Marano lagoon suggests that it was artificial, but it may also have been a Roman adjustment of a natural channel to deal with the problems of water stagnation in the western area of the city. Besides being used for commercial navigation, it also importantly collected water with the aim of preventing surface water stagnation.

A passage from the Roman architect Vitruvius' treatise *De architectura*, from the end of the first century BCE, speaks at length about cities built near the coast and in swampy areas and deals with the problems concerning the healthiness of such places and surface water:

Therefore, when a city is built in a marshy situation near the sea-coast, with a northern, north-eastern, or eastern aspect, on a marsh whose level is higher than the shore of the sea, the site is not altogether improper; for by means of sewers the waters may be discharged into the sea: and at those times, when violently agitated by storms, the sea swells and runs up the sewers, it mixes with the water of the

Figure 1.3 Aquileia. Satellite image of the city and its surroundings. At the left the Amphora Canal is visible with its straight course.

marsh, and prevents the generation of marshy insects; it also soon destroys such as are passing from the higher level, by the saltness of its water to which they are unaccustomed. An instance of this kind occurs in the Gallic marshes about *Altinum*, Ravenna, and Aquileia, and other places in Cisalpine Gaul, near marshes which, for the reasons above named, are remarkably healthy.[17]

It is clear from the Vitruvian passage that one of the purposes of this canal was to guarantee the *incredibilem salubritatem* to the built-up area, evidently combating the spread of diseases linked to stagnant water in the brackish areas between the lagoons and the city itself. In this sense, although projected out into the surrounding landscape, the Amphora Canal proves to be an infrastructural work serving, above all, the city.

To understand the significance of Aquileia in ancient times, we need to look beyond its immediate surroundings and consider the broader regional landscape. Aquileia is situated just a few miles from the Adriatic coast, where the Mediterranean Sea extends deep into the European continent (Figure 1.1). In ancient times, waterways were the primary means of transportation and communication. This made the northern Adriatic and Aquileia a crucial passageway between the rich Mediterranean world and the equally prosperous European continent. Aquileia's location on this transit route made it a key geographical hub, connecting the Mediterranean with Europe.

As mentioned, between the sea and Aquileia stretched coastal lagoons and watery spaces which allowed easy navigation. Indeed, the lagoons closest to Aquileia (Marano and Grado) were only the easternmost in a series of very similar lagoons that characterized the whole Adriatic coastline as far as Venice.[18] These vast 'inland sea' areas were connected by canals and waterways extending as far as Ravenna.[19] This allowed transport between Ravenna and Aquileia by water. Aquileia, being at the northernmost point, was easily accessible by water without having to venture into the open sea. This ensured the smooth transport of goods and people from Ravenna and even central Italy.

Access to the city from the lagoons and sea was via the river formed by the Natisone, Torre and Isonzo, along which the city had grown. Over time this led to the large river port being created at the point of where the river and city met, close to the urban area.

Yet, Aquileia and its port were not only a reference point for the maritime and Mediterranean areas. In fact, the same waterways that fed its river port were also the natural transit route for goods and people from the plains, Prealps, Alps and transalpine areas.[20] Aquileia is situated only a few kilometres from the edge of the Alpine ranges that were crossed by a series of valleys and passes used for easy communication with present-day Austria, Germany and Slovenia.

Aquileia's position, close to the northern shores of the Adriatic Sea and the southern base of the Alps, made it an exceptionally important centre for ancient trade and a key point of contact for the acquisition and distribution of goods coming from both the Mediterranean and Europe. This geographical position and its role were key to the exceptional importance that Aquileia had in antiquity.[21]

An important piece of evidence about the relationships between Aquileia and the various regions comes from a famous passage by the geographer Strabo. Strabo, a Greek by origin and culture but well-versed in the Roman world, describes the trade between Aquileia, the sea and the transalpine regions. He explains how the Illyrians reached Aquileia bringing and taking away all types of merchandise: 'Aquileia has been given over as an emporium for those tribes of the Illyrians that live near the Ister; the latter load on wagons and carry inland the products of the sea, and wine stored in wooden jars, and also olive-oil, whereas the former get in exchange slaves, cattle, and hides.'[22]

The advantages of the environment thus favoured Aquileia as a commercial hub. But we should not forget the other advantages that the city derived from its position on this large, fertile, alluvial and irrigated plain. Aquileia is located on the far eastern edge of the Po Valley, the biggest plain in Europe. It was already celebrated by Polybius; in the second book of the *Histories* the author states that it was difficult to describe the extraordinary fertility of the soils of this region, as demonstrated both by the cultivated crops and the wild produce.[23] The same author also extols the fertility of the Po Valley when recounting Hannibal's march into Italy.[24]

The Po Valley itself is also the object of numerous mentions by Roman authors such as Cato,[25] who extols the outstanding yield of the vineyards, Strabo,[26] Livy,[27] Vergil,[28] Pliny the Elder[29] and Pliny the Younger,[30] who mentions the *summa abundantia* of the north Italian plains. Tacitus too, in the first century CE, described the region between the Alps and the Po as the 'most flourishing region of Italy',[31] while Cicero referred to the north Italian plains as the 'flower of Italy'.[32]

Indeed, a rich collection of historical, archaeological and topographical studies has highlighted the potential and importance of these lowland settlements, including Aquileia. The primary and most significant activity was agriculture. This is demonstrated by the substantial evidence of agrarian divisions, which will be discussed in the chapter on the territory.

But the great plains that surrounded Aquileia also provided the ideal basis for a second activity that we know was practised at Aquileia: cattle breeding. Most important was the breeding of small animals, such as sheep, who could benefit from the presence of evergreen pastures both on the plains and in the pre-Alpine areas. Sheep breeding was the basis for the extraordinary wool production that the entire central and eastern Po Valley was famous for.

The most recent studies have also helped reconstruct the types of vegetation that characterized the plains around the town between the protohistoric and Roman periods.[33] Pollen analyses show that there was certainly good forest cover around the town, which remained unchanged between the protohistoric and Roman periods. Oaks and hornbeams as well as ash, elm and alder formed these wooded spaces, indicating the probable presence of moist soils. Spaces within the woods saw the growth of hazelnut, dogwood and cornelian cherry. These studies allow us to envisage the landscape and environment that preceded the formation of Aquileia, which became a stable human settlement from the ninth century BCE and survived until the Middle Ages.

One of the most interesting aspects of modern research is the possibility of studying the plant remains recovered during archaeological investigations and understand how people brought about important changes in the natural environment where they lived. The landscape of Aquileia was no exception in this respect, and the natural environment surrounding the city gradually changed due to the presence of humans.

Various methods, such as pollen analysis, carpological analysis (on fruit remains) and anthracological analysis (on the remains of carbonized plants), are used to understand how humans have historically changed the environment. These studies can identify the different species of grasses, shrubs and plants that grew around the city during various periods, helping us understand the human activities that significantly impacted the vegetation landscape. For the pre-Roman period, we have data from the excavation of the pre-Roman village (ninth–third centuries BCE), which will be discussed in the following chapter.[34]

These studies have demonstrated that even before the foundation of the colony, Aquileia's surrounding countryside had already been partially cultivated with the sowing of cereals such as barley and emmer, soft wheat, durum wheat and other varieties which are nowadays very uncommon, such as spelt. At the same time, much of the surrounding countryside was left in its natural state, covered by large forests and uncultivated areas where community activities (hunting, fishing, gathering wood) or free animal grazing could be practised. In contrast, it is likely that horticultural crops or fruit trees were cultivated near or within the settlement, as shown by the remains of fruits such as grapes, pumpkin, figs, apples, cornelian cherry, blackthorn and blackberries.

The environment must have changed progressively with the foundation of the Latin colony in 181 BCE, which will be discussed in chapter 3. As a result of population growth and the increasing presence of the Roman army, it is likely that the countryside was gradually became more inhabited and used for production.

For this period, we have the results of the most recent investigations carried out around Titus Macer's House in the Fondi Cossar (Figure 0.1, n. 7).[35] In this area of the city, a large *domus* of more than 1,200 square metres has been excavated that was active between the first century BCE and the sixth century CE. This long 600-year period saw Aquileia's greatest demographic and monumental growth, but also the greatest exploitation of the surrounding countryside. Plant finds from all phases of the urban settlement were collected during the excavation, and with them it was possible to gain an insight into how people modified the layout of the land.

Between the first century BCE and the first century CE, the landscape around the city was open, featuring temperate oak forests and damp woods.[36] Evidence suggests a significant human presence in the area, with activities such as cattle breeding and agriculture, including the growing of cereal and textile crops, as well as vegetable gardens. There were also extensive wetlands.

The forest and tree cover ranged from 19.4 per cent to 31.4 per cent, with deciduous broadleaf trees being the most common (from 15 per cent to 27.5 per cent). These included deciduous oaks like *Quercus cerris* (Turkey oak), along with black hornbeam, oriental hornbeam, common ash, manna ash, opium maple and elm. Shrubs like common hazel were also present. Conifers, represented by pines and some silver fir, made up less than 4 per cent of the vegetation.

Species typical of humid environments are present in significant numbers (12.4 per cent–25.2 per cent); species typical of damp woodlands include alders, poplar and willow. The scarce presence of hydro/elophytes indicates that areas of permanent standing water were few.

Human activity indicators are well documented (18.1 per cent–19.7 per cent), and cultivated plants, especially cereals, dominate (9.3 per cent–11.8 per cent), including barley, oats, wheat, spelt and common rye. Textile plants in the form of hemp and flax are documented. Although hemp had been cultivated from the Bronze Age, its use increases in the Roman period. Flax was grown both for its fibre, from which precious fabrics are made (e.g. the cloth of the Turin Shroud), and its seeds, producing flour and edible oil. Fruit species are well represented (on average over 1.1 per cent), including cherry, common walnut and olive. Among the shrubs, rosemary is found, a medicinal plant widely used in Roman cuisine. The presence of the common chestnut is probably linked to hillside plantations.

There is significant evidence of typical meadow/grazing plants, reaching values of over 42 per cent and indicating abundant livestock spaces. There are numerous *cichorieae* followed by spontaneous grasses, as well as peas, purple milk-vetch, medicinal herbs and clover.

During the height of the Roman Empire (second–fifth centuries CE), the landscape changed significantly due to human activity.[37] The number of trees decreased to about half of what it had been during the early Roman presence in Aquileia, with trees making up only 12.5 to 14.5 per cent of the landscape. The vegetation became more open and was heavily affected by human activities. Large areas were cultivated, with fields of cereals, vegetable gardens and fruit orchards. Agricultural spaces were divided by hedgerows and trees marking boundaries, alternating with meadows and pastures, and possibly fallow areas. This description aligns with Pliny's account of different species planted along canals and boundaries, which were protected by hedge barriers and fences. The significant number of pastures and meadows indicates widespread livestock raising.

The fact that the typical wetland plant species falls below 6 per cent is an indication that land reclamation and drainage of spaces around the city was likely taking place.

During the mid-Roman period, vegetables like chard, lettuce, chicory and parsnip became more common in gardens. Brassicas, including turnips, chamois cress and mustard, were also widely grown, sometimes making up as much as 38 per cent of the crops.

In Late Antiquity, the landscape began to change. While open spaces with modest tree cover remained, the abandonment of many city buildings led to an increase in meadows, pastures and fallow areas, while cultivated lands decreased.

From the end of ancient times (post-fourth century CE), human activity and the cultivation of plants and vegetables declined from an average of 25 per cent to 21.5 per cent.[38] The gradual abandonment of the area led to changes in the vegetation. Uncultivated areas increased and tree cover grew, while wetlands remained largely unchanged. There was an increase in meadows and grazing areas, while cereal cultivation remained constant. Large vegetable gardens continued to grow chard, chicory, lettuce, dill, parsnip and various brassicas.

Despite the challenges the city faced from the fifth century onwards, there is ample evidence of human presence, demonstrating the settlement's resilience and its ongoing relationship with the environment even after the fall of the Roman Empire and significant socio-political changes.

CHAPTER 2
AQUILEIA BEFORE AQUILEIA: THE INDIGENOUS EMPORIUM

Until a few decades ago, all historical and archaeological research agreed in placing the foundation of the city of Aquileia at the start of the second century BCE. This chronology was based on that most authoritative ancient source: the Latin historian Livy. In his chapter on the colony's foundation, Livy placed the city's establishment by Rome in 181 BCE.

However, during the second half of the twentieth century written sources were augmented by information from an increasing number of archaeological excavations. Over time, these historical and archaeological sources have been increasingly integrated. At Aquileia, progress in fieldwork has made it possible to revise Livy's important historical narrative based on new discoveries which have partly modified its meaning.

The many excavations conducted within the modern town of Aquileia and its surrounding area have unearthed traces of human presence that predate 181 BCE, showing that people frequented the area of the lower Friulian plain and the area of the town itself before the arrival of the Roman legions.[1]

Scattered human presences date back to much earlier times: people had been present in this part of the plain since the recent Mesolithic, as shown by studies conducted in the Belvedere area, which lies just south of Aquileia towards the Grado lagoon. The area was certainly inhabited in the more recent phases of the Bronze Age (second millennium BCE), as demonstrated by the remains of villages unearthed by archaeologists around Aquileia. Metal finds recovered from these dwellings and farms document the intense trade between the Alpine areas, the plains and the Adriatic coast. One of the most important villages that preceded the founding of Aquileia was located slightly to the west of the present town, in the piece of land traversed by the Amphora Canal. Here, in the locality of Ca' Baredi, archaeologists have found traces of a Bronze Age settlement from the fourteenth to thirteenth centuries BCE. Research indicates that it was a large village, surrounded by wooden defences. The settlement was located near the lagoon, which likely contributed to its defence and food supply through hunting and fishing.[2]

Recent studies have also shown that stable and well-organized settlements from the second millennium BCE lie under the city of Roman Aquileia. Even in this early period the settlements acted as a corridor for the passage of goods and people between continental Europe and the Adriatic Sea,[3] a role later taken on by Roman Aquileia. There was likely continuity through the millennia, with the area continuing to perform the same function into later times.

Evidence of human presence and the organization of villages become much clearer in the Iron Age and during the first millennium BCE. During this period, the entire eastern Po Valley, stretching from Lake Garda to the eastern Alps, underwent significant change in settlement patterns. After a period of crisis and major transformations at the start of the first millennium BCE, new developments marked the gradual emergence of the most important settlements that would later grow into urban centres. Many scattered villages began to cluster together, giving rise to small towns that eventually became large centres where people, goods and functions converged. This process led to the birth of cities.

Archaeological investigations show that a similar phenomenon seems to have begun around Aquileia, where an important settlement gradually grew, preceding the founding of the Roman city by many centuries.[4] The discoveries made have shown that the Roman city was established at the behest of the Roman Senate on a site where the local population had built an important settlement some centuries earlier. Unfortunately, we do not know its name, but scholars claim that the Roman name 'Aquileia' originated in a pre-Roman toponym and may have indicated this earlier settlement.

However, the archaeological investigation that revealed this important pre-Roman settlement was not particularly extensive and has only provided minimal information about it. The traces of the earliest town lie buried beneath the various Roman monuments and have been partly destroyed or hidden by the later buildings. Furthermore, the remains of the village are at a very low level (around 3–4 metres below the contemporary ground), which is now being affected by the underground water table. The fact that the remains are permanently submerged has made further investigations difficult and mostly ineffective.

Despite these difficulties, some parts of pre-Roman Aquileia have been excavated. The remains (Figure 2.1) have been mostly found in the northern part of the Roman city,

Figure 2.1 Aquileia. The excavation at the 'Essiccatoio nord' site (© Archives of Museo Archeologico Nazionale di Aquileia).

in the area known as 'Essiccatoio nord',[5] not far from the area that became the Roman forum (Figure 0.1, n. 4). It is not known how extensive the pre-Roman centre was: the few remains investigated are limited to the modest space that was investigated in depth, but certainly the early settlement must have extended far beyond the area to the north of the Roman forum. If we compare this to other centres active in this region at that time, we can imagine a village extending for a few hectares.

Archaeological investigations have uncovered the remains of a settlement primarily made of perishable materials. The remains include huts built using the typical construction techniques of wooden poles, clay and marsh reeds, with masonry or bricks only used in exceptional cases. The excavation also revealed that the village was built in waterlogged areas. To counteract this problem, the whole area was carefully drained using a construction system known throughout the ancient world. Large piles were driven deep into the ground and beams and planks were placed horizontally on the top of them. These formed a base for the floorings and walls that made up the rooms of the huts. The extensive use of wood for land reclamation and the construction in waterlogged areas was a widespread custom in the ancient world and pre-Roman times.[6] The physical properties of wood allow it to retain its structure in water-rich areas, as the presence of water and the lack of oxygen in wet soils prevents the decomposition of plant material. A similar technique was used at Roman Aquileia and for the medieval buildings of the Venetian lagoons, including the palaces of medieval Venice.

Other important information from the excavations concerns the huts' construction methods. It seems that these were four-sided wooden structures made with the branches of bushes covered with silty clay mixed with pottery fragments, which increased their durability and solidarity. There were also small hearths near the huts used for heating and cooking as well as the most basic craft activities.

The excavation of the pre-Roman village also showed that the buildings were precisely laid out in recurring patterns. This tells us that it was a settlement organized on a precise plan, which demonstrates the considerable organizational capabilities and knowledge of those who occupied the area before the Romans arrived. The same form of spatial planning has been found in many of the large settlements that were founded in the first half of the first millennium BCE in north Italy, particularly in the Veneto area. A small warrior statue preserved at the National Archaeological Museum shows that this settlement had artefacts of high craftmanship, perhaps the result of commercial activity with the Mediterranean regions (Figure 2.2).[7]

Scientific research has also made it possible to reconstruct many aspects of daily life in pre-Roman Aquileia.[8] Plant remains analysis has shown that there was extensive use of cereals for food, such as barley and emmer as well as soft and hard grains like spelt. Millet and panicum are also documented, albeit in smaller quantities. Opium poppies were used for their pharmacological properties as well as for food. Other edible plants used in pre-Roman Aquileia included grapes, pumpkin, figs, apples, cornelian cherry, plums and blackberries.

Village life was also marked by the presence of animals, used in a variety of ways, both as a labour force to till the land as well as a food source. Remains found during the 1990s

Figure 2.2 Aquileia. Statuette of a warrior (fifth century BCE) (© A. Chemollo).

excavations showed the presence of pigs, sheep, goats and cattle, used to provide meat, milk, wool, hides and bones.[9] Hunting was also practised alongside farming, as evidenced by the remains of wild boar, deer and birds, while fishing may have been practised in the nearby lagoons and waterways.

There were many production and craft activities in the pre-Roman village, documented by artefacts found near the huts investigated in the area to the north of the Roman forum. We know for certain that the inhabitants practised spinning and weaving wool and processed and fired clay to make pottery vessels for the preparation, storage and consumption of food.

Archaeologists have also unearthed some finds of worked metal,[10] which allows us to assume that metalworking, particularly of iron, was also practised in pre-Roman Aquileia. This detail is important as it indicates that already in this period there was a trade relationship with the Alpine and transalpine regions of *Noricum* (present day Carinthia in south Austria), from where came the worked and raw metal used in Roman Aquileia.

This complex pre-Roman village had a long life. Archaeological data suggest that it came into existence between the ninth and eighth centuries BCE and was fully active in the seventh century BCE.[11] However, life in the village cannot have been easy and the relationship with the natural elements was not always smooth. The management of the numerous watercourses must have been particularly tricky as they were often very full. In fact, village life was abruptly interrupted due to a violent flooding, evidenced by the layers of silt and sand that buried part of the oldest huts during the seventh century BCE.

This natural event must not have been very severe or widespread, as the village came back to life as early as the sixth century BCE, with the houses and general features of the village remaining much the same as before. From the study of material culture (objects, architecture and artefacts), we can say that the pre-Roman centre was part of a cultural *koinè* that spread throughout north-east Italy. The objects found are similar to those found in present-day Friuli Venezia Giulia and Veneto, where the important *Veneti* culture, one of the most highly developed of pre-Roman Italy, flourished. Pre-Roman Aquileia must have been inhabited by people belonging to the *Veneti* group, as suggested by a passage from the Latin historian Silius Italicus. He mentions the Adriatic city among the communities of *Veneti* auxiliaries present alongside the Romans on the eve of the Battle of Cannae (216 BCE).[12] These communities likely played an important role in the transport of goods and in maintaining relationships between different and distant peoples.

Excavations have also revealed that pre-Roman Aquileia suffered another flooding during the fifth century BCE, but findings from different areas of the city show that this was marginal and did not greatly affect the life of the settlement. In fact, during the fourth and third centuries BCE, ceramic materials and metal artefacts were still arriving in these areas, demonstrating that the future Roman Aquileia was the end-point for long-distance trade routes.[13] In fact, imports exist from the Venetian, Etruscan and central Italian areas.

These finds are particularly important as they demonstrate that the pre-Roman village on which the Latin colony was established in 181 BCE was already managing relations between the regions bordering the Adriatic Sea, central Italy and the Alpine and Balkan areas. Important finds related to this network of relationships include the small Etruscan and Central Italian bronzes used in religious rituals as votive offerings.

The long-distance trade involving pre-Roman Aquileia likely had very ancient origins. It has been suggested that already in pre-Roman times the Aquileia area imported amber. Amber, a fossil resin, was collected on the shores of the North Sea and after a long journey was traded in the Mediterranean. It is present in grave goods and many regions south of the Alps from protohistoric times.

Although the excavations at the pre-Roman site of Aquileia don't provide a complete history of the area, they are incredibly valuable for understanding the broader history of Aquileia. The presence of a thriving village between the ninth and third centuries BCE clearly explains why the Romans chose to establish the Latin colony of Aquileia in the same location in the second century BCE. This older settlement, with its commercial potential and international connections, must have been well known to those deciding on new Roman colonies and likely influenced their decision.

We don't have specific information about the changes the pre-Roman centre underwent when the new colony was founded, nor are there any archaeological or written records of destructive events. Instead, the well-documented friendly relationships between Rome and the centres of Venetian culture in north-east Italy suggest that the old pre-Roman centre was absorbed and integrated into the new colony.

It is also plausible that the creation of the new colony provided security and stability for the old settlement, especially in a region where historical sources mention threats from Gallic tribes. Interestingly, no Celtic material culture has been found from the pre-Roman phases of Aquileia. It is only from the second century BCE, with the founding of the Roman colony, that *Noricum* coins appear, indicating mature commercial relations with these peoples.

CHAPTER 3
THE FOUNDATION OF THE LATIN COLONY IN 181 BCE: LIVY'S STORY AND THE BIRTH OF THE ROMAN CITY

The founding of the Latin colony

In 183 BCE a lively debate took place in the Roman Senate.[1] The senators discussed the establishment of a colony, to be called Aquileia, in a territory to the north-east of Italy which had been invaded and occupied a few years earlier by Gallic populations from beyond the Alps. The Roman senators approved the project and decided to establish a Latin colony, something which was implemented in 181 BCE.[2]

This was one of the last new foundations carried out by Rome. Following the example of what was happening in the Greek and Hellenistic worlds, as early as the fourth century BCE the Roman state had also begun an expansionist policy in north and south Italy by creating new urban centres. Sometimes cities were built *ex novo*, where no inhabited centre had existed previously, but often new colonies were established by moving people into pre-existing towns.

From a legal point of view there were two types of colonies: the Roman colonies were in fact appendages of the state of Rome and comprised a few hundred families who were assigned small parcels of land; the Latin colonies were real centres with their own administrative autonomy to which thousands of families were sent and to whom very large parcels of land were assigned. The families of the Latin colonies often came from areas or centres of the Latin world allied with Rome.[3]

Aquileia was founded as a Latin colony and there were military and strategic reasons for choosing to found the city in north-eastern Italy. In the years preceding its foundation, the region had been the focus of numerous events and not entirely peaceful relations between the Romans, the Transalpine Gauls, the Histri and probably the Veneti.[4] In 186 BCE a Celtic tribe of 12,000 Transalpine Gauls, driven by the search for new territory, had moved from their usual settlements and *transgressi in Venetiam* through previously unknown routes to occupy a section of the lower Friulan plain and establish a stable settlement (*oppidum*) of their own in the eastern Friuli just where, five years later, Aquileia would be founded.[5]

The Roman Senate's reaction was not long in coming and a delegation was sent to the Transalpine Celtic community. The leaders of this community denied any involvement in the invasion and replied that it was a completely autonomous and independent initiative by a group of tribes. Livy adds no further details to the narrative of the following three years, but in 183 BCE we know that the Senate announced some new decisions. It was now considered a hostile and intolerable act to invade the territories south of the Alps, requiring an immediate response.

Consequently, the consul Marcus Claudius Marcellus was sent with the legions to attack the Celtic people who had attempted to expand their territories into the Friuli plains. The decisive and violent actions of the consul led to the destruction of the Celtic *oppidum*. Following this the Celts were pushed back across the Alps, into the regions they had originally come from. The military action concluded by sending a new Roman delegation to the Celtic tribes' headquarters. Here, the Roman ambassadors firmly told the Celtic tribes that the summit of the Alps would henceforth be a boundary that they must never cross in any way (*Alpes prope inexsuperabilem finem in medio esse*). The natural Alpine boundary thus became a military and political boundary.

Rome's ambitions and desire for conquest did not stop there and the consul Marcus Claudius Marcellus himself planned an expedition against the Istrian peoples in the following years.[6]

It is not known if this expedition took place. What is certain is that Aquileia was founded two years later. The time that elapsed between the Senate's decision and the foundation act was almost certainly due to the war that was being waged in the same year against the Histrians, who were trying to prevent the colony from being established. But there were also logistical difficulties, foremost among them being the need to enlist enough Roman citizens and Latin allies to be transferred to lands not yet fully pacified, distant from those of their origin and where their lives would be at risk.

From the Roman side the impetus for the foundation is much clearer: as mentioned in the previous chapter, this part of the plain was of fundamental importance for managing the commercial relationships between the Mediterranean, the Adriatic Sea and the Alpine and transalpine areas which provided crucial resources for Rome. But in the decision to found the colony the ancient relationship between the people of Rome and the Veneti may also have played a part. Indeed, it was the Veneti who inhabited the lands of north-eastern Italy and who had, almost certainly, founded the pre-Roman centre of Aquileia. Scholars have suggested that the friendship between Rome and the Veneti also contributed to the decision to found Aquileia as a bulwark to defend these lands and the interests of the Veneti themselves, which could have been damaged or threatened by the advance of the Celts into the eastern plains. It has been convincingly argued that a member of the Roman Claudii Marcelli family defended these territories due to the long-standing mutual interests they shared with the Veneti.

The Senate decided to send 3,000 settlers who were destined to become the lifeblood of the newborn settlement. Some historical studies have tried to trace the origins of the people who were moved to Aquileia to establish the new city.[7] This has been mostly possible through the names of the settlers, which are documented by numerous inscriptions from the earliest phases of the colony and compared to those from other regions of the ancient world. The study found that most of the new inhabitants of Aquileia came from central or southern Italy. The original legal status of these newcomers varied: some were full Roman citizens, while others were Latin or Italic peoples allied with Rome and came from both the central and northern Italian regions.

Interestingly, a substantial proportion of the new citizens of the Latin colony belonged to families from the same area as Aquileia and were almost certainly those who had lived in the pre-Roman village described in the previous chapter. These findings support the idea that there was a physical, political and demographic overlap with the earlier centre. It has been argued that many of the most important local families may also have played an important role in the new colony's institutions.

Together with the 3,000 foot soldiers and their families, an unknown number of centurions and horsemen also arrived in Aquileia. The colonists were assigned very large plots of land, almost certainly to encourage their transfer to the new and remote centre. Some 50 *iugera* were assigned to the foot soldiers (corresponding to around 12.5 hectares), 100 *iugera* to centurions (around 25 hectares) and 140 *iugera* to the cavalry (corresponding to about 35 hectares). These cultivable lands were in the immediate vicinity of the new city, but they must have occupied a substantial part of the low Friulian plains between the Tagliamento and Timavo rivers. The two classes of centurions and cavalry went on to form the ruling classes of the fledgling colony, which soon led to the appointment of local magistrates, assemblies and the necessary governing bodies of the small autonomous state.

The Latin colony was a sovereign state with its own governing bodies.[8] The large number of surviving inscriptions has made it possible to reconstruct the full picture of the local magistracies established after the foundation. The most important were the *quaestores*, the *aediles* and the *duoviri*, who were the magistrates with the highest authority in the colony. At a lower level stood the *censores*. All magistrates held office for one year, and after serving they joined the city council, called the *Senatus*. Decisions made in the colony were based on those made at the meetings of the citizens which took place in the *Comitium* (Figure 0.1, n. 6), which archaeological research has identified as being placed north of the forum.

The administrative framework only changed in 90 BCE when the colony was transformed into a municipality, where all inhabitants were granted full Roman citizenship.[9] To set up the administrative life of the colony, the Roman Senate appointed a special commission of three magistrates who were given specific responsibility for the colony's establishment.[10] The three selected magistrates were highly esteemed officials of the Roman state, comprising two former consuls, Publius Cornelius Scipio Nasica and Gaius Flaminius, and a former praetor, Lucius Manlius Acidinus. The latter had been part of the last Roman embassy to the peoples of the eastern Alps[11] and was also honoured in the city much later with a commemorative statue and an inscription (Figure 3.1) that honoured the most important citizens in Aquileia's history. This person must have been enormously admired by the city, to be remembered many centuries after his death.

Building Aquileia on top of a long-standing earlier settlement meant that the families and settlers must have absorbed this pre-Roman centre and improved it. It may be that at least some of the previous inhabitants welcomed the arrival of the new settlers, who guaranteed the growth and defence of the settlement under the protection of the growing

Figure 3.1 Aquileia. Inscription of the triumvir of 181 BCE L. Manlius Acidinus (J. Bonetto).

Roman state. Yet, the new city immediately experienced moments of crisis, caused by skirmishes with the Gallic peoples who in 179 BCE returned to demand land in exchange for submission to Roman rule.[12]

Furthermore, the city immediately became the setting for war against the Histri. Legions left Aquileia bound for those eastern regions under the consul of 178 BCE, Aulus Manlius Vulso; troops also arrived in Aquileia under the other consul, Marcus Iunius

Brutus.[13] In the following year, new troops arrived under Gaius Claudius Pulcher, who then led the final and victorious campaign of 177 BCE against the Histri.[14] All this also demonstrates that the foundation of Aquileia was intended to be the starting point for Roman expansion towards the east and north. Having a fortified centre at the northern end of the Adriatic Sea became essential for quartering troops destined for new, more ambitious conquests. These ongoing conflicts made the colony highly vulnerable and of great significance in Roman politics.

In 171 BCE the citizens of Aquileia turned to Rome with an explicit request for help. The messengers sent to the capital described their city as 'insecure and as yet insufficiently defended' and asked the Senate to send reinforcements to the city.[15] So, two years later (169 BCE), Rome sent a further 1,500 families of infantrymen-colonists to the shores of the Adriatic[16] to add to the previous contingent and in order to adequately and definitively reinforce the colony.[17] As with the initial transfer, three specially appointed magistrates were sent to oversee it: Titus Annius Luscus, Publius Decius Subulus and Marcus Cornelius Cethegus.

The reliability of Livy's text concerning the reinforcements sent and the new magistrates charged with reorganizing the colony was confirmed by a 1995 archaeological find from the city's forum (Figure 0.1, n. 4), the colony's civic square *par excellence*.[18] Here, the limestone base of a statue was uncovered bearing an inscription dedicated to Titus Annius Luscus (Figure 3.2), one of the magistrates sent by Rome in 169 BCE. The text was written several decades after the magistrate's work, in around 130 BCE, and recalls his activities in the colony. It is important because it explicitly mentions his actions, almost certainly in collaboration with the other two magistrates. It records that Titus Annius erected and dedicated the colony's first sacred building; it also attributes to the same magistrate the decisive act of drafting the colony's first laws and creating the list of the local city senate.

Rome's intentions with these repeated and forthright actions between 186 and 169 BCE was to garrison and control a part of Italy north of the Apennines that was becoming of interest to, and threatened by, the Celtic populations. At the same time, however, the central government's plan for the city was that it become an advanced starting point towards further, deeper penetrations to conquer the area of the Upper Adriatic, the eastern Alps, Istria and the Balkans.

Yet, its role as a commercial and economic bridgehead should also not be underestimated. Rome wanted to monopolize trade with those Alpine, transalpine and above all Danubian and Central European regions which, along ancient routes and trackways, used the Adriatic as the point of contact with the advanced and wealthy Mediterranean mercantile world.

As already mentioned, the chosen position for the new city followed that of the earlier pre-Roman centre. And like its precursor, this city enjoyed a privileged position in terms of relations with other areas of the ancient world. The new colony was built in a flat area a few score of kilometres from the foot of the Alps and about 11 kilometres from the open sea, to which it was connected by the Natisone river that ran along the eastern side of the city.

Figure 3.2 Aquileia. Base of statue for the triumvir of 169 BCE T. Annius Luscus (J. Bonetto).

The city walls

Thanks to Livy, we have detailed information about the birth of the colony. However, little is known about how the new settlement was shaped in terms of spatial organization and the construction of the first buildings.[19] The archaeological evidence relating to the earliest phases of the colony's life is buried beneath the newer buildings and has not been reached by archaeological investigations. Furthermore, many of the earlier buildings were also made of non-durable materials, such as wood, which prevented their preservation. Finally, many of the earliest buildings were certainly demolished to make room for later ones. For these reasons, very few remains of the early city have been unearthed and documented by archaeological investigations.[20]

An exception is the first fortifications that surrounded the space of the fledgling colony to protect it from the Celtic populations, whose threats first led to Aquileia's foundation.[21]

The military nature of the new settlement suggests that the need for effective fortifications was recognized from the very beginning. It is likely that construction started with a boundary to define and protect the city, following ancient Roman laws that required a symbolic definition of urban space for new colonies. According to the religious rules observed by Romulus when founding Rome, a sacred furrow, known as the *sulcus primigenius*, had to be dug around the urban area first. The city's earthen bank and walls were then built alongside this furrow, clearly marking the distinction between urban and suburban spaces.

This act of religious town-planning and strategic value must have taken place at the moment of Aquileia's foundation in 181 BCE and finds an evocative echo in a relief preserved in the National Museum of Aquileia (Figure 3.3). This panel depicts the digging of the furrow by a pair of cattle yoked to a plough and followed by Roman magistrates.

Large sections of the oldest walls of the city have been uncovered in repeated excavations conducted in the modern town from as early as the last century, mainly by the archaeologist G. B. Brusin in the 1930s (Figure 0.1, n. 1).

The reconstructed plan of the fortifications is that of a very elongated north–south rectangle.[22] The perimeter of just over 3,000 metres encloses an area of approximately 40 hectares. The length of the defensive circuit appears adequate for the number of settlers (3,000), as a rough theoretical calculation shows that protecting the city required one soldier for every metre of wall.[23]

The city wall dimensions were the same as those of other Latin colonies in Roman Italy which, larger than those of the Roman colonies, delimited areas of between 40 and

Figure 3.3 Aquileia. Slab of the *sulcus primigenius* (© slowphoto.studio).

60 hectares. Aquileia's perimeter, as with other Latin colonies, was adapted to the geography of the surrounding area. Its long and narrow shape was dictated by the course of the Natisone river that bordered – at about 20 metres distant – the entire eastern edge of the city, offering further protection. The river also explains the non-rectilinear and curved course of the north-eastern part of the walls, which clearly traced the winding watercourse.

The straight southern side of the fortifications was kept about 300 metres from the river, which curved decisively south of the city centre. There is no clear reason for this, so it must be assumed that there were problems with water in this area that discouraged the installation of defensive works.

The western side has a more regular, broken-line course, with modest changes in direction. It widens noticeably with a sharp bend where the Via Annia entered the city at the western gate. Finally, the defensive line was completed by the short northern side, which featured a gate allowing access into the city via the Via Postumia, built in 148 BCE.

Although Aquileia's first city walls were variously conditioned by river morphology along the east and south sides and the extra-urban road system to the west, the influence exerted by the internal urban organization appears marginal. In this way physical geography played a major part in the planning and executional phases of the fortifications.

The structure of the walls

The repeated excavations of the above-described republican wall have left us with a good knowledge of its technical features, many of which are particularly interesting (Figure 3.4).[24] Along the eastern edge the brick foundations rested on a layer of gravel which had a clear drainage function; brick was a highly innovative material at this time, which was being introduced into northern Italy. A short, excavated section of the western curtain wall was formed by a foundation consisting of superimposed layers of sand and gravel on which rested a mass of stone.[25] On this rested two well cut and rusticated blocks of Istrian limestone, which formed the base for the brick wall above.

The reason for the marked difference between the foundations of the eastern and western sides is probably to be found in the geomorphological characteristics of the different urban sectors.[26] As already mentioned in the chapter on the environment and landscape, the whole western area right up to the city walls was marshy. The use of sand and gravel, which are excellent for draining water, and Istrian limestone, which is ideal for preventing water from rising through the brick walls, can be explained by the presence of waterlogged soils.

The excavations of some sections of the wall (Figure 3.5) have shown that the upper part of the defence wall was approximately 2.4 metres thick, equal to eight Roman feet; the strength of the wall was doubled at two specific points in the south-eastern sector, probably in relation to the original presence of wooden stairs leading up to the wall-walk.

The wall was constructed entirely of unusually large, rectangular or square, fired bricks. Recent excavations on the south-eastern side of the wall uncovered square fired bricks measuring between 0.35 and 0.37 metres.[27] This brick size matches the five-palm

Figure 3.4 Aquileia. The walls of the colony at the Cossar funds/former railroad area (© Archives of Museo Archeologico Nazionale di Aquileia).

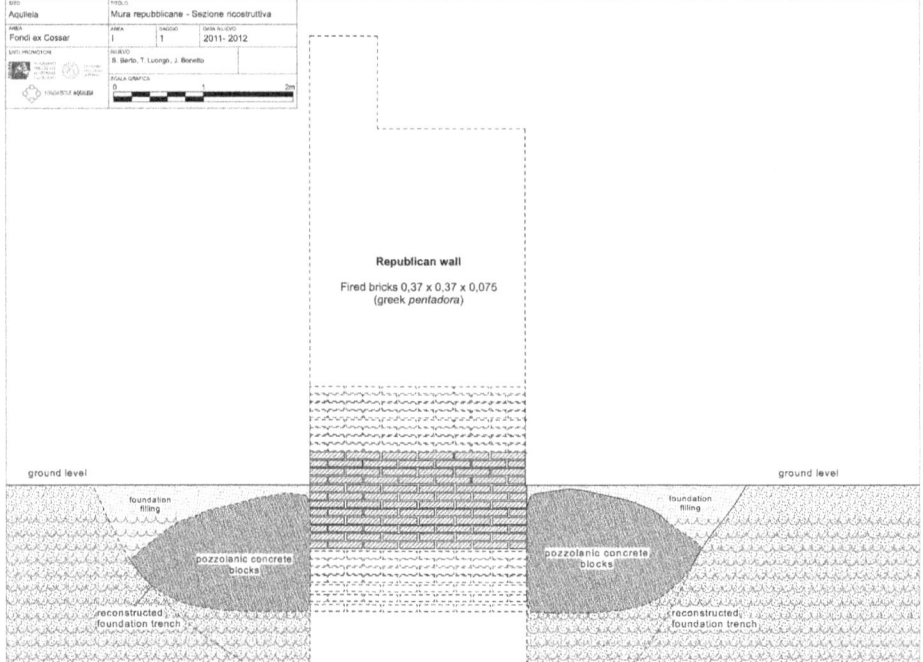

Figure 3.5 Aquileia. Reconstructed section of the republican walls at the Cossar funds (J. Bonetto).

measurement described by the Roman architect Vitruvius as typical of the *pentadora* brick,[28] which was used by Greek craftsmen.[29] Other sections of the city's oldest walls were also built with unusually large bricks (49–50 × 40–42 centimetres; 50 × 50 centimetres), which were not typical of the Roman measurement system but closer to those used in the Greek world. The construction of the oldest walls at Aquileia, including the gates and towers, seems to reflect Greek architectural models, which will be discussed later.[30]

In the meantime, it should also be noted that the extensive use of bricks was related to the abundant clay and silt deposits across the Friulian plain and the corresponding shortage of other types of building materials; the availability of stone from the Istrian quarries and the Trieste Karst was still limited, and it was only from the second half of the first century BCE that they were intensively exploited.[31]

The towers along the walls

The republican era towers are very interesting.[32] One of them, on the south-eastern corner of the perimeter, is square with 7.2-metre sides; its perimeter wall is 2.4 metres thick, the same as the curtain wall; and the internal space is the same 2.4 metres. Of the two other known towers, one was concorporated into the curtain wall near the port warehouses and the other formed the north-eastern corner of the perimeter.

Both have an unusual and interesting pentagonal (five-sided) or heptagonal (seven-sided) plan, with an outward-jutting corner. There is nothing comparable to this type of tower in the fortifications of Roman Italy, so it rather have its roots in the Greek-Hellenistic construction tradition. There is a mention of towers with corners jutting outwards in Philo of Byzantium's treatise written at the end of the third century BCE – not long before the construction of the Aquileian wall.[33] The particular polygonal structure, which was also considered the most efficient by Vitruvius,[34] was built for solidity. The lateral obtuse angles and the frontal projecting angle helped to deflect and reduce the impact of blows directed at right angles to the curtain wall.

There are clear reasons why the square and polygonal layout was used for the different towers. The most exposed sectors of the walls, that is, the northern side and the one facing the river, needed the most protection and consequently had the most solid polygon layout whilst along the more protected southern side the erection of a tower with a simpler square layout was considered sufficient.

The city gates

There must have been at least four city gates and one postern in the republican city walls of Aquileia.[35] From neither the eastern one, in the Monastero district – the knowledge of which only comes from first century BCE texts – or the southern one – fleetingly seen and not surveyed in recent years – do we have any architectural-building details. There is a similar lack of documentation for the minor gate seen during excavations along the western side of the wall, at the junction between the curtain and the *decumanus* that runs tangentially to the southern side of the forum. However, the layout of the two large gates along the northern and western sides is partially known. Most of our knowledge concerns the northern gate (Figure 0.1, n. 1.1), through which the Via Postumia – the main Roman road in the Po Valley, stretching from Genoa to Aquileia – entered the city. This gateway had been investigated in the nineteenth century (between 1872 and 1876) by Austrian archaeologists, and a portion was seen again by G. B. Brusin (between 1936 and 1937). The recent comprehensive study of the structure[36] is based on the discovery in the archives of the plan drawn up during the first and most complete excavation.

The gate was built with a sandstone foundation and brick elevation. This material, typical of the whole curtain wall, was used in pieces measuring 50 × 43 centimetres, which can be found in other sections of the republican wall.

The gateway, of which only the foundation remains, must have been very compact, with an almost square floor plan, and a maximum size of 28 × 30 centimetres. This imposing structure stood astride the walls and protruded both into and out of the city. On the outer side, the body of the gate was protected by two circular towers approximately 7 metres in diameter, whilst on the inner side there were two, almost square, bastions measuring 8.5 × 10 metres. The most striking aspect of the plan is the presence of a courtyard that separated the two gates which opened inwards and outwards from the walls; the courtyard had curvilinear inner walls that formed an elliptical/ovoid shape of about 16.6 metres.

This elliptical courtyard is a very important detail of this gate which opened towards the most important road that reached Aquileia from the Po Valley, devised with defence in mind, as it avoids the creation of 'dead' firing spaces at the corners and instead exposes any assailants who may have entered to the defenders' attacks. This layout originated in the Hellenistic age; the earliest examples to be found in the circular recesses in the Stymphalos gate (Greece), the 'Eletra' gate at Thebes and, in particular, the 'Arcadia' gate at Messene, whose layout is virtually identical to that of the north gate at Aquileia. The Aquileian example can be understood as a later Hellenistic type from the early second century BCE in a context where military and strategic concerns were of paramount importance.

The second gate in Aquileia's walls where structural details are known is the one located along the western wall circuit (Figure 0.1, n. 1.2), where the Via Annia entered the city. However, there is a lack of useful data for an architectural reading of the structure. It was probably investigated at the end of the nineteenth century and then re-excavated in 1939, but it was not until 1946 that a plan was made based on the excavation data, which, together with some archive photographs, is the only known documentation. Its foundation comprised some very large stone blocks and had a very simple structure, with a central square courtyard and two masonry sections protruding about 1 metre from the outer front.

These avant-corps could have been used to support part of the external façade's decoration, but they might also have been used to create support for the passage closing systems, as is the case with the 'Laurentina' and 'Romana' gates of Ostia, where similar structures were used to house the portcullis.

After its foundation in 181 BCE, Aquileia was thus defended by a mighty brick fortification with towers and gates. Two important issues need to be addressed concerning this great architectural project. The first concerns the time of its construction. Studies in the past have always assumed that the city walls were built at the time of the city's foundation in 181 BCE or a few years later. However, this interpretation has been derived from historical rather than archaeological data. Only recently have excavations been carried out close to the city's walls, around the Fondi Cossar in the south-eastern corner of the perimeter and in the area of the Fondo Comelli along the western side.

Although in neither case has it been able to fix the time of the construction of the walls, important insights have been gained. In both excavations the 14C dating of the wooden elements in the construction layers indicate that the defensive wall was likely built in the second century BCE. However, it seems highly probable that it occurred after 169 BCE, when the Aquileains asked Rome for new reinforcements, not when the city was first founded.

This hypothesis about the time difference between the colony's foundation and the construction of the first walls is not based on the time it took to build them. A recent study[37] quantified the man-hours needed to procure materials and build the republican walls at Aquileia, showing that construction might have lasted a very short time, between two and ten years, depending on the number of workers (estimated at between 100 and 400).

There might also have been other reasons for carrying out the work after the colony's foundation and reinforcement. The logistical organization of the building site, the procurement of material, the establishment of a production chain and the construction-related operations must all be set within the context of a settlement that was already developed from the point of view of territorial control, population size, equipment and other technical-logistical details. Establishing all these elements would have required a not inconsiderable amount of time in the aftermath of the colony's foundation and were all essential before the building site, itself short-lived, could be up and running. These considerations and the absolute chronological data suggest that there was a chronological hiatus between the date of the colony's foundation/reinforcement and the construction of the walls. The possible 'delay' found here is a well-known phenomenon affecting many new settlements in the Mediterranean.

In both Greek and Roman colonies, the time lag between the foundation and fortification of the nascent cities is frequently seen in the stratigraphic excavations of the walls. In these cases it has been suggested that the first phases of the settlement were accompanied only by structures that were particularly important to the *status* of the urban space, such as the gates, and that the urban boundary between these openings was only at first delineated by the digging of a *sulcus* or ditch with the use of palisades and embankments to give initial protection to the city while awaiting the building of a more substantial work such as a wall.

In a nutshell, absolute chronological data, assessments of the logistical and operational scenario of the colonial foundation and various comparative analyses seem to suggest that the walls of Aquileia were built a few decades after its foundation (181 BCE) and reinforcement (169 BCE).[38] In the meantime, and due to the decidedly hostile climate in which it was founded, it is highly likely that a *vallum* and *sulcus* were completed soon after its construction, as well as other defence works such as palisades and embankments, to give the fledgling colony some limited protection.

Another aspect of interest regarding the oldest fortifications is who were the key actors. Recent studies have revealed several architectural details which suggest the possible origin of the architects.[39] In fact, structural forms, such as the standardized wall body, the use of fired brick and their unusual size, explicitly indicate the technical-constructive culture of the Greek Mediterranean world, where similar applications can be found throughout the vast architectural panorama of Greece and Magna Graecia.

Various other details lead us back to Greek building traditions: for example, the technique of building with layers of sand and gravel, found in many Aquileian and north Italian contexts, can be traced back to examples from the Graeco-Mediterranean areas.[40] Another technical aspect linking the colony's fortification with the Greek world is the use of large stone blocks for the construction of the western section of the fortifications. There is an almost unique parallel in the Greek colony of Apollonia (Illyria) in present day Albania. This part of the wall's stonework also has a Greek origin. The use of the 'rusticated ashlar' at Aquileia[41] has its origins in the Classical Greek period but has also been increasingly found in Hellenistic walls and the Peloponnese (Gortyna (Arcadia), Dodona, Hyllarima).

Further indications of links with Greek builders can be gathered from the architectural features of the towers and gates of the republican wall. As mentioned, the circuit wall was protected by a pentagonal tower at the north-eastern corner and by a heptagonal tower along the eastern side. Both have an outwardly projecting corner. This type of tower structure dates to the Early Hellenistic age and the Greek world and is mentioned in Philo of Byzantium's treatise on siegecraft, written at the end of the third century BCE. Comparisons can be found in the eastern Aegean and western Asian Minor, where some cities had five- and seven-sided towers built into the curtain wall (Samos, Heraclea at Latmos, Hyllarima), just as in Aquileia. These examples date between the end of the fourth and the beginning of the second century BCE, and thus only a few decades before Aquileia was founded.

The two gates could be closed on two sides divided by a central courtyard and thus repeat a pattern that was well known in the Greek peninsula from the fourth century BCE onwards and which then gradually spread to Magna Graecia and Italian areas. The derivation from Greek-Hellenistic military architecture is clearer when looking at the layout of the northern gate with its circular entrance.

These observations lead us to believe that the great post-foundation Aquileian architectural projects involved Greek professionals attracted by the rapid rise of urbanization in this region and by the opportunity to put the great Hellenistic building traditions into practice. The archaeological evidence also shows that not only low-level labourers (typically employed in the production of material) but also medium- to high-profile workers (involved in the placing of the materials and even the buildings' design) were active here. Furthermore, the evidence points to there being many Greek workers who were organized into coordinated groups or 'enterprises', as suggested by the number of documents, the geographical extent of the evidence and, above all, the monumental scale of the buildings completed.

There is strong evidence of direct contacts between the northern Italian regions and the Aegean world in various spheres, including literary history, economic and commercial relations, and the artistic milieu. These connections can be traced back to the ancient relationships that linked the Greek emporia of Spina and Adria in the north Adriatic to the Greek cities of Sicily and Magna Graecia. For example, Dionysius the Elder, the tyrant of Syracuse, had colonizing ambitions in the north Adriatic world. Other centres, such as Ravenna and the pre-Roman settlement of Aquileia, also received Greek trade inflows between the fourth and third centuries BCE, confirming the existence of an ancient Adriatic route between the Greek world and northern Italy.

The division of the urban space

While the walls were one of the first and most important structures built after the colony's foundation to protect the people and armies of the city, other urban and architectural projects were also planned as early as the second century BCE.[42]

Like all ancient cities, one of the most pressing needs was to divide the internal spaces within the walls by creating a precise street system. Since the sixth century BCE, the Greek and Roman worlds had developed a refined understanding of how to divide urban spaces between public and private areas and areas with different functions. Architects and engineers developed highly functional urban plans based on a 'chessboard' layout of parallel and perpendicular streets, facilitating the regular division of urban areas and the movement of people and goods.

It is reasonable to assume that in Aquileia too, after its foundation in 181 BCE, there were plans to subdivide the space enclosed by the walls, as described above.

Although many scholars have tried to reconstruct the initial plan of the city (Figure 0.1),[43] they have all come up against the difficulty of tackling Aquileia's early street layout due to the limited archaeological information on the oldest part of the city.

Consequently, the reconstruction of a 'programmatic plan' has been proposed, formed by a series of extended road axes with a NW 22.3° direction, which is based on the archaeological evidence of stone-paved roads built in the Early Imperial Age (first century BCE–first century CE).[44] This proposal also seems convincing because the proposed scheme is consistent with some architectural features built in the early phases of the colony, such as the wall gates and the *Comitium*, the assembly square. This plan is further confirmed by research undertaken in the Fondi Cossar area, near the south-eastern corner of the city, where the existence of a series of roads with a NW 22.3° orientation have been found. These gravel and silt roads, which can be dated to the first century BCE,[45] were later upgraded with stone paving material (trachyte from the Euganean Hills and Aurisina marble).[46]

However, the results of this research still leave us with some doubts about whether the entire colony was completely and regularly subdivided from the start. This is still a possible hypothesis but unsupported by clear evidence and we cannot say with certainty that the urban planning was completed in 181 BCE. It is entirely possible that many parts of the colony were not densely populated in the first decades of its existence and that the infrastructure was organized around simple beaten earth tracks or coarsely filled paths, none of which were completely regularized in terms of layout.

The current archaeological data, therefore, indicate that the first republican road grid was built at the end of the second century BCE, or possibly even in the first decades of the first century BCE. Moreover, there was a lot of building activity at Aquileia at this time. It became a *municipium* following the new laws of 90–89 BCE (*Lex Iulia de civitate*) and underwent a significant public building programme, such as the reconstruction of a city gate, the construction of a *porticus duplex* and the building of the *macellum* at the forum. As the excavations in the Fondi Cossar itself have shown,[47] this is also the time when private buildings were given significant new features, with the construction of an atrium house, in line with central-southern Italian models. Some scholars link this moment to the construction of the first sections of a sewer system linked to the public road system being built in the central area of the city.

Other data is emerging from archaeological research conducted around the city[48] which shows that it was only by the first century BCE that the town space was becoming more and more occupied by buildings, suggesting that an extensive urbanization programme was underway, aimed at supporting a new urban layout. In short, the available archaeological data indicate that the first geometric subdivision of the city took place at the beginning of the first century BCE using earth and gravel roads and that at the end of the same century, or at the beginning of the following one, the street grid was upgraded by paving the roads and constructing a sophisticated water drainage system.[49]

This change over time from gravel tracks to stone-paved streets is typical of Roman urban infrastructural evolution in northern Italy. The presence of gravel roads below paved streets is well documented not only in Aquileia but also in other Po Valley towns such as Verona, Rimini, Bologna, Reggio Emilia and Trento.

The colony's first public and sacred buildings

As mentioned, little is known about the public and sacred architecture of the colony's early period, with the sole exception of the well-known city walls.

Few other buildings can be attributed to the republican period, between the second and first centuries BCE. The reason for this lack of evidence can perhaps be found in the building forms, which in this phase saw a major use of perishable materials such as wood and unbaked clay. Only for buildings of essential value (such as walls) were resistant baked bricks used. Stone from quarries in the eastern Alps was still little used.[50]

The only solid structure buildings we know of are those around the colony's main square, the forum (Figure 0.1, n. 4).[51] At its north-western corner stood one of the most important buildings used for trade. This building, known in the Roman world as the *macellum* (Figure 0.1, n. 5), had a square plan of over 30 metres long and was internally divided into a series of spaces arranged radially around a central courtyard. These rooms served as workshops and storerooms and were paved with baked clay bricks. Outside the shops, the corridor was paved with small bricks arranged '*di taglio*' that better resisted the wear and tear of footsteps. The function of the *macellum* in Aquileia was to accommodate sellers and buyers in the exchange of goods arriving from the port or from the city's countryside. Although the type of goods that were traded in this market is not known, it is possible that they were both foodstuffs and handicrafts. Recent excavations suggest that the *macellum* was built in the final years of the second century BCE.[52]

Even closer to the forum was a second important building: the *Comitium* (Figure 0.1, n. 6). This building, used for holding political meetings, is always found near the forums of the Latin colonies. The location, at one corner of the forum, reflects the close link between the political functions of the *Comitium* and the various meetings of the citizen body that took place in the open space of the forum in front of it.

The Aquileia *Comitium* had a square outer perimeter and a circular inner ring characterized by an open space and a series of steps on which seats were placed to accommodate those who took part in the town's assemblies. The building was constructed a few decades after the foundation of the colony and almost certainly shortly after the middle of the second century BCE.

In the Late Republican era, the large city forum space in front of the *Comitium* was also established. During these early phases, the public square was paved with bricks and featured a series of small holes that served as temporary installations to organize citizens during periodic voting (*comitia*). Its dimensions of 142 × 55 metres (including the gullies) were similar to those of the forum in the Imperial Age.

We have limited information on the religious buildings of the colony during the republican period.[53] The central area of the city likely housed the temple erected by T. Annius Luscus,[54] as mentioned in the inscription found in the forum in 1995. It is hypothesized that some moulded elements (frieze, pediment, roof decoration) dating to the second half of the second century BCE belonged to this building.

In the urban area, another temple building must have been located in the north-eastern sector of the colony (Fondo Gallet), just north of the forum. It is very likely to have been a temple again built in the second century BCE with four columns on the front facing east, towards one of the minor thoroughfares.

Other evidence documents the existence of other buildings that must have comprised elements of the urban landscape that have unfortunately completely disappeared. Thus,

Figure 3.6 Aquileia. Terracotta telamons, which may have decorated the urban gates of Aquileia in the republican period (© A. Chemollo).

in the north-eastern sector, in the Monastero locality, the remains of a clay pediment with cult statues have been recovered,[55] suggesting the presence of an extra-urban temple in this area. In the centre of the pediment stood three standing deities, one male and two female. The dedication of the temple is possibly related to the victories the Romans achieved in 177 and 129 BCE against the Balkan peoples.

Equally significant are the remains of the ornamental parts of the city gates consisting of large clay elements. Among them are two large clay statues, each over 2 metres high, depicting telamons (Figure 3.6). These statues likely adorned the entrances during the republican period and are now exhibited in the museum.

CHAPTER 4
THE CITY AND ITS TERRITORY: THE CENTURIATIONS, THE AMPHORA CANAL AND THE ROADS

The Aquileia territory and its borders

As mentioned in chapter 3, the colony was provided with a large agricultural area, parcels of which were allocated to the new families that made up the new community. Each of the 300 families of foot soldiers was allocated about 12.5 hectares, the families of centurions 25 hectares and members of the cavalry as much as 35 hectares.[1] Many more thousands of hectares were allocated to the 1,500 colonists sent to resettle the colony in 169 BCE.

The large amount of the land available for the new colonists was partly due to Aquileia's geographical context. Behind the city stretched a wide and fertile plain whose distant physical boundaries were set by the base of the pre-Alpine foothills. At the time of its foundation, Aquileia was the only administrative centre allied to the Roman state in this area and therefore it could justly (as far as Rome was concerned) claim all the territory between the sea and the Alps.

Because of this, the city's territorial boundaries were very wide but, at the same time, difficult to define precisely. While it is certain that the whole plain from the sea to the base of the mountains to the north and east belonged to Aquileia, some recent discoveries show that the territory controlled by the city extended into the mountains and even reached as far as the Ljubljana area of Slovenia.

As time passed (from the mid-first century BCE), the emergence of new autonomous centres, such as *Tergeste* (Trieste), *Forum Iulii* (Cividale del Friuli), *Iulia Emona* (Ljubljana), *Iulium Carnicum* (Zuglio) and *Iulia Concordia* (Concordia Sagittaria), limited the extent of Aquileia's territory. In the Imperial Age the border was marked by the Tagliamento river, beyond which lay the agricultural land (*ager*) of *Iulia Concordia*, founded in 42 BCE. To the east its land extended as far as Aurisina in the direction of Trieste and as far as the base of the pre-Alpine foothills to the north. However, an inscription found about twenty years ago describes the 'borders between the Aquileians and the inhabitants of *Emona*' near the course of the Ljubljanica river, located between ancient *Nauportus* (Vrhnika)[2] and *Emona*. This shows us that at the height of the Roman period, the city's *ager* extended over areas far from its centre.

Thanks to its vast territorial assets Aquileia was able to avail itself of the important resources that the region offered. Firstly, the control of the plain guaranteed an exceptional agricultural production, which exceeded the needs of the city itself and generated wealth for Aquileia through the sale of its surplus. Furthermore, the possession of huge Alpine and pre-Alpine areas also gave the city access to the mountain resources, especially tall timber, which in ancient times was fundamental for building projects and shipbuilding. Finally, the direct management of a territory that extended beyond the Alpine watershed allowed Aquileia to control those important land routes, which will be discussed shortly, that connected the city and its river port to the regions of Central and Balkan Europe.

The Amphora Canal

Several needs had to be met in this vast territory in the years following the colony's foundation. The first was ensuring that the urban and suburban areas were healthy for human settlement.[3] Of key importance here was the state of the surface water on the plain. The areas immediately outside the city centre were the object of special attention, leading to the creation of one of the most important hydraulic structures known in antiquity[4] – the Amphora Canal.[5] This canal made a significant contribution to guaranteeing the healthiness of the lowland areas between the city and the coastal lagoons.

This Amphora Canal is famous amongst the hydraulic works of Roman northern Italy and was already known to studies from the twentieth century on and considered to be one of the most important engineering works of the Friulan lowlands. It connected the Upper Adriatic emporium directly with coastal lagoons, the Adriatic Sea and Ravenna. The canal (Figure 4.1) is still partly active today and studies by the Austrian Archaeological Institute prove that it began immediately to the west of the republican walls,[6] proceeding in a straight 6-kilometre line towards the Marano lagoon. Its artificial nature can be gleaned from various clues, not least by the way it seems to have regularized a natural watercourse and its use as a boundary for the cultivated *ager*; indeed, its course seems to coincide with one of the main axes of the Aquileia centuriation, as discussed below.

The canal had some very interesting technical features: a scholarly report of 1820 indicated that the Amphora Canal was distinguished from others in the area by its bed and sides being lined with large stone slabs. This characteristic, confirmed during a 1978 inspection at the western end of the canal,[7] not only facilitated the regular inflow/outflow of water but also the cleaning and maintenance of the canal bed, preventing it from progressively silting up. A more recent investigation ascertained that the bottom slabs were 5 to 6 centimetres thick and made of Istrian stone, which is particularly resistant to the effects of brackish water. Other sections of the canal were not lined, as shown by other excavations (in 1978 and 2004–5) conducted on the section east of the Terzo river. At this point the canal's banks and bed were carved out of the sterile clay. A further important technical aspect was the consolidation of the banks, using an alignment of circular or square cross-section wooden piles, driven into the clay to protect the banks from erosion.

The width of the canal varied along its route. Luisa Bertacchi observed that the canal gets gradually wider from the area closest to the city to the lagoons (16.4 metres, 25.4 metres, 30.4 metres and 40.4 metres).[8] Whilst the difference in width is quite evident from one end to the other, the depth remains substantially uniform, though there is a

Figure 4.1 Aquileia. Zenithal aerial view of the Amphora Canal.

modest slope along the whole route. Exchange of water between the lagoon and hinterland must have depended on the tidal pressure forcing the brackish water up to Aquileia's western suburbs.

On the other side, the outflow of surface water from the countryside was facilitated by the Amphora, which served as the main channel into which many of the north–south flowing secondary watercourses, including probably the Terzo, drained. Amongst these was the one crossed by the bridge discovered by G. B. Brusin that flanked the southern bank of the Amphora.[9] The fact that the Amphora Canal, flanked by a service road on the left bank, was used for transport is evidenced by the remains of one or two sewn boats found in it. Trade must have developed along the waterway, directed to a port which was probably found in Aquileia's western suburbs.

The date of the canal's construction has long been debated. Some scholars have suggested a first century BCE date, but others think that the ditch may date back to the second century BCE, built by one of the three magistrates of the second colonial reinforcement of 169 BCE (M. Cornelius Cethegus), who was active shortly after the reclamation of the Pontine marshes (160 BCE).[10] Recent excavations offer some faint clues to the canal's construction period. It started to be used as a dump for unwanted material, according to the customary use of waterways as dumps, at the end of the first century BCE, meaning that the work must have been completed by then. The canal remained in use until the Late Imperial period. The gradual silting up of at least part of the canal is likely to have occurred at the beginning of the fourth century CE and was completed by the middle of the same century (361 CE), when a new city wall appears to have been built, whose construction over the old canal shows that it was, by then, closed.

The centuriations and the agrarian organization

While the Amphora Canal guaranteed excellent water drainage and an efficient transport system for the areas immediately outside the city, it was still necessary to provide for the areas further away from the centre. Therefore, the citizens and governing bodies planned reclamation works on a larger scale, aimed at improving the healthiness of the vast territory as well as its productive capacity through the cultivation of crops needed to sustain the population and livestock.

The cities of the Mediterranean world had been addressing the issue of how to organize the countryside since the Greek era and even from the fifth and fourth centuries there are documented plans to subdivide the land through roads and canals. As a whole, these works ensured optimal water management, agricultural production, wild livestock management and road communication.

The Roman world developed increasingly refined systems to achieve these conditions through the practice known as 'centuriation' (*centuriatio*). This entailed dividing land areas by plots of land called *heredia*, of approximately 0.5 hectares, that were allocated to individual settlers and grouped into larger units of 100 *heredia* called *centuriae*. The *centuriae* corresponded to squares with a side length of 710.4 metres and a surface area of approximately 50 hectares. This organization of the land – which could also have different shapes and patterns from the one described – was carried out by a body of specialist technicians called *Agrimensores* or *Gromatici*, who have left us with a series of very important treatises which can help us reconstruct the methods and procedures of Roman land management.

Thanks to these technical accomplishments, a widespread and regular organization of the agricultural spaces was also carried out in Aquileia. The city's centuriations have been the subject of many studies and various reconstructions,[11] sometimes turning out to be quite complex, since the land divisions have not always remained clearly visible. The Friulian plains have been transformed over the centuries by both natural (floods and river outflows) and human (urbanization and infrastructure projects) causes, which have partially cancelled the ancient traces. Despite this, some reconstructions are possible.

Traces of lines which may represent ancient roads and ditches have been noted above the spring line, where the impact of the watercourses is less strong. Maps of the area around Gradisca di Sedegliano near the Tagliamento river show the recurring presence of stretches of country roads, ditches and modern agricultural boundaries that may follow ancient divisions.[12]

This farming landscape of the upland plains has also been crucial in uncovering signs of the past in the southern areas. Scholars have identified a possible extension of the Aquileia centuriation, known as 'Classical', towards the sea. The *centuria* square is defined by the intersection of its perpendicular and parallel axes, forming squares with sides of 710.4 metres, as noted. A series of axes are oriented NW 22.3°, exactly the same as those in the city that subdivided the urban area, as described in the previous chapter. This alignment appears to be significant and not coincidental.

In fact, it seems that the surveyors (*agrimensores*) wanted to construct a physical and symbolic relationship between the city and its territory, giving the same orientation to both the city roads and the farmland divisions. The *kardo maximus*, that is, the north–south axis, continued along the centuriation, thereby connecting and simplifying all urban and extra-urban road systems. However, it is not easy to identify the centuriation's second axis, the *decumanus maximus*, at right angles to the *kardo*. According to a recent suggestion,[13] this axis might be revealed by an important public road (Via Annia), discussed below. If this is indeed the case, the junction of the *kardo* and *decumanus maximus* would have been at the present-day locality of Strassoldo.

The Amphora Canal was an essential part of the farmland division. It functioned as a large ditch and served as one of the main axes dividing the farming plots. This so-called 'Classical' centuriation covered a vast area, with major axes extending about 40 to 50 kilometres in both directions. While the extensive network of roads and ditches is well documented, other parts of the territory might have been organized using smaller divisions and different methods. For instance, some scholars have identified possible farmland divisions of 20 × 24 *actus* (710.4 × 852.4 metres) in the middle and upper Friulian plains, between Tricesimo and Udine. However, there is currently limited evidence to support these findings, and they have been set aside for future research.

The villas

Outside the colony itself the territory was progressively marked by a series of settlements and single buildings.[14] Our knowledge of these is incomplete, since most of the remains of the ancient settlements have been lost. Yet, some information can be gleaned from the archaeological excavations that have been conducted at various points of the territory and from surveys carried out looking for ancient settlements and their material remains. Written texts can also provide us with some useful information on the secondary settlements in the territory. For the first century BCE, written texts inform us that there were two small *vici* (small rural settlements) near Aquileia: Vrhnika (ancient *Nauportus*)[15] and Zuglio (*Iulium Carnicum*).[16]

Other archaeological data suggest that there were other settlements in the rest of the Alpine, pre-Alpine and lowland areas. For example, recent studies have revealed a human presence in the areas of modern Codroipo, Palazzolo dello Stella,[17] San Canzian d'Isonzo and San Giovanni di Duino.

As far as isolated structures are concerned, there were two types of buildings that differed in size, shape and function. The first was what the ancients called a villa: a complex and economically active settlement used both as a residence and a productive estate which managed the surrounding farmland. Small craft industries often sprang up around such constructions, producing specific products such as baked clay bricks for building (roof tiles, shingles and bricks). An interesting piece of evidence is the wreck found in the Stella river, near Precenicco. It was carrying a cargo of tiles and roof tiles to be transported from an unknown production point on the plain to Aquileia and from there to cities on the Adriatic coast to meet the needs of the many first-century CE construction sites. The second type of building was like a modern farm, housing a single family managing a self-sufficient agricultural smallholding.

Isolated settlements can be found throughout the whole of Aquileia's territory, between the upland plains and the lagoons from the Tagliamento to the Timavo, as far as the easternmost border of Aurisina's *ager*.

There is no evidence of villas being built at the time of the colony's foundation, as in those early uncertain times, occupying the surrounding countryside must have been a challenging undertaking. The first evidence of villas appears towards the end of the second century BCE, and an interesting case is the settlement on the lower plain near Planais in Carlino (Udine), about 10 kilometres west of Aquileia. Near the Via Annia a number of walls have emerged beneath the later villa which can be dated to the second and first centuries BCE. Other finds attesting occupation from the end of the second century BCE have also come to light between the upper and middle plains, in Pradamano (Udine). Here, an early ironworking plant has been documented. Its favourable position along the road to *Noricum* (the main source of ore) ensured its involvement in trade between Aquileia and *Noricum*, already underway by the second century BCE.

From the end of the first century BCE onwards, the *villa urbana et rustica* began to appear, often built near simpler rural buildings. At a building in the Planais locality, just a few rooms facing a courtyard have been excavated; one of them, of considerable size (9 × 4 metres), opened with a threshold onto a garden with trees or with a pergola which was embellished with a semicircular structure interpreted as a monumental fountain; another room had an underfloor heating system. Although this villa primarily had an economic function, it was already equipped with prestigious architectural features, with the use of imported stone testifying to the high social status of the owner.

A large settlement at Pavia in Udine, a few kilometres north of Aquileia, has been extensively investigated. This villa is on the direct route to *Noricum* and along the ancient course of the Torre river. It comprises several units separated by open areas, with a main building for residential and farming use, facilities for the production of bricks and an ironworking workshop. The extensive excavations have allowed us to picture the layout of the main building, which was constructed on a raised area: it was centred on a vast courtyard (40 × 29 metres), porticoed on three sides and open towards the west, to ensure the optimal exposure of the building and adapt it to the terrain. Behind the northern portico were a few simple living quarters, one of which was paved with black and white mosaics and one with large terracotta tiles formed by cut roof tiles. On the eastern side was the farming sector. The numerous bronze and iron artefacts (agricultural tools, a bronze cup handle decorated with bird heads) attest to the villa's involvement in commerce between Aquileia and *Noricum*.

A significant concentration of villas from the second half of the first century BCE has been found in the area known as *Lacus Timavi*, between Monfalcone and Duino and about ten miles east of Aquileia.[18] This basin was separated from the sea by coastal strips and islands (the *Insulae Clarae*) and fed by a secondary branch of the Soča/Isonzo river and the *Timavus*. This watery territory and the slopes of the Karst behind it offered both beautiful scenery and multiple economic opportunities, due to the variety of local resources (wine, wool, fish) celebrated by the ancient authors. Of the dozen or so villas investigated in the recent past, near the inner bank of the basin and on the first of the *Insulae Clarae*, it is mainly the residential sectors that have been brought to light, marked by high quality workmanship, such as marbled mosaic floors. Besides providing residential accommodation, they also had economic functions, as shown by the presence of production facilities, centred on fishing, and probably also a *fundus* for wine and oil production.

Investigations carried out between 1970 and 1973 on the villa della Punta by L. Bertacchi, or more recently on the villas of the Mandrie and via Colombo, provide us with a general idea of the complexities of these compounds: they were never very large (1,000–1,500 metres squared) and basically built on a geometric plan, sometimes on terraces sloping down to the basin and centred on an open area. The same care was taken in the construction of the residential sector of the Staranzano and Ronchi dei Legionari villas, both located behind the *Lacus Timavi*.

For the Roman Imperial Age (first–fourth centuries CE), the best documented centres are the villas of Joannis and Vidùlis. The former, just ten miles north of Aquileia, was part of the centuriation network. The investigated sector extended for at least 70 metres in a north-west–south-east direction and opened towards the west onto a cobbled courtyard. This wing of the villa included a residential sector to the north and a farming sector to the south, dedicated to wine production.

In contrast, the large urban-rustic villa of Vidùlis[19] stood on the north-western periphery of the Aquileian countryside, where traces of another possible agrarian division have been identified. Despite its marginal position (it was over forty miles from Aquileia as the crow flies), the straight road from Concordia to *Noricum* and the nearby Tagliamento river ensured that the settlement had easy connections with other urban centres. Over 1,700 square metres (70 × 23 metres) of the villa have been investigated, which comprised two centres around an open area, interpreted as a courtyard. It is likely that the western sector housed the *pars urbana* and the eastern the *pars rustica*. The fact that this landscape was not very suitable for agriculture and has always been used for livestock suggests that the main economic role of this large villa was sheep breeding, the processing of wool and textile manufacture.

Settlement patterns continued to be scattered between the second and third centuries, with villas mainly distributed along rivers and especially along the important road routes (to Trieste, *Emona*, *Noricum* and Concordia) and with a greater density between the lowlands and the coastal strip. Overall, the villas transformed or maintained their production facilities while the residential areas were reduced,[20] phenomena that indicated a continuity of use, but also possible changes in the way they were managed, now perhaps functioniong as part of larger estates or even imperial property. A certain economic decline can be noted. In the *Lacus Timavi* area most villas seem to have already been abandoned in the third century CE, perhaps due to environmental changes. An interesting fact is that most of the villas renovated between the second and third centuries CE survive until the fourth century. Aquileia's strategic role as a north Italian defensive bulwark, with numerous troops stationed in the area and the nearby *claustra Alpium* defence system, clearly had a positive impact from an economic-productive point of view, giving a new stimulus to the economy. An emblematic case is that of the Carlino villa (Chiamana), where a brick production kiln, active since the first century BCE, was industrialized in the fourth with the creation of three new kilns and ancillary structures to produce glazed pottery, intended to meet the needs of the troops stationed in the area. Similarly, Vidùlis kept its production area active and even expanded the residential sector in the Constantinian Age (fourth century CE), with the construction of monumental baths.

It was only after the critical political and military events that followed at the turn of the fourth and fifth centuries CE, and the consequent economic and demographic crisis, that the area was generally abandoned, with moves probably first towards the city and then towards the safer coastal areas. The few surviving villas are concentrated mainly in the southern area.[21]

It should be remembered that the villas frequently had their own burial grounds, which we must assume were connected to the small farmsteads or villas described above and distributed throughout the territory. Small cemeteries of this type have been excavated in Basaldella, Pozzuolo del Friuli, Codroipo and Castions di Strada.[22]

The roads

Roads had a paramount strategic military and commercial importance, both in terms of Rome's expansionist policy towards all conquered regions and of the life of the colony itself. This is shown by the fact that one of the first operations that the Roman government undertook in northern Italy and Aquileia in the second century BCE was the construction of an extensive road system (Figure 4.2).

Two major roads reached Aquileia from the west: the Via Annia and the Via Postumia. These great thoroughfares were laid out by Roman engineers and legions to connect Rome and the Po Valley with the colony at the republic's easternmost point. Along these roads, people, goods and armies could be transported to this remote corner of Italy. The great novelty was their design. They ran in straight lines, touching all the major centres of the territory along the route that provided the fastest communication. Most important was

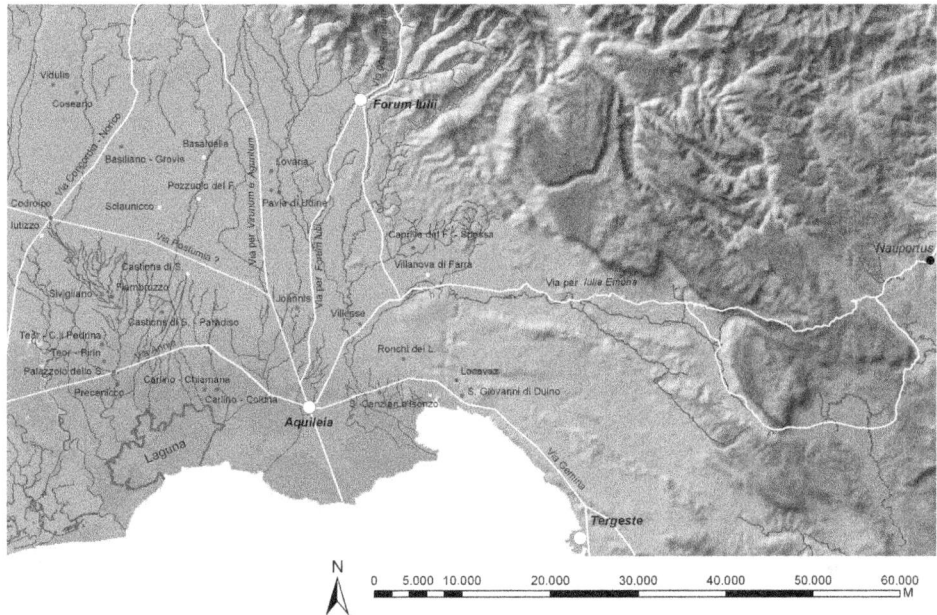

Figure 4.2 Aquileia. Map of roads connecting the city and the nearby regions (D. Riccobono).

the technological innovations that they brought. These great roads were built with enormous effort and equipped with drainage systems, gravel coverings, lateral ditches and bridges over watercourses, so they could be used for most of the year. Compared to the pre-Roman period, when the territory was criss-crossed by impractical earthen tracks, the plain and Aquileia were now endowed with a valuable infrastructure. This is why a rich body of literature has developed on this subject, making these roads, that entered the Aquileia territory from the west over the Tagliamento river, very well known.[23]

The Via Annia

The Via Annia[24] takes its name from its builder, who, at different times, has been recognized as the 153 BCE consul Titus Annius Luscus, the 131 BCE praetor Titus Annius Rufus, or the 128 consul BCE, namesake of the 153 BCE magistrate. The most recent studies[25] and the discovery of a stone column near Ferrara, which contains some important information concerning the route, leads us to believe that the first of these was the builder and that the construction of the road took place in 153 BCE. The discovery of the column has allowed us to reconstruct a route that started in Rome and finished in Aquileia. The fact that it was decided to create a direct route linking the capital with the colony so soon after its foundation indicates the enormous importance that Rome attached to Aquileia.

Recent excavations along the road show that it reused an older pre-existing route,[26] illustrating how Rome's government was conscious of the already existing infrastructure system where it was present.

The road came from *Patavium* (Padua), the most important centre in the Po Valley. Beyond *Patavium* the Via Annia reached Altino, on the edge of the Venice lagoon and then *Iulia Concordia*. After crossing the Tagliamento river it entered the areas directly owned by the colony. More precisely, it passed through the villages of Chiarisacco and Palazzolo dello Stella, following the direction of today's main road 14, along a route on which there are many milestones. It then passed near Torviscosa and reached the *Alsa* (Aussa) river, which it crossed by means of what is known locally as the 'Orlando' bridge, and continued onto the interestingly named San Martino di Terzo, which lies at the three miles (4.5 kilometres) from Aquileia. The road entered the latter from the north-west through a gate in the western section of the walls (Figure 0.1, n. 1.2).

The most recent excavations carried out along these stretches of the road, from Altino to Aquileia, have shown that it ran close to the shoreline[27] in a not perfectly straight line due to having to adapt to the geography and particularly to the slight bumps in the ground. The roadway was made of beaten gravel placed on top of a low earth embankment. It had two wide ditches on either side (Figure 4.3). Recent research has shown that there

Figure 4.3 Aquileia. Zenithal aerial view of the Via Annia in the countryside east of the city (P. Maggi, F. Oriolo).

were also different types and sizes of bridges that allowed the Via Annia to cross the various rivers and streams flowing down to the coastline at any time of year.

The road remained in use into Late Antiquity and beyond, as demonstrated by the fact that the road between *Patavium* and Aquileia is mentioned in the Antonine Itinerary, the Bordeaux Itinerary and the Peutinger Table (*Tabula Peutingeriana*), which are the most important documents describing the ancient road system, written in the fourth century BCE. In particular, the Antonine Itinerary mentions the section of road as part of the description of a route connecting Bologna and Aquileia.

However, during the Imperial Age the road experienced a series of disruptions and problems due to the changes in the layout of the land. Some texts document that between *Iulia Concordia* and Aquileia the road was damaged by lagoon-water floods, which necessitated some restoration work in the third and fourth centuries CE. This work was commemorated in several columns placed along the route. In this phase of Aquileia's history, the road must still have been used frequently because it was the gateway to Italy for the legions fighting in the turbulent Balkan provinces.

It was only from the fifth or sixth centuries, particularly after the Lombards entered Italy, that the road lost its strategic and economic importance. Along with the decline of the urban and road systems in eastern *Venetia*, the Via Annia fell into disuse, surviving for a few more centuries as a secondary route.

The Via Postumia

The second major thoroughfare that passed through the territory was named after its builder, the 148 BCE consul, Spurius Postumius Albinus, who is remembered by an important inscription originally placed along the road and preserved in the Maffeiano Museum in Verona.[28]

This road was built for strategic and military purposes: to control the entire Po Valley and connect the Tyrrhenian and Adriatic coasts. Its starting and finishing points were Genoa and Aquileia respectively. It immediately became the main east-to-west connection route and was of considerable importance for the Romanization of, and the historical events affecting, northern Italy. Thus, for example, a bronze tablet found in 1506 in Liguria (*Tavola di Polcevera*) reports the settlement of border disputes (117 BCE), citing the Via Postumia as the dividing line between landed estates. And again in 69 CE, the historian Tacitus[29] describes the battles for control of the imperial seat, mentioning the Via Postumia several times as an important hub for strategic movements in the Cremona area.

The road reached the territory of Aquileia from the west, constantly maintaining a route along the upper part of the plain, very close to the pre-Alpine foothills. After leaving Vicenza, the Via Postumia took a northeasterly direction along the foothills and then continued eastwards with some very long straight stretches that are still recognizable in today's roads. The Roman engineers decided on this route for reasons of stability, as it allowed the road to run along the part of the plain north of the spring line. This is a strip of land only a few kilometres wide, along which groundwater resurfaces and gives rise to boggy springs or rivers that then flow down to the lower plain. The route of the Via Postumia avoided these wetlands and their related watercourses. For greater safety, the road ran along an embankment that was slightly elevated above the plain to guarantee travellers good visibility and complete safety from possible flooding.

Before reaching Aquileia's territory, the road passed through the centre of Oderzo and crossed the Tagliamento river at Codroipo;[30] from here it headed along the S.S. 252 (*Stradalta*) towards Aquileia and entered the centuriation at Sevegliano. Finally, it reached the town from the north, entering the urban area through the northern gate (Figure 0.1, n. 1.1).[31]

Shortly before entering the city, or just after passing through this gate, a sort of road junction branched off from the Via Postumia, providing direct access to one of the colony's most important mercantile areas. A second-century inscription (Figure 4.4), now preserved at the National Archaeological Museum in Aquileia, records the presence of a road outside or inside the walls that allowed direct access to the city's *forum pecuarium*: that is, the market area for small livestock.[32] This is an important piece of evidence attesting to how carefully the road system was planned between the territory and the city. In fact, we learn that the Via Postumia was used to transfer cattle coming from the countryside of Aquileia towards the city, but from this document we also understand that special road sections were built to make the herds converge towards the market, avoiding city spaces intended for other functions.

Over the centuries, as the settlement and economic framework changed, the Via Postumia lost its importance, surviving only in the sections that were incorporated into a new system, in which the Milan–Aquileia route came to play a crucial role.

The road towards Illyria and Pannonia (Slovenia, Croatia, Hungary)

Besides the Via Annia and the Via Postumia, the territory of Aquileia was crossed by other important roads that led towards the Alpine and transalpine regions, both in the direction of Central Europe and the Balkans.[33]

One road was called the Via Gemina. The name is mentioned in two inscribed texts datable between 235 and 238 CE (reign of Maximinus Thrax).[34] This road must have played a very important role since it started from Aquileia and headed towards the extreme eastern edge of Italy where the city of Trieste is located. The Via Gemina exited the eastern gate of the city walls and after a few kilometres reached the present-day town of Monfalcone. The Peutinger Table indicates that there was a rest station near here, where the road ended. This station was located 12 miles (about 15 kilometres) from Aquileia and called *Fons Timavi*. At this point, the emergence of groundwater had created a lake area which was very popular in ancient times. The Timavo river rose here and after a short distance flowed into the sea. After crossing the Timavo, the Via Gemina reached Trieste and from here continued along two different routes towards Istria and the towns of Pula and Rijeka.

The two epigraphic texts which mention the road were found just outside the eastern side of the walls (near the site of the old Benedictine monastery – Monastero

Figure 4.4 Aquileia. Inscription of the road derived from the Via Postumia (© O. Harl).

neighbourhood) and are particularly important because they mention the emperor's order to reconstruct the road between Aquileia and the bridge over the Timavo. This shows how important the Via Gemina was even in the full and Late Imperial Age when the situation in the eastern and Balkan provinces was becoming particularly problematic, for both the history of Aquileia and in general the Roman Empire. Indeed, Emperor

Maximinus Thrax, who ordered the reconstruction of the road from Aquileia to the Balkans, came from the eastern provinces.

Unlike the routes mentioned so far, we do not know the name of the road that crossed Aquileia's territory in the direction of the eastern Alpine passes and the regions called Pannonia in ancient times (Slovenia and Hungary).

This road is implicitly referred to by the geographer Strabo[35] when he speaks of transporting goods by wagon from Aquileia to *Nauportus*, across the Karst; and it seems to have been described by the historian Tacitus[36] when he says that in 14 CE soldiers of the Pannonian army were sent to build roads and bridges along this route.

The Via Gemina was an important communication route between Aquileia and the Baltic countries bound by the Sava and the lower Danube. It retraced a prehistoric and protohistoric track used in the long-distance amber trade. The Roman section was probably built between the beginning of the first century BCE and the Augustan period, when it was given definite form following Octavian's military campaigns in Pannonia (35–33 BCE).

The route of the road out of Aquileia can be reconstructed through the remains of the burial areas that lined it in the countryside starting from the Monastero area. The route is still traced by the modern provincial road, which over time acquired the epithet via 'Pedrata', due to the presence of the ancient Roman cobblestones. It then continued towards the modern Gradisca d'Isonzo, where the cobblestones of the paved road were still preserved in the 1930s. Located here was the horse-changing station *ad Undecimum*, as named in the Bordeaux Itinerary. At Mainizza, where the road reached the Soča river, the remains of thermal baths have been found. The road crossed the river over a large bridge near the settlement, the remains of which can been seen during droughts. This bridge was destroyed by the Aquileians in order to halt the advance of Emperor Maximinus Thrax (235–8 CE), and they only rebuilt it later.[37] After crossing the Soča river, the Roman road continued for a long stretch along the left bank of the Vipava river to present-day Ajdovščina. At Mernala, the road entered today's Slovenian territory, before reaching the *Fluvio Frigido* rest stop (today's Hubelj river). After that it crossed the ridge of the Julian Alps by two routes: one through the Piro Pass (the rest stop called *ad Pirum summas Alpes*), the other by a longer route through the easier Predil Pass. From here the road entered Pannonia and then ended in Ljubljana (*Iulia Emona*).

The Via Gemina was, therefore, an extraordinary corridor between the Adriatic Sea, its Aquileia port and the rich regions of eastern Europe.

The roads to Raetia and Noricum (Austria)

Other routes left Aquileia and headed north and to the transalpine regions.[38] Although the names of these roads are lost, their routes are known well enough. The main stages of one of these were recorded in the Antonine Itinerary, which also clearly indicates that the end point was Veldidena (modern day Wilten), near Innsbruck. This road was the route to *Raetia* from Aquileia and, according to scholars, was constructed permanently at the beginning of the first century CE over a track that had crossinged the Plöcken Pass to the Hallstatt region since protohistoric times.

Three still partially legible stone inscriptions were found at this pass which provide information on the conditions under which the road was passable and on the maintenance undertaken by its keepers between the second and fourth centuries CE.

From Aquileia the road passed through Terzo (a toponym indicating the distance from the start) and Sevegliano, before arriving at the eastern outskirts of Udine. Then it reached the first stage mentioned in the ancient Itineraries, *Tricesimum* (modern Tricesimo), which lay 30 miles from Aquileia.

Tricesimo was an important hub for traffic heading north, as confirmed by an epigraph recording the construction of a defensive wall with access gates (*portas/muros*), erected to guard the road at the rest station.

Beyond Tricesimo, the road passed through Artegna, where the Roman paving stones can still be seen. Here, it must have met with a road coming from *Iulia Concordia*, heading for the *Noricum* region (Austria).

The road then reached Gemona (ancient *castrum Glemona*) and proceeded to the present-day station for Carnia. From this point the road divided: eastwards a branch led to the Alpine pass of Tarvisio and then into *Noricum* territory, where it passed through gold- and iron metal-rich regions; westwards, a second branch reached today's Tolmezzo, then entered the Bût river valley and climbed northwards to the important town of *Iulium Carnicum*, modern Zuglio. From here on, following a series of narrow and steep hairpin bends, it led up the mountain slope to the 1,360-metre-high Plöckenpass before entering the Roman province of *Noricum*. After this it continued to Lienz, Toblach, Fortezza, the Brenner Pass and the end point, Wilten.

These roads ensured that Aquileia looked out towards the regions of continental Europe and their natural and political resources.

CHAPTER 5
AQUILEIA IN THE IMPERIAL AGE:
PUBLIC ARCHITECTURE AND TRADES

Aquileia in the Early Imperial Age

The famous naval battle of Actium (31 BCE), where Octavian's fleet led by the loyal Agrippa defeated that of Mark Antony and Cleopatra, brought an end to a long period of civil war and laid the foundations for the birth of the Roman Empire.[1] A few years later, in 27 BCE, the Senate conferred the title of Augustus on Octavian, who thus became the first Roman emperor. He managed to establish a long period of peace and prosperity, but this was only possible after a series of demanding military campaigns. These included the Pannonian War, during which Aquileia served as a logistical base for military operations conducted by Tiberius between 12 and 9 BCE.[2] It was in Aquileia, in 11 BCE, that the latter had a stillborn son by his wife Julia, daughter of Augustus. Augustus himself, who had probably already stopped in Aquileia during his military campaigns in the Illyrian regions (35–33 BCE), certainly stayed there in those years, as in 10 BCE he received Herod, king of Judea, who joined him with his sons. The imperial family's residence is generally identified as a magnificent suburban villa, located south of the river *Natiso cum Turro* (*Fondo Tuzet*; Figure 0.1, n. 22).

The Augustan Age (27 BCE–14 CE) in Aquileia, which in the meantime had lost its status of *municipium* to acquire the title of *colonia* (while retaining its previous rights and institutions), was marked by the beginning of a process of architectural renovation,[3] which lasted throughout the whole Julio-Claudian phase (27 BCE–68 CE). This process of monumentalization was also taking place in the same period in many cities of Roman Italy, which were adapting their monumental structures and urban decor to the bright prospects of the new political path. This was especially the case for Aquileia, which could boast solid ties with both Rome itself and imperial power. Indeed, even in the absence of clear epigraphic evidence, it is likely that Augustus and Tiberius were, to some extent, decisive in giving impetus to Aquileia's urban renewal.

The forum[4] was the focus of these building works (Figures 0.1, n. 4; 5.1). It was paved throughout and provided with raised side porticos, behind which, on the long sides, were placed two rows of shops (these are better known on the eastern side). Despite some quite convincing suggestions, the exact location of the sacred buildings is still unknown. Beneath the paving of the square, and longitudinal to it, was a culvert belonging to the aqueduct.[5] At the time that the slabs were laid, a particular republican installation had already been removed: this was a series of small pits placed at the sides of the square and used to define the space organized for electoral meetings. Their abandonment is a clear indication of the loss of autonomy by the local communities in the interests of an

Figure 5.1 Aquileia. View of the forum (© Guido/Adobe Stock).

imperial policy that was increasingly invasive in every aspect of public life. The same applies to the defunctionalization of the *Comitium* on the northern side, symbol of the now obsolete republican colonial institutions, on whose remains a new structure with an uncertain function was built.

In contrast, the civil basilica was a fully functional type of building (Figure 0.1, n. 16), which, already at the outset of the Augustan Age, stood on the short side of the forum, preventing access from this side. The construction of the basilica had a twofold effect: on the one hand, it contributed to updating the facilities and functionality of the city's main public complex, and on the other, it interrupted the transit through the square in a southerly direction, along the city's main road axis. The forum, well delimited by the lateral porticos, was thus in the process of being transformed into an increasingly exclusive monumental space, destined for political and administrative functions, ceremonies, the custody of the city's historical memories and the celebration of imperial ideology. Instead, vehicular traffic and trade tended to be directed elsewhere, for instance to the large building that replaced the republican food market (*macellum*),[6] north of the forum.

The *praefectus fabrum* Caius Aratrius,[7] a member of an important brick-producing Aquileian family, was involved in some of the basilica's building works and other structures in the vicinity. His intervention is recorded on an inscription.[8] The state of preservation of this inscription does not allow us to establish whether it was an initiative carried out as a magistrate or an episode of private munificence (euergetism), in this case offering a public work to the town community at one's own expense. Aratria Galla, daughter of Caius, belonged to the same family of wealthy entrepreneurs. In her will she left a bequest of money for the paving of a city street adjacent to the forum (Figure 0.1, n. 11). The event is recorded in two inscriptions dated to the first decades of the first century,[9] which present several points of interest. Firstly, an act of euergetism is reliably recorded, this time by a woman, probably continuing the work of her father. It is also noteworthy that, as in other cities of the same period, some of Aquileia's streets were being paved, making them more decorous (and less dusty). Finally, we should highlight the use of the Latin term *decumanus* to describe the street affected by the works, corresponding to an east–west oriented city street. This term is generally used when talking about the territory outside a town, in relation to the centuriations, while it is very rare in the urban context. The Aquileian case seems to be due to the fact that the layout and orientation of the urban sector was fully in line with that of the agricultural land surrounding the city.

Returning to the forum, a series of plinths decorated on the front with individual heads of Jupiter Ammon and Medusa can be dated to the end of Claudius' principate (41–54),[10] just after the middle of the first century. They were arranged, in an alternating pattern, between the slabs of the plutei in the attic of the forum porticos; only those belonging to the western portico are preserved today. This figurative scheme is often found in the forums of the Adriatic, northern and eastern areas, inspired at least in part by the decoration of the attic of the side porticos of the forum of Augustus in Rome. Complementary to each other, the two images symbolically evoked the universal power of Rome, in the space of a forum increasingly focused on the exaltation of imperial ideology.

It should also be remembered that several statues and official portraits, all unfortunately decontextualized, of various members of the Julio-Claudian family come from Aquileia. In particular, these sculptures (Figure 10.2) include a togated *velato capite* (with veiled head) statue depicting the *Genius Augusti*, variously dated to between the Tiberian and Claudian ages; a headless female statue, possibly identifiable with Antonia Minor (Claudius' mother), dating to the Tiberian or Claudian ages; and a statue dressed up in military costume, datable no earlier than the Trajan era, into which an older head of Claudius was inserted, itself probably reworked from a portrait of Caligula.[11] It is possible that these three statues originally belonged to a celebratory cycle from the Julio-Claudian period, perhaps placed in a space dedicated to the imperial cult.

Beyond the walls: the river port and the first entertainment buildings

Aquileia achieved a leading economic role at the start of the Imperial Age,[12] taking full advantage of the extraordinary mercantile potential offered by its geographical position, straddling both the Mediterranean basin and the transalpine regions. After almost two centuries when the city had distinguished itself for the strategic role it had played in politico-military terms, it then consolidated its position as a commercial hub, encouraged by the establishment of a stable period of peace. Clear proof of this is provided by the very frequent archaeological evidence of the production, importation, consumption and redistribution of all kinds of raw and processed materials, foodstuffs and artefacts. The situation is well described in a passage by the geographer Strabo:

> Aquileia, then, which is the nearest to the inlet of the Adriatic, ... serves as an emporium for those Illyrian peoples who live along the Danube: they come to take products from the sea, wine, which they put in wooden barrels loaded onto wagons, and also oil, while the people of the area come to buy slaves, livestock and skins.[13]

To maximize the efficiency of the commercial activities, at the end of the first century or in the first decades of the following century, the large port facility along the navigable course of the *Natiso cum Turro* was expanded (Figures 0.1, n. 14; 5.2)[14] in the small space between the western bank of the river and the mid-sections of the eastern republican city walls. The river port was equipped with riverbank structures; quays with mooring holes organized on two different levels; a dense sequence of warehouses behind, extending for a total length of about 300 metres; as well as the necessary connecting ramps to the urban road system. This was probably Aquileia's main harbour complex, integrated with other structures on the eastern bank and along the following stretch of river, connecting the city with other coastal ports. However, there were also other landing places along the navigable waterways that surrounded the urban centre to the north and west, in turn communicating with the Amphora Canal, linked to the present-day Marano lagoon. It was therefore a highly developed port system, based on an extensive infrastructure.

Figure 5.2 Aquileia. Aerial view of the river port and the modern Via Sacra; in the background is the Christian basilica (© N. Oleotto).

To make space for the large river port, it was necessary to demolish several structures that had previously stood just outside the walls. This is not surprising, as already during the first century BCE the republican city walls (Figure 0.1, n. 1), while maintaining their defensive function, had begun to be a physical impediment to the natural needs of a rapidly expanding city such as Aquileia.[15] This phenomenon, common in Roman Italian cities, increased notably with the start of the long period of peace and prosperity guaranteed by Augustus' policy. On the one hand, this gave a very strong impulse to urban development, and on the other it made it superfluous to maintain obsolete defensive works around the built-up area, which consequently began to be at least partially dismantled, or at least surpassed, as a result of the urban expansion. An exception was the city gates, which were often maintained and restructured as a 'visiting card' to the city centre for those who entered it from the outside, sometimes loading them with propagandistic references to imperial politics (think, for example, of Augustus' Arch in Rimini).

Thus, at least formally, the memory of the ancient city walls was preserved, although their functionality was often compromised, in violation of those principles that wanted them to be both unassailable by enemies and inviolate and impassable by building works. Moreover, the development of commercial traffic had led to such sharp economic and demographic growth within Aquileia that repercussions were quickly felt in terms of both private construction and the urban layout itself. The bypassing and at least partial defunctioning of the republican walls are especially evident in the vast southern and south-western suburban sector, where a large strip of land was available for potential building development without being constrained by nearby watercourses. The city was thus able to expand by implementing an urban plan consistent with the orientation, road system and general layout of the inner wall area. In the southern sector, between the walls and the river, a predominantly residential quarter developed. In the south-western sector, on the other hand, a vast area was created for public use. This 'entertainment district'[16] extended between the *Natiso cum Turro* to the south and the initial stretch of the Amphora Canal to the north. Although different in terms of their use, the two sectors shared the unusually long new strip of southern city blocks, perhaps in anticipation of the future construction of the amphitheatre. This would seem to indicate that this vast extra-urban activity was part of a single urban plan, implemented over several decades.

The theatre[17] (Figure 0.1, n. 9) was the first large building erected in the 'entertainment district', just outside the walls and not far from the forum. It was built in the second half of the first century BCE or, at the latest, within the first two decades of the following century, most probably in the Augustan Age. In this period, theatrical architecture began to enjoy great popularity with the powers and city elites, who saw in it an excellent vehicle for imperial propaganda, carried out through the installation of sequences of statues and inscribed dedications. Similarly, theatre performances offered an opportunity to exercise a form of control, in that seats were divided, by law, according to the spectators' social order. The location of Aquileia's theatre was carefully chosen, since it was built in a prestigious urban context in the immediate vicinity of the forum, almost in the centre of the town, without having to touch an already built-up area, which would have entailed higher costs and probable expropriations that were as onerous as they were unpopular. Size-wise, it is an imposing building, with a diameter of approximately 95 metres, which is similar to the largest Roman theatres in the Veneto-Istrian region (*decima regio*). Located in a totally flat area, the cavea (the curvilinear sector with the tiers of seats for spectators) rested on vaulted, internally hollow, substructures, supported by a regular pattern of radial walls. In the centre was the semicircular space for the orchestra, over which the front wall of the *pulpitum* faced, punctuated by a series of decorative niches. Behind the stage was a high and massive *scaenae frons* wall, probably decorated with statues, in the centre of which was a wide semicircular exedra, framing the doorway through which the leading actors entered the stage (*valva regia*). The two main entrances to the theatre (*aditus maximi*) faced north, towards the continuation of the Decumanus of Aratria Galla, and south, on the opposite side.

Further south, shortly after the middle of the first century and probably still in the Claudian period (41–54), the monumental bulk of the theatre was flanked by that of the amphitheatre (Figures 0.1, n. 10; 5.3).[18] This was a large, elliptical building (148 × 112 metres) with a north–south orientation, which in the *decima regio* was second in size only to the famous Verona Arena. Like the theatre, it was built on hollow substructures supported by radial walls. The cavea was delimited at the base by a high podium that separated it from the central area of the arena, on whose sand-covered surface gladiator fights (*munera*) and wild animal hunts (*venationes*) took place. The peripheral location of the amphitheatre, at the south-western limits of the settlement, did not equate to a marginality of its functions. In fact, the amphitheatre was often built on the outskirts of the city for several practical reasons. First, constructing such a large structure required a vast plot of land, ideally well-connected by main roads and free of obstacles. Second,

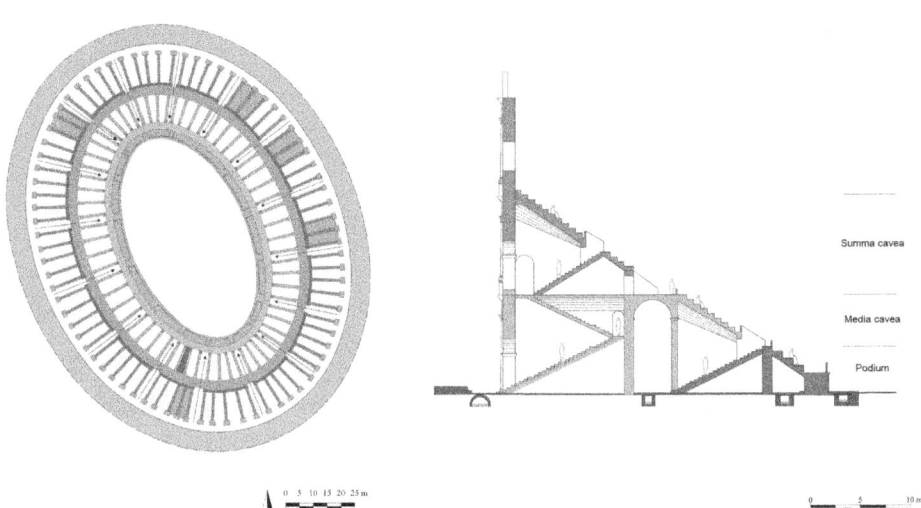

Figure 5.3 Aquileia. Reconstructive plan and section of the Roman amphitheatre (P. Basso, V. Grazioli and F. Soriano, Università di Verona).

given the popularity of amphitheatre events, it needed to accommodate large crowds quickly, drawing people from the city, countryside and neighbouring towns. Lastly, due to the intense and sometimes violent nature of the games, it was important to manage the excited spectators and maintain public order. The amphitheatre's peripheral location, visible to those arriving in Aquileia by water from the south-west, allowed for easy access, efficient crowd management and better maintenance of public order.

On the other hand, it is still unclear whether, in this period, there were other entertainment structures within this district. In fact, this very extensive area has so far only been partially investigated.

Aquileia in the Middle Imperial Age

Historical sources about Aquileia between the second half of the first century and the first half of the following century are rather limited. This, however, should not be interpreted as a sign of the city's decline. On the contrary, in this period Aquileia was the essential hub of an extensive infrastructural and commercial network, straddling the Mediterranean and Central Europe and reaching as far as the Danube. Happy Aquileia (*felix Aquileia*, as the poet Martial defined it)[19] was a city experiencing continuous economic growth, thanks to extensive trade development encouraged by a prolonged period of peace. It is interesting to note evidence of an episode of euergetism in this phase by the Emperor Trajan (98–117), who in 105 completely rebuilt an unknown public building (likely a bathhouse) in Aquileia.[20] However, as well as individual building projects, the entire town was also undergoing an extensive urban planning development,[21] as revealed by the gradual expansion of residential areas across the *Natiso cum Turro* river, east of the port and in the Monastero area.

In the second half of the second century, probably in 167, the sudden descent of the Quadi and the Marcomanni into *Venetia* brought about an abrupt disruption to the long period of stability. They even attacked Aquileia itself.[22] The two emperors Marcus Aurelius and Lucius Verus (diarchs from 161 to 169), who set up their headquarters in Aquileia, moved directly to confront the enemies and restore the violated borders. During the clashes, the city suffered both the strains of a long siege by the invaders and the effects of a dreadful epidemic (known as the 'Antonine plague') that raged across the Roman Empire at that time, carried by soldiers returning from the East. In Aquileia the terrible disease was particularly virulent, to the point that Marcus Aurelius found it necessary to summon the famous physician Galen to try to deal with the emergency.

But even these difficulties were overcome. From an architectural point of view, the last quarter of the second century saw some significant work in the forum[23] (Figure 0.1, n. 4). In fact, the eastern portico was restructured with the addition of new capitals, a new entablature and, in the attic above, a new series of plinths with depictions of Jupiter Ammon and Medusa,[24] modelled on those from the Claudian period (Figure 5.4). Between these plinths were the pluteus slabs, decorated with garlands supported by *amorini* and eagles and surmounted by the heads of satyrs and maenads.

Figure 5.4 Aquileia. Virtual reconstruction of the eastern portico of the forum in the Middle Imperial Age (© Fondazione Aquileia/Ikon/Nudesign).

While the work on the eastern portico can probably be dated to the Late Antonine period, the reconstruction of the basilica[25] (Figure 0.1, n. 16) with more monumental architecture seems to date back to the later Severan period (193–235). The building had a rectangular ground plan (90 × 29 metres), with two large apses on the short sides, not visible from the outside. Internally, the basilica space was marked by a peristasis of sixteen by six columns; four columns were arranged in front of each of the two apses. The main entrance from the square was through a forepart with a short propylaeum and through the southern portico, along the longitudinal axis of the forum; two other smaller openings were at the back.

Recent research suggests that the remaking of the architectural decoration of the *scaenae frons* wall of the theatre (Figure 0.1, n. 9)[26] also took place in the Late Antonine period or at the beginning of the Severian period. It is therefore plausible that Aquileia's recently renovated theatre was the venue for performances of the mime artist Bassilla, whose memory is preserved thanks to the funerary stele in the National Archaeological Museum.[27] Dated to the Late Severan period (218–35), the upper portion of the stele features a half-length portrait of the deceased, wearing a tunic and cloak; the lower portion carries an elegant epigraphic Greek text, dedicated to her by the company leader Heraclides and her fellow actors.

The siege of Maximinus Thrax and the period of military anarchy

The year 238 was a very important one in the history of Aquileia.[28] We are in the Middle Imperial Age; the long Severan phase had just ended and the period of crisis known as 'military anarchy' (235–53) had just begun. The emperor that year was Maximinus Thrax (235–8), an army officer of humble 'semi-barbaric' origins. To support the costs and demands of the war the Romans were waging on various fronts, Maximinus had increased the tax burden, mainly on wealthy landowners. The Senate of Rome detested the emperor, to the point of declaring him a public enemy of the state. In 238 a revolt broke out in Proconsular Africa that brought to power two other emperors from the senatorial order: Gordian I and Gordian II. Despite the initial defeat of the two Gordians, who were promptly replaced by Pupienus and Balbinus (with the very young Gordian III as Caesar), and who were on the Senate's side, the revolt against Maximinus continued and extended into Italy, forcing him to face the situation directly. Having crossed the eastern Alpine arc, he quickly reached the Friulian plain. But his advance had to reckon with Aquileia, the impregnable bulwark of the empire, whose heroic resistance is narrated in detail by the historian Herodian.[29]

Right from the start, Aquileia proved to be firmly loyal to the Roman Senate and immediately closed its gates against Maximinus' military vanguard. The ancient republican walls (Figure 0.1, n. 1), suitably reinforced for the purpose,[30] were quickly put back into operation, and from there all attacks were repulsed with stones, javelins and arrows. Maximinus then tried to negotiate. His army included a tribune of Aquileian origin, who was sent to the city to seek an agreement with his fellow citizens. The proposal was simple: the city would surrender, averting the risk of being destroyed, and in return obtain the emperor's magnanimous pardon. But the Aquileians refused the offer, urged on by Crispinus, one of the two men appointed by the Senate to organize the city's resistance. The wrath of Maximinus, a rough man of military ways, could not be contained: Aquileia had to be conquered, sacked and razed to the ground. His soldiers set up a temporary camp and, after overcoming many difficulties, the emperor's army finally managed to cross a river (probably the Isonzo), swollen with water due to the spring thaw, thanks to a bridge of wooden barrels tied together. This ingenious stratagem was necessary to solve the problem of the missing masonry bridge, previously destroyed by the Aquileians to prevent enemy passage.

After ravaging and looting the undefended suburban properties, the army was deployed around the city walls. Once the preparations were complete, the siege began. The united Aquileians defended themselves valiantly, repelling attacks from the war machines and attempts to break through the walls. From the heights of their defences they hurled stones and poured a devastating rain of sulphur, bitumen, pitch and boiling oil onto their enemies, which had the effect of depriving them of much of their weaponry and inflicting terrible burns; the war machines were hit and burnt by volleys of incendiary arrows. Day after day, the Aquileians gained confidence in their methods, while the attackers were increasingly exhausted and demotivated. Trust in the emperor also began to waver, both due to the failure of the military action and his violent and counterproductive tirades against his own officers.

The longer the siege went on, the stronger the Aquileian position became, based on their robust defensive systems, abundant supplies of foodstuffs and an inexhaustible supply of drinking water, as well as their own strength and determination. Moreover, according to Herodian's account, Aquileia was protected by the god Belenus, a local deity identified with Apollo, who fought in defence of the city. Maximinus' army, on the other hand, had plundered the countryside, denuding it of its resources, and was now also beginning to suffer the effects of Rome's supply blockade. Even the river water had become undrinkable, due to the corpses thrown into it by the Aquileians. The besiegers were effectively isolated, while Aquileia resisted and Rome waited for events to unravel. The turning point came thanks to an ambush by some rebel soldiers, who surprised Maximinus and his son (who had been given power as Caesar by his father) near their tent, treacherously killing them and desecrating their lifeless bodies. The two severed heads were then sent to Rome as evidence of the execution.

The conflict that began with the siege of Maximinus Thrax and ended with the death of Maximinus in 238 has passed into history as the *bellum Aquileiense* or the siege of Aquileia. In addition to the series of warlike episodes outlined above, the epilogue of the whole affair, also handed down by Herodian, is particularly significant. The soldiers peacefully approached the walls of Aquileia to announce the death of the emperor and the end of hostilities. The people of Aquileia did not immediately open the gates but, firstly, demanded that the army acknowledge and accept the Senate's choice of emperors. Secondly, they organized a market on the walls, where the former enemies could buy every necessity (food, drink, clothing, footwear, etc.) that, despite the recently ended siege, the city was able to offer in abundance. The soldiers then realized how prosperous Aquileia's economy was, and that they could never have succeeded in conquering a city so abundantly resourced. The siege of Aquileia was thus resolved in an unexpected climate of appeasement.

But in addition to the two directly involved actors (the besieged city and Maximinus' army), the third player in the background was undoubtedly Rome – in particular, the Senate of Rome, the oldest and most prestigious institution that, even during the Imperial Age, continued to represent the interests of the aristocracy, sometimes in opposition to imperial power. For Rome and its Senate, Aquileia was the most prized and indispensable ally – both because of its critical strategic location, defending Italy on its north-eastern flank, and its constant and unquestioning loyalty to the Roman institutions. In other words, defending Aquileia meant defending Rome and the whole of Italy. As long as Aquileia resisted its enemies, the power and authority of Rome was guaranteed. This concept is well illustrated in the side relief of a votive altar, preserved in the National Archaeological Museum, dedicated to the Capitoline triad and Mars, *pro salute et victoria* of the Augusti Pupienus and Balbinus and the Caesar Gordian III.[31] In this relief, Aquileia is personified kneeling before the enthroned Roman *res publica*.[32]

Despite the official propaganda, the political situation in Rome and the empire was far from stable. In Aquileia, during the mid-third century, signs of urban decay were evident, reflecting the city's struggles.[33] Control over the surrounding territory had been weakening for some time, as shown by the neglect of the Via Annia and the Via Gemina, which had required repairs by Maximinus himself, and the gradual silting up of the Amphora Canal to the west of the city. The early decline of the district across the river, east of the port, also dates to the third century. In the second half of the century, some residential buildings within the city were clearly deteriorating. Additionally, the post-Severian crisis is indicated by the rare architectural and decorative updates and the almost complete absence of new dwellings in Aquileia during the central decades of the third century.

Diocletian's reform and the great Aquileia of Constantine

Towards the end of the third century, Emperor Diocletian (284–305) implemented a very necessary and radical territorial and administrative reorganization of the Roman Empire, guaranteeing greater political and military stability to a territory that had become far too extensive. Firstly, he appointed Maximian (286–308) as the second Augustus, associating him with the throne and entrusting him with the functions of co-emperor in the western part of the empire. Secondly, in 293, he instituted an innovative form of government, called the tetrarchy (government of four). In this way, imperial power was divided between four individuals, united by a pact of mutual loyalty. The tetrarchy comprised two Augusti and two Caesars. The two Augusti (Diocletian and Maximian) were the de facto emperors in office; associated with them were the two Caesars (Galerius and Constantius Chlorus), who assisted the Augusti and would succeed them – as new Augusti – after a period of rule, appointing in turn two new Caesars.

The imperial territory was also divided into four parts: Diocletian ruled over the eastern provinces, with the capital *Nicomedia* (modern İzmit, Turkey); Galerius over the Balkan provinces, with the capital *Sirmium* (modern Sremska Mitrovica, Serbia); Maximian over Italy and most of the African provinces, with the capital *Mediolanum* (modern Milan, Italy); Constantius Chlorus over the western provinces, with the capital *Augusta Treverorum* (modern Trier, Germany). Each of these four parts was subdivided into dioceses, which in turn were subdivided into provinces (the number of which was increased significantly compared to earlier). Rome, the city par excellence (*Urbs*), remained the seat of the Senate and the absolute point of reference for the entire empire.

At this point, as part of the *Italiciana* diocese, Aquileia became the capital of the *Venetia et Histria* province, heir to the ancient *decima regio* established in the Augustan Age. The Upper Adriatic city thus obtained a new administrative role,[34] which led to the establishment of a close relationship with the imperial capital *Mediolanum* (Milan). Not surprisingly this was a period of prosperity for Aquileia, which was given a mint around 295/296[35] and, amongst other things, became a focus of political life. The governor of the province, the officials of the new ruling class, local notables and other wealthy members of the aristocratic elites close to the imperial power and keen to show off their status all habitually resided in the city. On several occasions the emperor himself and all his retinue stayed there, thus reaffirming its contemporary geopolitical importance.

It is believed that, perhaps between 293 and 296, the future emperor Constantine (306–337) met the very young Fausta, daughter of Maximian and his future wife, in Aquileia's imperial palace (see next paragraph), receiving from her the gift of a precious gold helmet. This scene was depicted in the Aquileian palace, but it is doubtful whether the event really took place there or indeed anywhere else. In the context of the clashes over his rise to imperial power, which followed the Tetrarchic power struggles, the relationship between Aquileia and Constantine was initially conflictual. Consistent with its professed loyalty to Rome, the Upper Adriatic city had in fact sided with his rival Maxentius, son of Maximian and resident in Rome, while Constantine was seen as a sort of usurper supported by the army. The turning point came in 312, after the Battle of Verona, which saw Maxentius' troops surrender to Constantine's, presaging the final outcome of hostilities, which occurred shortly afterwards with the well-known Battle of Ponte Milvio, near Rome. Besieged, Aquileia shrewdly preferred to surrender and switch to the side of the pre-announced victor, thereby avoiding the worst and, indeed, obtaining in return important benefits thanks to the emperor's magnanimity. This further strengthened the already close relationship between Aquileia and the imperial power.

Consequently, it was no coincidence that in the Tetrarchic and Constantinian eras, and throughout the entire fourth century, Aquileia established itself as one of the greatest cities of northern Italy and, indeed, of the whole Roman world (Figure 5.5).[36] It was a landmark in terms of urban space, monumentality, the variety of architecture, urban decor, population (tens of thousands), the complexity of the civic structure, trade,

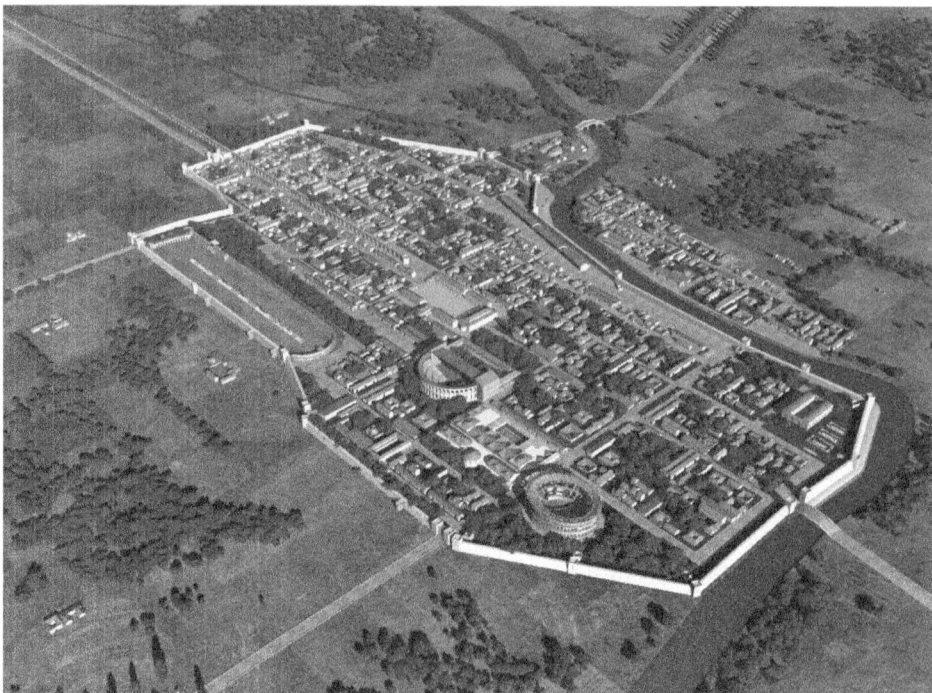

Figure 5.5 Aquileia. Virtual reconstruction of the city in Late Antiquity, view from the south-west (© Ikon).

economic vitality, and political, strategic and military importance. Nor, in the wake of the Edict of Milan in 313, should we overlook the sudden and almost prodigious emergence of the Christian Church in Aquileia and the growth of the city's episcopal complex under the leadership of Bishop Theodore, who could claim a close relationship with Constantine himself (see chapter 8). For his part, the emperor visited Aquileia on several occasions and even issued some constitutions from there. He visited twice in 318 (spending more than two months on the first occasion), twice more in passing in 326 and he may have returned in 333.

The Late Roman walls and the western district

To adequately protect such an important city, it was necessary to build a completely new, solid city wall[37] (known in the literature as M2; Figure 0.1, n. 2), of almost 4 kilometres in length. This single project was on a much larger and more demanding scale than the localized reinforcements carried out in the first century BCE and later during Maximinus' siege. Not since the building of the republican defensive circuit had the city been required to undertake such a huge building project.

The new walls, equipped with towers, encompassed an urban area double the size of that of the republican colony: approximately 83.5 hectares compared to the initial 41 hectares. For the first time the walls incorporated some vast residential areas that had developed over time outside the original urban perimeter, in particular in the north-eastern sector (with the exclusion of the neighbourhoods east of the port and Monastero) and the southern and western sector, which would soon be the subject of major building initiatives. The northern urban boundary remained unaltered and the defensive role of the waterways surrounding the city was further emphasized, in particular that of the *Natiso cum Turro* on the eastern and southern sides, which brought the wall line along the riverbank. The inclusion of several monumental complexes within the defensive perimeter was strategic, both to preserve their integrity and functionality and to prevent them from falling into enemy hands. To this end, on the eastern side, a long stretch of the new walls was built along the edge of the river port quays, while on the western side they included the theatre and the amphitheatre, two imposing public buildings that otherwise, in the event of an enemy siege, could have been transformed into dangerous offensive footholds close to the city.

A large amount of used building material was recycled in the construction of the new city walls, including numerous architectural elements and inscriptions. These probably include two honorary bases dedicated to the Emperor Gallienus and his wife Salonina, whose names were erased due to the *damnatio memoriae* (condemnation of memory) established in 268.[38] This date can therefore be considered a useful *post quem* indication of the construction of the new city walls, which recent studies believe to be have been a consequence of a Tetrarchic imperial initiative, with later reinforcements of a different architectural nature.

Moreover, the same imperial initiative can also be linked to a series of challenging building works that radically monumentalized the western sector of the city,[39] highlighting the undisputed importance acquired by Aquileia in the Tetrarchic Age. Recent investigations have in fact made it possible to identify both the construction of the Great Baths and the circus, two imposing public building complexes, whose monumental architecture, decorations and specific functions were ubiquitous in the main cities of the period, especially in imperial seats such as *Mediolanum* (Milan), *Arelate* (Arles) or *Augusta Treverorum* (Trier).

The Great Baths (Figure 0.1, n. 12)[40] was an enormous bathing facility built between the amphitheatre to the south and the theatre to the north, occupying an area of more than 2 hectares. Typologically, it falls into the category of the 'great imperial baths' found in Rome and the major cities of the Roman world. As was customary, the building was probably surrounded by a fence and developed symmetrically along a central axis, from east to west, based on the following sequence of rooms: a centrally placed large *frigidarium* (unheated room for cold baths), with a great apse on the east side and numerous baths; a *tepidarium* (warm room); a large *calidarium* (heated room for hot baths), with an apsidal end wall on the west side. The latter faced west to enjoy more sunshine during the afternoon hours. On either side of the central axis was a series of spaces, symmetrically duplicated: entrances, changing rooms (*apodyteria*), baths, rooms for sporting activities, rooms for body care, corridors, porticoed courtyards and more. The grandeur of the layout was matched by the equally sumptuous decoration, partial evidence of which remains not only in the selection of precious marbles used in the architectural elements and cladding, but also in the quality of the mosaic floors and statuary. Particularly noteworthy are the polychrome mosaics of the two chambers located on either side of the *frigidarium*: in the northern one, mythological references to the marine world and a series of portraits of athletes predominate; in the southern one, allusions to the theme of hunting are dominant. Also noteworthy is the system of functional structures for hypocaust heating and the management of all those services that ensured the smooth running of such a complex facility.

Chronologically speaking, the planning and first building likely originated in the Tetrarchic period.[41] It is highly significant that, in northern Italy, the bath complex in Aquileia can be compared to Milan's Herculean Baths, built by the Emperor Maximian. However, as was the case in Rome for many ongoing building projects, the construction of the building in Aquileia must have been completed in the Constantinian Age. This is implied by the inscription on a statue base dedicated to Constantine, found near the *frigidarium*, in which the name *felices thermae Constantinianae* recurs;[42] the dedication was probably placed between 324 and 337 by two high-ranking officials in charge of the construction. It is interesting to note that the Diocletian's Baths and the Baths of Constantine in Rome were also used the formula *thermae felices*. A fragment of another dedication, to Constantine himself, recalling the emperor's role in the restoration of some decayed buildings, probably refers to a different Aquileian bath.[43]

The circus (Figure 0.1, n. 13),[44] built to the north of the theatre in the western district, is the other large building complex constructed in this period. This area was previously crossed by a north–south watercourse, which, according to geophysical surveys,[45] must have flanked the north-western section of the republican walls and then connected at right angles with the initial section of the Amphora Canal. The original suburban area adjacent to the waterway was probably transformed into an industrial and residential district. Archaeological investigations have shown that between the end of the third and the beginning of the fourth centuries, the section of the Amphora Canal close to the city, already partially silted up, was finally filled in (see chapter 4). Consequently, the connecting waterway, which ran along the north-western section of the ancient city walls, must have been decommissioned at the same time. Based on what has been reconstructed so far, this was a preliminary intervention connected with the urbanization works on the adjacent land, once suburban and now in the process of being included within the new Late Roman walls. Once the pre-existing buildings had been cleared and the road system of the terminal section of the Via Annia modified, a large flat area was created which extended in a north–south direction and which, free of obstacles, was suitable for the construction of the circus.

Horse-drawn chariot races were held in the circus. They emerged from the starting pits (*carceres*) and raced seven laps of the track around a long central spine. Spectators watched from the stands lining the sides. At the end of the race, the winner, acclaimed by the crowd, left the track through the triumphal gate, generally placed in the centre of the short side opposite the *carceres* (in the case of Aquileia, the south-facing side). The dimensions of these buildings were generally enormous. Although little is known from an archaeological point of view, the circus of Aquileia was no exception: as far as we have been able to reconstruct, it reached a total length of 460/470 metres and was about 95 metres wide. The entire length of its western wall coincided with the corresponding section of the new city wall, meaning that the circus and the M2 wall had to have been built at the same time, as part of a single urban project of the Tetrarchic Age, organized according to the orientation and general layout of the settlement.

Looking at the entire western urban sector, we can see that this planning led to the doubling of the already extensive 'entertainment district', with recreational and leisure facilities. Following this expansion, the amphitheatre, the Great Baths, the theatre and the circus were arranged in sequence from south to north. These were four monumental buildings dedicated to entertainment, care of the body and soul, socializing and leisure. Furthermore, it is widely known that in Late Antiquity the circus enjoyed particular imperial favour, as, during competitions, it allowed the emperor to disseminate imperial ideology and garner popular consent in a direct and immediate way. In the capital cities and other imperial seats in this period the relationship between such buildings and the emperors' residences became more pronounced. The nearest example is again Milan, where the circus formed a unified whole with the imperial palace.

Based on a passage in a 307 panegyric,[46] it is believed that there was a palace (*Aquileiense palatium*) at the disposal of the emperor when he stayed in Aquileia. Perhaps it was the residence of the *Venetia et Histria* provincial governor or a palace built specifically for the purpose. Archaeological evidence suggests that here, as in Milan, this building complex was in the immediate vicinity of the circus, probably along its eastern side.[47] From this area, albeit from different locations, come several significant finds. These comprise one or two series of marble clypei with busts depicting the Twelve Gods,[48] dated to the first half of the fourth century; the earlier-mentioned group of three larger-than-life marble statues (*Genius Augusti*, Claudius and, perhaps, Antonia Minor), partly reworked and reassembled and probably transferred from their original context to the new prestigious site; and an inscription, dated between 326 and 330/333,[49] linked to a statue base and celebrating Constantine's victories. The same western district might also have housed the mint,[50] active – albeit with some intervals – from 295/296 to 425.

The forum and commercial structures in Late Antiquity

Next to the new 'imperial district' in the western sector of the Late Roman city, the city centre had for centuries housed a place where Aquileia's political and administrative life converged. This was the forum[51] (Figure 0.1, n. 4), with its square, buildings and commemorative monuments. Periodically updated both in terms of its architecture and in its decoration, over time the ancient forum had acquired the charm of a sort of prestigious 'historic centre', in which the community of Aquileia recognized itself and saw in it the ideal location for preserving and celebrating the city's glorious history. For example, the creation of a sort of gallery of *summi viri* (illustrious men) was the result of a civic initiative, rather than being commissioned by the emperor. A series of inscriptions bearing the names of Aquileia's important historical figures bears witness to this development: from *Lucius Manlius Acidinus*, *triumvir* of the first colonial settlement in 181 BCE, to Emperor Maximian, Augustus of the Tetrarchic government. In order to carve these inscriptions, it was necessary to partially erase the upper frame of the garlanded slabs of the attic of the forum's portico; these statues (unfortunately not preserved) thus stood above the carved-out cartouches.

Other fourth-century embellishments of the forum were commissioned both by wealthy members of the local aristocracy and imperial officials. These were, after all, the most prominent personalities in contemporary Aquileia, the same ones who resided in the most prestigious urban dwellings, often equipped with monumental reception rooms. The initiative implemented shortly after the mid-fourth century by Septimius Theodulus, *corrector* (governor) of the *Venetia et Histria* province, exemplifies this trend. Intent on adorning the town square and despite being a Christian, he had a series of statues of traditional Roman deities placed on some reused bases.[52] This act, while apparently contradictory, is actually representative of the changes taking place in society and religion of the time. In this period, the practice of reusing the statues of pagan deities as ornaments in public places by taking them from temples and effectively depriving them of their cultic significance was widespread and tolerated. Such actions enabled notables of the Christian faith to display their loyalty to Roman institutions and at the same time reaffirm their religious beliefs.

Commercial activities had long moved from the prestigious spaces of the forum, now used for less mundane activities, to other specialized market areas. To the east of the forum, towards the harbour, a new building, probably a food market,[53] was constructed during the fourth century. The location of this building is quite logical, if we consider that the nearby harbour area was very busy even in Late Antiquity[54] and after the construction of the M2 wall, which overlay part of the quays' edge along the river. The inclusion of the port buildings within the new defensive wall was an effective way to protect the port (Figure 0.1, n. 14) without compromising its use. In fact, the warehouses behind the quays were considerably enlarged, perhaps in the Constantinian Age, to adapt them to the growing volume of trade with the entire Mediterranean basin, well evidenced by the conspicuous quantity of imports from Africa and the East. Having made the appropriate adaptations to the landing system, the smooth unloading of goods was ensured through two openings facing the river, which allowed a connection with the buildings behind.

In addition to this best-known river port, it is highly probable that other ports were active along the waterways that encircled the settlement. For instance, another is believed to have been located at the bend of the *Natiso cum Turro*, in the south-eastern urban sector. Recent studies show it was located in the immediate vicinity of a vast building complex used for the sale of foodstuffs (fish, meat, cereals, etc.),[55] consisting of a series of market squares (Figure 0.1, n. 19) with arcades and shops and built within the new city walls between the end of the third and beginning of the fourth centuries. Immediately to the north stood the imposing block of the *horrea* (Figure 0.1, n. 21),[56] intended for the storage of grain and other commodities, replicating the architectural model of similar buildings in the imperial capitals *Mediolanum* (Milan) and *Augusta Treverorum* (Trier). Consequently, it is believed that the construction of the great Aquileia *horrea* should also be attributed to the tetrarchic central power, probably to support the crucial strategic–military functions played by Aquileia in this historical period.

All that glitters is not gold: Aquileia during the fourth century

In the *Expositio totius mundi et gentium*,[57] whose first edition is dated to the time of Emperor Constantius II (337–61), Aquileia and the imperial capital *Mediolanum* appear together as *splendidae civitates* (splendid cities) in the context of *Italia annonaria* (one of the two vicariates into which the *Italiciana* diocese was divided). But not all that glitters is gold. Although Aquileia had developed significantly, it owed this title, above all, to its strategic position and military role, close as it was to the diocese's boundary and located behind the defence system of the Julian Alps (*claustra Alpium Iuliarum*). In the course of the fourth century, the town would experienced several blood feuds, the ambition of temporary usurpers and a number of siege attempts.[58]

In 340, the final clash between Constantine II and the troops of his brother Constans took place in the vicinity of Aquileia, ending with the death of the former, whose decapitated corpse was thrown into the waters of the *Alsa* (Aussa). Aquileia, however, remained uninvolved in these events. Ten years later, Constans himself fell victim to a conspiracy hatched by the usurper Magnentius (350–3), who in 350 and then between 351 and 352 made Aquileia his headquarters; it was here in 352 that he was surprised by Constantius II, who surrounded the city while his rival was watching the circus races, forcing him to flee to Gaul, where he committed suicide.

A decade later, between 361 and 362, Aquileia at first vigorously resisted the siege by the Emperor Julian 'the Apostate's' army (360–3), but ultimately surrendered with the rebel troops barricaded inside only when the death of Constantius II, considered to be the legitimate ruler, was announced. The new M2 walls (Figure 0.1, n. 2) withstood the attack. As narrated by the historian Ammianus Marcellinus,[59] the attack was first carried out overland by encircling the city; then from the river, using a system of wooden towers mounted on boats; then by interrupting the flow of the aqueducts; and finally by adopting the ingenious stratagem of diverting the course of the river itself. Leaving aside Julian's siege, this last measure had the effect of altering the water system of the *Natiso cum Turro* itself, permanently changing the relationship between the city and its river. It is likely that as early as the second half of the fourth century, some of the newly built defensive towers erected along the eastern side of the walls rested on the very ground that had partially filled the riverbed.[60]

It was also in Aquileia, in the second half of the century (388), that the usurper Magnus Maximus' reign (383–8) came to an end, defeated by Emperor Theodosius.[61] The poet Ausonius commemorated the city's role in these events with the lines: 'Raised by recent merit, thou shalt be named ninth among famous cities, O Aquileia, colony of Italy, facing toward the mountains of Illyria and highly famed for walls and harbour [*moenibus et portu celeberrima*].'[62] In 394, Theodosius himself defeated the usurper Eugenius in a tough battle near the river *Frigidus*, reaching Aquileia after a hard-won victory.

Sudden political upheavals and military instability were practically the order of the day. We can therefore reasonably assume that the events referred to so far and the general political climate created a deep sense of insecurity and unease in the Aquileian community, despite the recent glory of Constantine's great Aquileia and the *splendida civitas* of Constantius II. Some comfort was provided by adherence to the Christian faith, which was becoming more important in the society of the time. However, we should not overlook the fact that, at that time, the Church in Aquileia was riven by bitter theological disputes, linked to the spread of Arianism, which contributed to the climate of conflict and was only really resolved with the Council of 381 (see chapter 8).

Despite these problems, for a few decades in the second half of the century, Aquileia enjoyed a certain internal equilibrium, thanks above all to the authoritative leadership of bishops Valerian and Chromatius. This was especially the case after Emperor Theodosius (379–95), together with Gratian and Valentinian II, had proclaimed Christianity the state religion of the Roman Empire in 380. Theodosius himself visited the city several times, in 388, 391 and 394. Evidence of the strong bond that was established between Theodosius and Aquileia is provided by a monument with statues of the emperors Valentinian II, Theodosius and Arcadius[63] erected in the forum or some other prestigious location[64] on the authority of *Valerius Adelfius Bassus, consularis Venetiae et Histriae* (a provincial governor position that replaced that of *corrector* after the middle of the century).

The general trend, however, was one of progressive decline in the quality of public building, the management of infrastructure and in the overall nature of urban decoration. When the M2 walls were being built in the Tetrarchic period, the new defensive structures involved a massive reuse of architectural elements and inscriptions. This is a clear indication that several monumental creations had been dismantled to deal with far more pressing emergencies. However, the panorama must have been quite varied. On the one hand, many buildings gradually fell into neglect (think, for instance, of the state of disuse of the amphitheatre in the second half of the fourth century), but on the other hand there was no lack of renovation, as in the case of the public building restored under Constantine. There are also examples of buildings that changed function, such as the theatre (Figure 0.1, n. 9), whose substructural rooms began to be partly employed for the accumulation of marble fragments and partly for metalworking activities (Figure 5.6).[65] Other monumental complexes retained their functionality: take the forum, for example, the undisputed seat of the city's institutions, albeit increasingly squeezed between the 'imperial quarter' to the north-west and the emerging episcopal complex to the south-east.[66]

Figure 5.6 Aquileia. The blacksmith's workshop installed in the Late Antique period in the substructural rooms of the theatre (© A. Walczer Baldinazzo).

Even in the late fourth and early decades of the fifth century the *Notitia Dignitatum* still recognized Aquileia's significant role.[67] However, this precarious equilibrium was to break down when, in 402, the Emperor Honorius (395–423), who succeeded his father Theodosius in the western empire, shifted the imperial court from Milan to Ravenna, thereby effectively altering the geopolitical balance of northern Italy. As we will see in chapter 7, this was the beginning of a particularly difficult fifty years for Aquileia, culminating in Attila's devastating sack in 452.

CHAPTER 6
LIVING AND DYING IN AQUILEIA: *DOMUS*, NECROPOLISES, ARTISTIC PRODUCTION

Residential construction in Aquileia: the state of the art

Residential building in Roman Aquileia is a particularly rich field of research,[1] thanks to a vast number of finds unparalleled in the rest of northern Italy. This is often associated with the study of the numerous mosaic floor coverings found inside dwellings, investigations of which enjoyed great popularity during the twentieth century. Although many domestic buildings remained undiscovered, others were open to the public through the creation of special visitor routes, after the restoration of the wall structures and the consolidation of the flooring directly *in situ* (Fondo CAL and Fondo Beneficio Rizzi, Fondi Cossar, crypt under the Christian basilica). However, even in the best-preserved or best-known cases, general knowledge of private building in Aquileia was hampered by the fact that none of the excavated houses were completely known. This serious limitation was partly due to the contingencies of the individual finds (incomplete documentation, emergency excavations, interruptions imposed by current property boundaries, etc.) and partly due to the absence of precise information on the entrances and how the layout developed in the various dwellings. For the dozens of domestic buildings found in Aquileia, the situation revealed by the excavations showed a series of adjoining rooms, but it was impossible to establish whether they belonged to one or more houses.

Research in recent decades has aimed to deepen our knowledge on the subject and to improve accessibility to and understanding of Aquileia's archaeological remains. Important publications have focused on the subject of domestic construction in Aquileia by considering the wider Cisalpine context, and, more specifically, focusing on the examination of individual residences such as Titus Macer's House (Figure 0.1, n. 7),[2] *domus delle Bestie ferite* (House of the Wounded Beasts;[3] Figure 0.1, n. 17) and *domus dei Putti danzanti* (House of the Dancing Putti;[4] Figure 0.1, n. 18). This research led to innovative reconstructions by the Fondazione Aquileia. A notable example is Titus Macer's House, which opened to the public in 2020. This house is a prime example of a historically accurate restoration of an ancient Aquileian home, with roofing systems and internal layouts that match the original design.

Titus Macer's House, in the Fondi Cossar, is also the first Roman house in Aquileia to have been completely investigated. Its plan and interior layout have been reconstructed, its relationship with the road networks and neighbouring buildings analysed and its transformation from construction to abandonment has been traced. Outlining a brief summary of its architectural and town-planning history is particularly useful in illustrating some salient features of residential buildings in Aquileia.

Residential building in the republican period: the example of Titus Macer's House

Titus Macer's House (Figure 0.1, n. 7) was built at the beginning of the first century BCE in the south-eastern urban block,[5] close to the republican walls. According to a recurring pattern in the urban layout of Aquileia, the relevant block (*insula*) measured 4 × 2 *actus* (1 *actus* = 120 *pedes* = 35.52 metres) and was originally divided longitudinally into two equal sectors by a long intermediate wall. The longitudinal sectors, 1 *actus* wide, appear to be divided transversely into modular parcels of land, oriented approximately east–west, and almost 6 metres wide (20 *pedes*). Such parcels make up the smallest units, often grouped in multiples to form building plots of a suitable size for house construction.[6] The same pattern is found elsewhere in Aquileia, such as in the 'Wounded Beasts' *insula* and in other areas of the city.[7] In the case of Titus Macer's House, the plot where the building was constructed consisted of two adjoining plots with a total width of almost 12 metres (40 *pedes* = ⅓ *actus*). The perimeter walls were shared by neighbouring dwellings, thus resulting in an apparently uninterrupted sequence of domestic rooms that, to our eyes, often makes it difficult to distinguish the boundaries of the individual dwelling units. In this sense, Titus Macer's House is a happy exception, due to the presence of a narrow alley (*ambitus*) flanking it on the southern side and because of its characteristics, which facilitate the reconstruction of its size and overall layout.

The *domus* had an atrium plan, corresponding to a well-known Roman housing type, but one never previously documented in Aquileia. Access, next to a shop (*taberna*), was from the street on the western side. After passing through the entrance hall (*fauces*) with a vestibule (*vestibulum*), you entered the atrium, initially without columns to support the roof (*atrium tuscanicum*), which had a well next to the central *impluvium* and extended into two lateral *alae* at the back. To the left of the atrium there were two small bedrooms (*cubicula*), while on the right side there was a secondary entrance connecting to the side alley. At the back, arranged along the central axis of the building and visible from the entrance, was the house owner's room (*tablinum*), completely open to the atrium. In these spaces, which make up the heart of the traditional Roman atrium house, the archives, images of ancestors and memories of the family (*gens*) were kept, and the owners' business was conducted. Next to the *tablinum* was a dining room (*triclinium*) and, on the opposite side, a passageway led to the vegetable garden behind (*hortus*), equipped with a basin.

The layout and decorative scheme of Titus Macer's House was extremely restrained. This can be seen especially in the mosaic flooring of the atrium and the *alae,* which were completely black with white tile borders and thresholds. The *tablinum*'s geometric mosaic was more elaborate, while that of the *triclinium* had a central *emblema*, unfortunately not preserved. Its overall size (426 metres squared) and interior layout shows that the *domus* was built using a well-codified plan, frequently found in the towns of central Italy. However, from a chronological perspective, the Aquileian version comes from the end of the evolutionary development of this type of *domus*, when in central Italy atrium dwellings with a rear peristyle had already been widespread for some time, in accordance with the Hellenistic influence then in vogue.

Titus Macer's House is the best documented example of a republican residential dwelling in Aquileia. Overall, structural or pavement remains pertaining to about ten houses from this period have been identified in the city, distributed fairly uniformly across the various urban sectors. As noted in the previous chapter, the physical limit of the republican walls had already been breached for residential purposes during the first century BCE.

Residential building in the Imperial Age: the example of Titus Macer's House

The full development of residential building in Aquileia took place during the first century CE, starting in the Augustan Age. Archaeological evidence comes from across the whole city, with a greater concentration in the northern and southern sectors, which were also experiencing a phase of extensive expansion outside the republican walls, particularly towards the south, inside the river bend. As elsewhere at that time, this phase of domestic building development in Aquileia reflected the conspicuous economic potential of the city's elites, derived from the flourishing trade network in which Aquileia was a principal node connecting the Mediterranean and transalpine regions. There are about twenty luxury urban dwellings from this period, better documented from a structural point of view than more modest houses. They are a type of extensive single-family building, generally constructed over large areas and developed on the ground floor, although in some cases there may have been some rooms on the upper floor. However, there is no evidence of multi-storey blocks of flats or other forms of intensive multi-family housing.

Within these noble houses, significant attention was given to the elegant porticoed peristyle around which the living and entertaining areas were arranged, following a well-known Hellenistic architectural model. This concept was first adopted and reworked in the central Italic area and later spread to northern Italy. In some instances, the central space of the peristyle was kept as a garden whilst in others, particularly in Aquileia, this space was paved. More numerous and larger than the average northern Italian Roman dwelling, the peristyles of the houses in Aquileia (including the central open area and side porticoes) sometimes covered areas up to 200 metres squared. However, there was no shortage of dwellings whose central core comprised smaller courtyards.

A particular case in point is Titus Macer's House (Figure 6.1),[8] characterized by a distinctive atrium layout in the Italic tradition. Around the middle of the first century, between 25 and 75, the layout of the house was radically altered, following the acquisition of the bordering plot to the east, which was merged into a single building extending as far as the street that flanked the block on the eastern side. This operation involved a large section of the block itself, between the two parallel streets that flanked it on the long sides. When the work was completed, the size of the *domus* had almost tripled compared to the original (from 426 to 1,260 metres squared). In the old existing house, the insertion of four columns around the *impluvium*, which supported the roof of the atrium (transformed into an *atrium tetrastylum*), and the elimination of the old *hortus*, sacrificed to allow for the connection with the newly built area, are of particular note. In this sector, connected to the previous one but quite distinct from it from a visual and functional point of view, a large courtyard kept as a garden, surrounded by a closed and windowed portico (in place of the more common columned peristyle) took on a central role, probably to cope with the effects of the cold and humid climate typical of the Veneto-Friuli plain. Around the courtyard were numerous rooms with different functions, the most prominent of which was a grandiose reception hall (*oecus*) of about 90 metres squared, paved with a white mosaic bordered by a black band, whose entrance was aligned with an ornamental pool located in the garden. Next to this room, which was intended for larger receptions, was a *triclinium* for more limited functions, with a pool lined with marble slabs on the back wall. Its tricliniar function is confirmed by the subdivision of the pavement into three decorative units, in bichrome geometric mosaic, flanked by a lateral band in white mosaic tesserae. At the eastern end of the building, along the portico opening onto the street, was a row of four shops (*tabernae*), one of which was likely a bakery.

The considerable dimensions that the *domus* took on in the Early Imperial Age, the multiplication of the rooms, the inclusion of a prestigious reception hall, the lavishness of the mosaic flooring, the presence of columns and water features, but also the respect shown for the ancient atrium are all indications of a high-ranking client, perhaps a descendant of the original owners. According to one appealing theory, at this time the house belonged to a certain Titus Macer, whose name appears engraved on a stone weight found in one of the workshops on the eastern side of the building.

The prestige of the house remained unchanged even during the Middle Imperial Age (second–third centuries). Contrary to what has been observed in other Aquileian

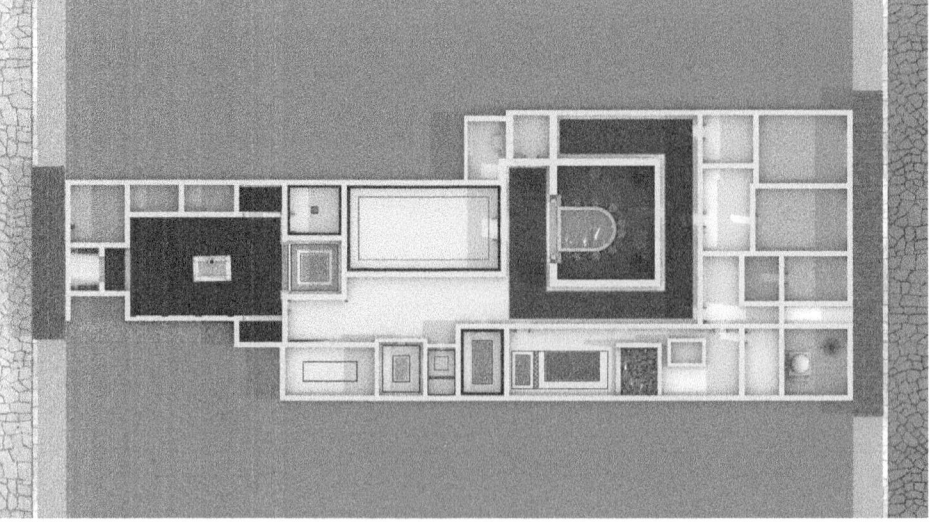

Figure 6.1 Aquileia. Reconstruction of Titus Macer's House in the Early Imperial Age, view from above (© A. Ciancio).

dwellings, this house was not provided with larger reception rooms at that time, since both the *oecus* and the two *triclinia* were already of considerable size. On the other hand, the decoration of numerous rooms was updated by laying new mosaic floors (overlying the previous ones) and some changes were made to the pool in the garden. There was also no lack of utilitarian building work, including a reorganization of the workshop sector on the eastern side of the building.

Significant changes were made to Titus Macer's House in the fourth century.[9] While the front sector of the house, centred on the ancient Late Republican atrium, retained its austere appearance, with the layout, internal routes and the function of the individual rooms remaining substantially unchanged, the central sector was variously modified according to the taste of the time. Here, a series of renovations took place that involved, among other developments, the closing of the northern arm of the courtyard portico, according to a Late Roman trend; the paving of the courtyard itself, once kept as a garden; and the laying of a new polychrome floor mosaic inside the *oecus*, which overlay the previous tessellated one. The new mosaic floor, raised almost half a metre above the original floor, displayed a composition of irregular octagons and adjacent crosses, further embellished by a rich repertoire of animals depicted within the octagons themselves, and a central fishing scene, alluding to the sumptuousness of the banquets or the wealth of the sea, perhaps the origin of the owner's fortunes. In keeping with Late Roman sensibilities, the *oecus* seems to be the end of an access path that wound through the domestic spaces, reaching the internal paved courtyard before ascending to the great hall, at the culmination of a short upward sloping section. This solution made it possible to physically raise the figure of the master of the house (*dominus*) and, at the same time, achieve the effect of symbolically emphasizing his role in the eyes of the guests admitted into his presence.

Yet, the desire not to alter the now obsolete layout of the entrance, atrium and the entire front part of the building is clearly conservative. Moreover, although there was ample space, the owner did not follow the fashion of constructing an apsidal room with representation and reception functions, unlike other contemporary Aquileian dwellings (House of the Wounded Beasts, northern and southern *domus* of the Fondo CAL, building near the Violin's Stable, etc.).[10] The decision to introduce a prestigious environment with such characteristics into one's own dwellings, richly decorated and aimed at self-representation of one's role and achievements, was part of a climate of mutual emulation among the members of the city's elites. Evidently, however, this mode of ostentation was not of interest to the owner of the *domus*, who did not even install the luxurious and refined opus sectile flooring that was quite fashionable at the time (even in the limited number of Aquileian records). We almost get the impression that he was more interested in preserving the austere imprint of the house than to assert himself competitively, thus limiting himself – so to speak – to renovating the mosaic flooring of the already existing *oecus*.

In the same archaeological area of the Fondi Cossar, a useful comparison can be made with the neighbouring house to the north. Towards the end of the fourth century, the owner of this house had a large rectangular reception room paved with a colourful mosaic known as the 'Good Shepherd in Singular Costume', flanked by animals. In Late Roman aristocratic imagery, this pastoral scene in a residential setting symbolized the master immersed in an idyllic rural environment. At first, this scene, similar to the colourful mosaic in the apsidal room of the northern *domus* of the Fondo CAL (Figure 0.1, n. 8), was interpreted as Christian. This led to such rooms being considered Christian oratories. This is no longer the case.

Domestic buildings' decoration: mosaics and paintings

Current knowledge of private building decorations in Aquileia[11] mainly concerns floor surfaces, primarily (but not only) mosaics, and, to a lesser extent, wall coverings, generally consisting of layers of painted plaster. There is also no lack of data on luxury furnishings (furniture, *appliques*, *oscilla*, small statuary, etc.) and various household artefacts.

The entire corpus of Roman pavements in Aquileia has recently been collected and analysed,[12] finally providing an organic and systematic image of the hundreds of remains brought to light in the Upper Adriatic city. Before outlining the evolutionary framework of Aquileia's famous mosaic production, particularly in the domestic sphere, it is worth pointing out that the floor coverings surveyed include not only the numerous tessellated coverings (mosaics) and the less frequent ones in marble inlays (*opus sectile*), but also those of the so-called poor techniques, such as the brick and cement pavements.

Unlike the second century BCE, from which very few pavements have been found (none of them mosaic), a good number of remains come from the period between the first century BCE and the middle of the following century. Over this period the cement pavements, especially those with a clay base, seem to be fully in line with the central-Italic tradition. From the decorative point of view, the Aquileian clients were more inclined to use stone or marble inserts than tessellated ornamentation, even if there is no lack of evidence of mixed techniques being used, with a cement base supplemented by limited portions of tessellates. The valuable *opus sectile* pavements, however, are quite rare. A couple of cases exist with tessellated border bands, a decorative type that was also widespread in central Italy.

In the same period, there is much more evidence of tessellated floor coverings, often distinguished by considerable skill of experienced workshops. This is particularly evident in the famous polychrome mosaics of the Nereid on a sea bull and the *asaroton* (an unswept floor with the remains of a banquet scattered on the ground), both from the area of the Fondi Cossar and datable to the second half of the first century BCE, which directly followed the Hellenistic tradition and are attributed to foreign craftsmen. From the same area also comes the highly refined polychrome mosaic of the Vine Branch with Bow, coeval with those noted above and distinguished by its ornamentation. A further example, from the first century, is the polychrome *emblema* (a mosaic '*quadretto*' made separately and then inserted in the centre of the pavement) of the *domus* of Lycurgus and Ambrosia, depicting a teeming marine fauna.

Geometric mosaics were heavily influenced by the central Italian tradition, and Aquileia is known for producing a wide range of decorative schemes, particularly from the Augustan Age onwards. Clients in Aquileia, aiming to align their home decoration with trends from Rome, likely sought the expertise of central Italian itinerant workshops. These workshops contributed to the establishment of a local mosaic production culture that incorporated techniques and models from the Campania–Latium area.

During the Imperial Age, the workshops in Aquileia were known for their remarkable artistic activity, especially evident in the quantity and quality of mosaics produced. The range of geometric patterns expanded, with new motifs reworked into unique forms. One of the most famous examples is the mosaic of the Flowered Carpet (second–fourth century) (Figure 6.2) at the House of the Dancing Putti, which features an elegant 'vegetalized grid' pattern inspired by ceiling paintings. Black-and-white bichrome compositions, reflecting the austere urban and central-Italic taste, were common until the end of the second century. After that, there was a noticeable shift towards polychromy from the Severan Age onwards, although some continuity in the use of colour is also recorded in Aquileia during the Early Imperial Age. Starting in the Severan Age, it became common to decorate entire floor spaces, often incorporating figurative themes within intricate geometric patterns. *Opus sectile* and mixed technique pavements, combining tessellated and *opus sectile* or clay elements, were also popular during the Imperial Age.

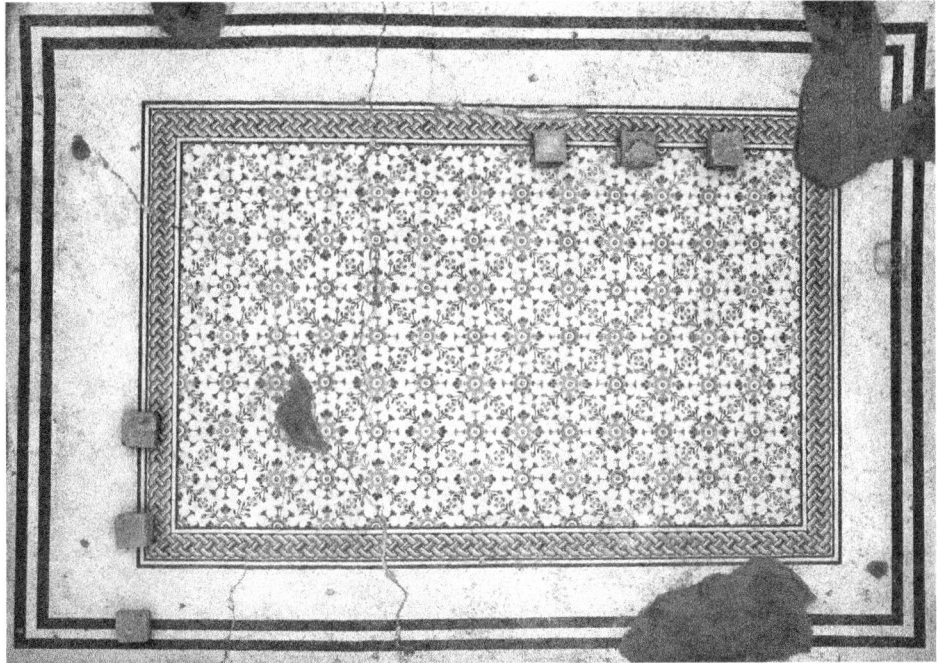

Figure 6.2 Aquileia. Mosaic of the Flowered Carpet (© Archives of Museo Archeologico Nazionale di Aquileia).

There was a notable increase in mosaic production in Aquileia during the Late Roman period, and particularly in the fourth century thanks to it being the capital of the newly established *Venetia et Histria* region. Mosaic decoration was widely used in domestic architecture, especially by the ruling class and city elites, but also within newly constructed important public and sacred buildings, such as the Great Baths (see chapter 5) and Christian basilicas (see chapter 8). Changes in decorative techniques are clearly shown in the increasingly complex schemes, the decorative redundancy, the predominance of polychromy and the use of figurative scenes to meet the demands of the wealthiest patrons, who probably relied on specialized craftsmen to decorate their state rooms. Thus, certain themes typical of aristocratic self-representation developed, with subjects inspired by sport, hunting and amphitheatre *venationes* (mosaic of the Wounded Beasts in the *domus* of the same name), fishing (mosaic of the *oecus* in Titus Macer's House) and the rural-idyllic world (mosaics of the 'Good Shepherd' in the *domus* of the same name and in the northern *domus* of the Fondo CAL), or alluding to the female virtues of the *domina* (mosaic of the 'Lady of the Roses', again in the House of the Wounded Beasts) or to the social role of the couple who owned the house (mosaic of the *domus* of Calendio and Iovina, in which the two are represented as Cupid and Psyche). Alongside this exceptional mosaic production, the use of precious *opus sectile* finishings also spread widely in Late Antiquity.

The extensive documentation available on Aquileian mosaics allows for an interpretation that highlights the close relationship between the decorative elements of domestic spaces and their intended use.[13] In the study of Roman period private architecture, understanding the relationship between decoration and the function of house spaces can effectively complement the studies of house plans. A clear distinction can be made based on the materials employed, with 'poor techniques' typically used in service or passage rooms, while marble is indicative of luxury in more prestigious areas. The arrangement and decoration of the numerous mosaics offer valuable insights. This method is particularly effective for geometric mosaics, where the selection and organization of decorations can suggest the layout, hierarchies and usage patterns within residential structures.

Looking at a few examples, we see that monochrome backgrounds (white or, more often, black) and repetitive decorations, such as simple dotted or other motifs, often recur in passageways (entrances, corridors, porticoes). This approach, well documented in Aquileia in the courtyard portico of Titus Macer's House, enjoyed long success in the Imperial Age; different arrangements are only found in Late Antiquity, for example in the porticoes of the villa in the Marignane locality, where we find a series of panels decorated with a variety of geometric patterns.

Living and reception rooms were different, intended for static rather than dynamic usage, hence they present a distinct internal arrangement. As for *cubicula* (bedrooms), in the Early Imperial Age their mosaic flooring is frequently bipartite in order to distinguish the antechamber, which is more decorated, from the bedchamber. In Aquileia, some clear examples of this are offered by the two *cubicula* in the *domus* beneath the Christian basilica and a *cubiculum* of Titus Macer's House.

Study of the *triclinia* (dining rooms), which evolved progressively in their decorative arrangement, is also informative. At least until the first century, the floors of these rooms feature a partitional band (e.g. the aforementioned mosaic of the Vine Branch with Bow) separating the antechamber from the dining space, as can be seen in the most recent of the two *triclinia* in Titus Macer's House. At a later stage, a different floor layout, in the shape of a 'T + U', became common, corresponding to the arrangement of tricliniar beds along the walls framing the central space designated for banqueting, such as in the fine example of the *triclinium* in the Lycurgus and Ambrosia *domus* (late second–early third century). From the end of the third and then in the fourth century, the single semicircular-shaped bed (*stibadium*) finally became widespread, which was well suited to the curvature of the apses in certain Late Roman reception rooms.

When compared with the excellent knowledge we have of the floor coverings, and despite continuing research,[14] the reconstruction of the wall and ceiling decorations in Aquileian private buildings becomes challenging. This is mainly due to the difficulties involved in recontextualizing the painted plaster fragments found on archaeological excavations, which are rarely discovered in situ or in a collapsed state. Despite the gaps in the surviving documentation, recent studies on the paintings of the suburban villa of the *Fondo Tuzet* and of some urban *domus* are particularly important in shedding light both on the technical aspects and on the reconstruction of the decorations.

The *Fondo Tuzet* villa (Figure 0.1, n. 22), decorated to the highest standard, was a prestigious Early Imperial Age residence (see next paragraph). Evidence of the high quality of its decorations can be found in a series of plaster fragments painted with III style motifs, stucco elements and fragments of wall mosaic. In the urban area, a careful analysis of the *Beneficio Rizzi domus* (Figure 0.1, n. 8) found painted plaster fragments relating to different building phases. The first group of fragments relates to a ceiling decorated with free vegetal composition (first half of the first century). A portion of the wall reproducing a highly illusionistic *scaenae frons* relates to the renovation phase (first half of the second century). Some wall fragments, painted with vine shoots and bunches of grapes and probably other items that were part of a ceiling with a 'vegetalized lattice' composition, were probably part of a later replastering project.

From the second half of the first century, Aquileian craftsmen began developing their own style within the framework of an innovative pictorial production, capable of assimilating and reproducing the decorative solutions of the so-called Pompeian styles. The frescoes in the *domus* under the Baptistery demonstrate the use of a wall scheme with panels and interpanels decorated with 'umbrella candelabra', a scheme that became widespread in the transalpine area. In the mid-Imperial period, decorating the plinths of painted walls with red-purple splashes on a white background or with reproductions of faux marble slabs became common. Imitation marble facings later became widespread in Late Roman Aquileian painting, as seen in the decorations of the Theodorian complex (see chapter 8).

The *suburbium*: necropolises and funerary monuments

The walled circuit of Roman cities was generally surrounded by a strip of land called the *suburbium*, which designated the gradual transition of, and mutual interaction between, the built-up area and the countryside. This highly mutable peri-urban zone was often crossed by important infrastructural works (roads, canals, bridges, aqueducts, etc.). In this zone, cultivated land, suburbs, scattered villas or buildings, workshops, commercial spaces and sacred and funerary areas could all coexist.

Aquileia was no exception.[15] For example, in the Republican Age, a cattle market probably operated in a suburban area linked to the Via Postumia by a special road junction (see chapter 4). Also in the republican period, probably in the north-eastern suburbs, on the right bank of the *Natiso cum Turro*, a temple was built from which came the well-known clay pediment found in the Monastero locality. This temple, with a marked 'anti-barbaric' connotation, was perhaps associated with the celebration of important military victories won on the eastern front. Further away from the city, but still linked to it, were two other republican places of worship, situated in topographically important locations. The first was located along the Via Annia near Ponte Orlando, northwest of Aquileia, near the bridge over the river *Alsa* (Aussa) and a four-sided arch erected on the edge of the suburban necropolis. The second was located in the Panigai locality, south of the city, not far from the present mouth of the river Natissa. Even in more recent times, although we know little about Aquileian sacred topography, it is likely that various places of worship were located in the suburbs, such as that of Belenus, in Beligna, south of the city. In the peri-urban area, particularly the southern one, various production activities were also to be found, constructed outside the built-up area in order both to reduce the inconveniences (noise, traffic, smells, etc.) and fire hazards associated with the use of furnaces and other workshop facilities and to facilitate the supply of raw materials and distribution of products across the roads and waterways.

The area surrounding the city was also home to several important suburban villas,[16] both working and residential. They were probably built on landed estates belonging to the city elites, as was likely the case with the villa in the Strazzonara locality, about a mile east of the city. On the other hand, two prestigious villas located just outside the town were purely residential. These were the villa at the *Fondo Tuzet* (Figure 0.1, n. 8),[17] immediately south of the *Natiso cum Turro* river, and the villa in the Marignane locality (Figure 0.1, n. 20),[18] west of the circus. The first, noted for the grandeur of its layout and for the exceptional quality of its decoration (paintings in III style, stuccoes, wall mosaics, architectural terracottas known as 'Campana reliefs'), can perhaps be identified with the residence of Augustus, Tiberius, Julia and other members of the imperial family during their stay in Aquileia between 12 and 9 BCE. The second, embellished with fine mosaic floors, was initially believed to possibly be the Late Roman imperial palace (see chapter 5); however, this suggestion seems unlikely as the building – although luxurious and close to the circus – was located outside the Late Roman city wall, thus extremely exposed to possible dangers.

The vast funerary areas are well documented in the Aquileian suburbs.[19] These were placed within a radius of about three miles (4.5 kilometres) from the city. In the Roman world, ancient and authoritative legal provisions forbade incinerations, inhumations and the building of tombs within settlements. The archaeological evidence confirms that these prescriptions were scrupulously observed in daily practice. The *ustrina* and *busta* (areas for cremations), *sepulcra* (tombs, sepulchres) and *monumenta* (funerary monuments) were part of the cities of the dead (necropolis), which were usually developed outside the urban perimeter, quite distinct therefore from the cities of the living. However, the two realities were complementary, including in terms of social self-representation by the different households residing in the settlement.

In Aquileia, from the final decades of the first century BCE onward, tombs were generally gathered within funerary enclosures belonging to different family units.[20] Similar (but not equal) in size and aligned with each other, even in several parallel rows, such enclosures were regularly arranged along the road axes that radiated from the city into the surrounding area. The best known necropolises correspond to the following areal distribution: from the locality of Marignane-Scofa to Ponte Orlando, along the Via Annia, in a northwesterly direction; in the localities of Santo Stefano, Morona and Zuccherina, along the Via Postumia (coinciding in this section with the road to *Noricum*), in a northerly direction; in the localities of Colombara and Sant'Egidio, along the road to *Emona* (Ljubljana), in a north-eastern direction; from the Casa Bianca locality to Roncolon, along the Gemina road, in an easterly direction; in the locality of Beligna and beyond, along the road toward the sea, in a southerly direction; and in the localities of Dorida, Bacchina and Panigai, along another, more westerly, direction toward the sea. The necropolis in the Santo Stefano locality seems to be the oldest of them all.

The only Roman funerary area currently accessible in Aquileia is the 'Sepolcreto' necropolis (Figures 0.1, n. 15; 6.3),[21] which extends out of the city along a secondary road heading southwest. Recently investigated and restored, it is one of the best-preserved necropolises in northern Italy. Presently, five funerary enclosures are visible, each

Figure 6.3 Aquileia. The sequence of funerary enclosures of the 'Sepolcreto' (© N. Oleotto).

corresponding to plots of varying width but equal depth, belonging to five Aquileian families (Statii, anonymous family, Iulii, Trebii and Cestii). These enclosures were used by the same families for several generations starting from the first century, housing numerous tombs along with their respective grave goods and funerary monuments. The long-term use of this necropolis allows us to observe the transition from the prevalent rite of incineration (where the burnt remains of the deceased were collected in urns or ossuary vessels) to inhumation (where the body was buried), well exemplified by the Late Roman sarcophagi in the fourth enclosure.

Numerous funerary artefacts have been found in Aquileia. Among the oldest is a *cippus* in the form of a small column surmounted by a helmet, variously dated between the second and first centuries BCE. While *cippi* are rather rare, urns, of various shapes and types, are much more common, as are stelae, which often bear images of the deceased, or, in other cases, reproduce the 'gate of Dis', with an obvious allusion to the passage into the realm of the dead. Also widespread are funerary altars, both cylindrical and, more frequently, rectangular in shape. Among the latter, the funerary altar of the soldier Quintus Etuvius Capreolus (late first century), from the necropolis in the Sant'Egidio locality, is of monumental dimensions. From the second century, sarcophagi are also found, particularly the 'chest' and 'architectural' types.[22]

Some funerary monuments took on architectural forms, typically of the aedicule type. A notable example is the monument of the Curii, dating to the first half of the first century. Originally from the necropolis in the Colombara locality, it is now housed in the garden of the National Archaeological Museum (Figure 6.4). This monument features an

Figure 6.4 Aquileia, National Archaeological Museum. Funerary monument of the Curii (© Esedra).

aedicule on a podium with three Ionic columns, containing a headless female statue. It is topped by a pinnacle with hollowed sides, culminating in a Corinthian capital crowned with a pinecone. The monument was set within an enclosure, with the front slabs bearing a long funerary inscription and bordered by four pinnacled urns. Several Aquileian funerary statues, including that of the so-called Navarch (see next paragraph) were likely placed in similar monument.

Finally, mention must be made of the Great Mausoleum[23] which, despite extensive and questionable restorations, is one of the most impressive funerary monuments visible in Aquileia today. Found in the necropolis in the locality of Roncolon, it was improperly reconstructed in 1955 within the town, not far from the forum, at the expense of the Candia family (hence its name, 'Candia Mausoleum'). The monument, reconstructed to a height of 17 metres, consists of a plinth, flanked by two apotropaic lions, on which rests a relief-decorated dado, which in turn supports a circular aedicule with Corinthian columns, surmounted by a pinnacle roof and crowned by a pinecone. Inside the aedicule is a headless togated statue of the deceased.

Sculpture

There are numerous sculptural works from Aquileia,[24] most of which are housed in the National Archaeological Museum.[25] Many of these were intended for funerary contexts like those just illustrated, while others were for public, sacred or private settings.

The oldest evidence includes some interesting examples of terracotta sculpture (coroplastics), from Aquileian sacred and public republican buildings. Regarding sacred architecture, there are some decorative elements from two, not yet identified, temples dating to the second century BCE. The remains of the pediment found in the Monastery locality was part of one of these.[26] Another set of architectural terracottas concerned a different temple, possibly located in the forum.[27] Terracottas like this are frequent in the cult buildings of the republican-era colonies. As far as public buildings are concerned, two groups of large terracotta telamons (first half of the first century BCE) (Figure 3.6)[28] should be mentioned, which probably ornamented one or more of the city gates.

During the first century BCE, Aquileia developed its own autonomous sculptural culture, with the emergence of local workshops that worked the hard limestone extracted from the nearby Aurisina quarries. These artisans produced numerous funerary monuments, whilst those for public use are much rarer. Some of these have come down to us headless (e.g. the maiden with pomegranate, now dated to the Augustan Age), but fortunately others are intact, such as the married couple originally placed in a funerary aedicule in the necropolis in the Sant'Egidio locality (Augustan Age). The field of funerary sculpture includes a large number of male and female portraits fully in the round (Figure 6.5), made mainly of limestone (and only exceptionally of marble) between the second half of the first century BCE and the first half of the next century. These statues typically represent individuals of high social standing who wished to portray themselves according to contemporary Roman models. These portraits are

Figure 6.5 Aquileia, National Archaeological Museum. View of the collection of portraits (J. Bonetto).

chiefly characterized by the 'intaglio' style and by physiognomic depictions of the subjects, emphasizing individual features, often unidealized, and displaying faces marked by old age. At the same time, among the urban middle class, a similar realistic rendering of faces, albeit in more schematized forms and types, is found in portraits carved in relief on funerary stelae, as well as on some funerary altars. In many cases these are high-quality products, made by local workshops.

Some of the highest-quality marble sculptures were imported even though some of the Aquileian workshops were probably capable of sculpting in marble or at least refinishing it. The well-known headless statue of the so-called Navarch of Cavenzano (second half of the first century BCE), in Greek marble, was originally placed in a Aquileian funerary monument, probably a mausoleum. The work, in the Hellenistic tradition, depicts a victorious admiral, reprising a type of statuary adopted by the Roman aristocracy for the heroized dead. A series of statues and official portraits of emperors and the Julio-Claudian imperial family (see chapter 5) are assumed to have been imported from Rome or other specialized centres or to have been sculpted in the city by itinerant craftsmen.

A quite exceptional find is a bronze *applique* with the head of *Boreas* (personification of the wind blowing from the northeast), of uncertain date, which might have belonged to a monument in the forum. The forum was the most prestigious urban setting for the display of honorary statues, of which several inscribed bases are preserved. The decoration of the attic of the forum porticoes, with a series of plinths decorated with heads of Jupiter Ammon and Medusa, has already been discussed in chapter 5.

Several historical reliefs are also attributed to the Early Imperial Age. Prominent among these is the famous relief of the *sulcus primigenius* (Figure 3.3), the sacred furrow, depicting the city's foundation ritual through the definition of its perimeter by a pair of yoked cattle. The scene takes place in the presence of *triumviri* following the plough (see chapter 3). The relief, originally placed in an important public building, possibly the forum basilica, can be dated to the first decades of the first century. According to some scholars, it reproduces the Latin colony's foundation rite (181 BCE), whilst others believe it to be the symbolic act of the colony's re-establishment (once the municipal phase had ended); still others view it as a scene related to an agricultural festival.[29]

Sculpture from the Imperial Age, both idealized statuary and local funerary portraiture, holds particular interest. After a sharp decline between the second half of the first and the entire second century, these products experienced a revival from the Severan Age and throughout the third century. The funerary purpose is evident in the case of stelae (e.g. the stele of the mime artist Bassilla) and sarcophagi featuring portraits and whole figures, carved in relief. However, it is also likely, as already found in the Late Republican and High Imperial phases, that many limestone and marble full-relief heads of both men and women also had such a funerary function. Such artefacts often reflect the characteristics of official portraiture of the period, marked by distinct volumetric features and a certain expressive realism. The only bronze portrait from Aquileia dates from the middle decades of the third century. It is a gilded bronze male head, probably depicting an, as yet unidentified, emperor.

One or two series of marble clypei with busts of deities depicting the twelve gods and dated to the first half of the fourth century probably belonged to the Late Imperial palace (see chapter 5). Aquileian portraits in the round or in relief on sarcophagi or funerary stelae (many of which belonged to military personnel) also continued to be produced during the Tetrarchic Age and the fourth century. The subjects' rendering reflects the figurative language of the time, marked by distinct volumetry and a certain abstraction in the facial features, whilst retaining their expressive intensity. A notable example from this period is a finely crafted marble head, probably not made in Aquileia and dating between the late fourth and early fifth century. It is believed to portray a member of Theodosius' or Honorius' imperial court.

Artistic craftsmanship

Aquileia has been famous for centuries for the frequent discovery of precious artefacts,[30] many of which can be admired in the National Archaeological Museum. As discussed in the previous chapter, Aquileia was a central hub for an efficient trade network which both guaranteed the arrival of raw materials and ensured the wide distribution of finished products, all facilitated by their easy transportation. This excellent location encouraged the development of sumptuary workshops, whose products were widely distributed across Italy and the transalpine provinces.

Aquileia was a flourishing and important centre for glyptics,[31] second in the West only to Rome. The city and its surrounding region received large quantities of raw ore or pre-shaped gemstones, which were then processed and finished by local workshops to be set into rings or other jewellery. The gems often featured images of protective deities, auspicious symbols or the names of the owners; for rings used for sealing, the names were engraved in reverse to be read correctly in wax impressions. Engraving activity in Aquileia began relatively early, as evidenced by some Italic-style gems produced as early as the second century BCE. A significant period of artistic flourishing occurred at the onset of the Imperial Age, marked by high-quality products that drew inspiration from Hellenistic models and themes or from motifs reworked from imperial ideology. Concurrently, the serial production of glass gems began, both as imitations of translucent or zoned stones and in coloured bands. Aquileia's glyptic industry saw substantial growth between the first and second centuries, achieving considerable commercial success, before experiencing a decline in the second half of the subsequent century. A modest revival occurred during the Constantinian era and the fourth century, with the creation of pieces featuring Christian subjects or symbols. Compared to engraved gems, which have been found in large quantities in funerary contexts and as lost items from urban areas, the number of hard stone cameos from Aquileia is much more limited. However, glass paste cameos that imitate zoned stones are more numerous.

In Roman times, Aquileia had a virtual monopoly for amber processing.[32] This valuable material arrived raw or semi-finished from the Baltic Sea, along the ancient 'amber route'. In Aquileia it was meticulously crafted into various and sometimes striking-looking artefacts, primarily intended for women. These included personal ornaments such as rings, necklace beads, pendants and *appliques*; toiletry items like cups, various vessels, spatulas and mirrors; and spinning tools including spools and spindle whorls as well as trinkets, figurines and gaming pieces such as astragals and dice. Additionally, other objects were intended for children, notably small necklace charms (*crepundia*), the sound of which were believed to ward off the evil eye. In fact, amber was believed to have prophylactic power over those who wore jewellery or amulets made of it; a beneficial effect enhanced by the apotropaic significance of the figures represented on the artefacts themselves. According to this belief, these special properties were also exerted by amber objects included in grave goods.

Aquileia was also the major centre of luxury glass production.[33] However, no definitive evidence of buildings used for manufacturing glass have so far been identified, either in the city or in the suburbs. The numerous Aquileian glass artefacts, sometimes intact (particularly from funerary contexts), are distinguished by a diversity of shapes, decorative motifs and colour combinations (Figure 6.6). In some cases, the extreme refinement of execution, achieved by resorting to different techniques over time, is startling: polychrome moulded glass ('mosaic glass'), in its different variants, sometimes distinguished by vivid colour combinations; 'gold-band glass'; blown glass, of more recent introduction, either coloured or naturally coloured or discoloured. At the beginning of the Imperial Age

Figure 6.6 Aquileia, National Archaeological Museum. View of the collection of glass artefacts (© A. Chemollo).

the prestigious 'cameo glass' vases, with white relief decoration on a blue background – linked to Aquileia by a few significant fragments – were very popular among the higher social classes.

Due to technological innovations, glass became cheaper in the second half of the first century and was widely used for making vases, various containers and other items. During the Late Roman period, production became more uniform and simplified, although valuable artefacts such as vases with engraved or gold-leaf decoration, probably of urban origin and intended for up-market clients, still circulated in the city. Notably, two fragments of cups among this output depict biblical scenes (the sacrifice of Isaac, the miracle of the spring of Moses), indicating the importance of Christianity in contemporary Aquileian society. Additionally, there is evidence of at least one diatreta cup in the city, characterized by cage decoration and iridescent dichroic glass, traditionally made by specialized Rhenish craftsmen.

Finally, artefacts and ornaments made of precious metals have been found in Aquileia,[34] though it cannot be confirmed that they were locally produced. Among the gold items, in addition to jewellery such as rings, necklaces and earrings, mention should be made of the notable discovery in a female tomb of 203 fly-shaped gold *appliques* that decorated the garment of the deceased. Regarding silverware, from the end of the Republican Age (or the beginning of the Imperial) we have the exceptional 'Aquileia plate', a masterpiece of Roman metalwork preserved in the Kunsthistorisches Museum in Vienna. This non-functional object features on its inner surface a complex relief depiction which plausibly merges Eleusinian and Isiac mythological traditions in an allegory of fertility alluding to the union between Mark Antony and Cleopatra. Additionally, numerous silver, gilded or silver-plated bronze artefacts from Late Antiquity mainly related to military ornamentation (cross fibulae, buckles, etc.) have been found. Some fine examples of table silverware, such as the gilded silver cup with niello decoration from the Fondi Cossar, and objects of Christian religious use can also be dated to the Late Roman period.

CHAPTER 7
ATTILA AND THE HUNS: THE TAKING OF AQUILEIA AND THE URBAN TRANSFORMATIONS BETWEEN THE ANCIENT AGE AND THE MIDDLE AGES

Aquileia in the first half of the fifth century

The change in geopolitical balance due to Emperor Honorius' moving the Western imperial court from Milan to Ravenna in 402 had some inevitable repercussions for Aquileia, leading to its progressive marginalization compared to the leading role it had played in the previous century.[1] For example, the emperors' sojourns were interrupted for the entire first quarter of the fifth century, and it is fair to assume that the imperial officials themselves had become noticeably scarcer in number by that time. From a military point of view, the situation had also been quite complicated for some time. In the north-eastern Italian territories, repeated incursions by the Goths and other barbarian contingents occurred during the first decade of the century: under the leadership of Alaric in 401, Radagaiso in 405–6 and again Alaric in 408. Although Aquileia was not directly affected by military operations at this point, the general climate was becoming increasingly uncertain and unstable, especially following the dramatic sack of Rome in 410 by Alaric's Visigoths. Lacking the enlightened leadership of Bishop Chromatius, who died in 408, the people of Aquileia saw the first quarter of the century end with two events that must have further fuelled a feeling of unease and inexorable decline: the outrageous torture of the usurper Joannes, beheaded in the circus in 425, and the closure of the mint in the same year.[2] Also in 425, the very young Caesar Valentinian III and his mother Galla Placidia resided in the city for about four months, marking the last recorded imperial stay in Aquileia in Late Antiquity.

The city must have still retained quite a monumental appearance, even if some ancient public buildings had by then changed function or, having fallen into disuse, been dismantled to obtain useful building material. From a construction point of view, alongside the proliferation of Christian sacred buildings (see chapter 8), priority was given to those works that maintained the effectiveness of the fortifications. In the first half of the fifth century, perhaps on the initiative of the Eastern Emperor Theodosius II (siding with Valentinian III), the defensive works were strengthened by erecting a new stretch of wall (known as M3; Figure 0.1, n. 3).[3] The new curtain wall ran parallel to the M2 defensive wall in the southern half of the urban perimeter, making it not an independent walled circuit, but an external reinforcement added to the existing walls, keeping a close distance from them and following the riverbank for a long stretch.

In providing this double curtain wall, the desire to protect the southern urban sector, where much of the social, religious and commercial life of Late Antique Aquileia was based, is clear.

In the eastern sector, the M3 walls extend for a certain distance above the – now closed – ancient riverbed, whose width had been reduced by the diversion of the watercourse carried out during Julian's siege in 361–2. Further south, at the bend, recent archaeological investigations[4] have shown that the wall structure included a series of openings connected to corresponding access ramps to the river, along which were landing points useful for loading and unloading goods. The most recent curtain wall thus combined the strengthening of defensive functions with the maintenance of commercial ones, practised behind the Late Roman markets (Figure 7.1) and close to the great *horrea* and the episcopal complex (Figure 0.1, n. 23). This was now the heart of Aquileia's public life.

Aquileia thus maintained the characteristics that had always distinguished it: an impregnable stronghold on the one hand and an emporium with broad commercial interests on the other. These were almost two solid literary tropes, extolled by Ausonius himself a few decades earlier, which still applied despite the increasingly precarious political and military situation. The general situation was constantly changing, and it should therefore come as no surprise that in Aquileia, as in other parts of Roman Italy, very different or even contrasting architectural and urban realities could coexist, sometimes even within the same urban districts. This phenomenon had already been observed in the previous century in terms of public buildings (see chapter 5). Influenced by the changed social order of the fifth century, investment in private buildings also began to decrease, resulting in a decline in architectural and decorative quality.

Figure 7.1 Aquileia. Virtual reconstruction of Late Antique walls, *horrea* and markets (© Fondazione Aquileia/Ikon/Nudesign).

Living in Aquileia in the first half of the fifth century: the case of Titus Macer's House

An interesting example of how housing was evolving in Aquileia in the first half of the fifth century is offered by recent excavations at Titus Macer's House (Figure 0.1, n. 7; see chapter 6).[5]

In the first quarter of the century, the building was still used for domestic purposes, did not show significant signs of degradation and had not been divided between different owners as is sometimes seen in coeval archaeological contexts. On the contrary, it underwent an organic and unified plan of renovation adapted to new functional needs and lifestyles. The overall image is that of a respectable house, inhabited by a family group with comfortable living standards and probably well integrated into Aquileian society.

In transforming the domestic building in this phase, the atrium, *tablinum* and other references to a now distant past were rejected in favour of a series of more contemporary spaces intended for the conduct of daily life. The brick repaving of almost the entire front part of the building was part of this transformation. Whilst, at least in this period, this was undoubtedly a rather unusual type of floor covering for the private sphere, it can be compared to the utilitarian brick floor that paved the city's Late Roman food market, east of the forum.

The front of the building was accessible both from the public street, whose paving was by then beginning to be covered by a substantial layer of soil, and from a side alley, also made of beaten earth; further communication with the outside was provided through the new service area on the northern side, equipped with a canopy under which a cart or other tools could be stored. All this, however, does not seem enough to suggest signs of an incipient process of the 'ruralization' of the urban space, characterized by the diminishment of residential contexts, the spread of cultivated areas between the walls and the progressive disappearance of urban life. In fact, Aquileia, at the beginning of the fifth century, was highly urbanized.

Alongside the 'rustic' space discussed above, the more dedicated residential rooms were reduced to one of the two original *cubicula* and, above all, to the core unit comprising the two rooms of the former *tablinum* and the former *triclinium*, now linked with each other. Even here, the change from the previous phases is noticeable. Though there was no change in the overall plan, the contraction of the residential spaces demonstrates a different conception of the domestic building, which no longer corresponded to the layout of the wealthy Imperial Age dwelling. Although radically transformed, the house maintained a space to adequately represent the role of the owner, identifiable in the large room with the 'mosaic with a fishing scene', which already existed in the innermost part of the house.

A marked change occurred in the second quarter of the century. The floor mosaic inside a living room was partially destroyed, with a subsequent accumulation of rubble, leading to the room being temporarily out of use. It was then transformed into a small domestic ironworking forge.

The reuse of living spaces for the purpose of conducting artisanal activities, primarily metalworking, is something that is increasingly found in Aquileia in this period. The archaeological dating of these changes is particularly interesting. The fact that, in this house, the beginning of the phenomenon turns out to be slightly before mid-century is particularly significant. The coexistence of living quarters and craft spaces within the same domestic building cannot be considered an indirect consequence of Attila's sack, but rather a reflection of social changes already underway before 452.

Attila's siege and its consequences

It is difficult to distinguish between history and legend in the most famous episode of Late Roman Aquileia: its destruction by Attila's army in 452.[6] After having crossed the Alps, the armed Huns besieged the solid walls of the Upper Adriatic city for three months. Yet, it proved to be an impregnable stronghold, living up to its inhabitants' expectations, as had already happened in previous centuries when it had withstood long and exhausting sieges. Every attempt to conquer the city had failed. Attila, now resolved to give up, suddenly received a premonitory sign that he interpreted as favourable: according to the account of the historian Procopius of Caesarea,[7] a stork suddenly took flight with its young, abandoning its nest on one of the towers of the walls to head towards the countryside. Seizing this as an omen of victory, Attila inflamed the spirits of his men and unleashed the decisive attack. On 18 July, an ominous day, Aquileia succumbed to the Huns' assault. The invincible bulwark of the empire had fallen into the hands of the Barbarians. What a grim augury for Rome!

A well-established tradition has it that, once fallen, Aquileia was sacked, set on fire and devastated by Attila's hordes who were responsible for the complete destruction of the city, from which it would never recover. The literary trope of the impregnable city[8] was replaced, as early as the early Middle Ages, by the common belief that the Hunnic sack of 452 represented a clear watershed in the history of Aquileia, whose inhabitants were largely forced to leave the city. Hence the tendency in certain literature to uncritically apply the suppositions of the so-called 'Attila theorem',[9] according to which every trace of fire or destructive episode from Aquileia in this period is attributable to the intervention of the Huns, while any building work must have taken place before the mid-fifth century. The limits of such a rigid approach are all too evident, more so if it is applied *a priori* to a historical phase marked by profound transformations such as those taking place between Late Antiquity and the early Middle Ages, from a political, military, economic, social, religious and cultural, not to mention climatic and environmental, point of view. A less simplistic approach, as in current studies, to such a complex subject considers that the dramatic events of 452 must be considered alone, albeit within the framework of a process that had already begun some time earlier, refraining, on the one hand, from from asserting a 'catastrophic' interpretation and, on the other, from being too 'reductionist'.

Recent archaeological research has shown that Aquileia survived the terrible episode in question.[10] Certainly, the city suffered a severe setback, but once Attila's army had left, the situation returned, albeit with some difficulty, to normal, especially when several Aquileian prisoners were able to return to their homes, as recorded in a letter sent by Pope Leo the Great to Bishop Nicetas in 458.[11] One way or another, the city came back to life, whether due to the resilience of its population, the leading role exercised by the Christian religious authorities, or an economic recovery founded on the vitality of commercial traffic. Indeed, recent investigation has shown that the large Late Roman market complex was still in use in the second half of the fifth century. The south-eastern urban sector, in the vicinity of the episcopal complex (Figure 0.1, n. 23), confirmed itself as the main centre of public life in Aquileia in this historical phase. However, there is no lack of information from other contexts as well, such as the Great Baths (Figure 0.1, n. 12), which underwent restoration until the middle of the fifth century, without forgetting, of course, the establishment of Christian sacred buildings (see chapter 8).

Despite these positive signs, there were significant concerns on the political and military fronts. The inevitable decline of local institutions was evident, symbolized by the deteriorating city forum. Additionally, the impending fall of imperial power became increasingly clear and troubling, especially after the devastating sack of Rome by Genseric's Vandals in 455.

Surviving in Aquileia in the mid-fifth century: the case of Titus Macer's House

In the mid-fifth century (425–75), research at Titus Macer's House (Figure 0.1, n. 7) reveals a fascinating historical and archaeological picture,[12] rich with building transformations reflecting the rapid changes of the time. This case study offers a unique opportunity to distinguish which transformations occurred before, during or shortly after the pivotal year of 452. While this snapshot of life in Aquileia doesn't represent the entire urban reality, it does allow us to closely examine some intriguing aspects of this controversial historical transition.

Firstly, the interior of the building was drastically restructured, upending the accepted approach to spatial use up to that time. The main changes involved the installation of small provisional structures, the defunctionalization of numerous rooms, the decommissioning of the forge and the contraction of the living space to within the front section of the building. This transformation seems to have taken place around the middle of the century, perhaps in relation to the sack of Attila or in the years immediately following that event. The sudden changes to the domestic building might therefore reveal a sudden change of ownership of the building during this dramatic period, which had led to the deportation of part of Aquileia's population into captivity. However, there seems to be no traces of fire or other violent destructive acts; on the contrary, some sporadic signs of maintenance can be discerned in the positioning of beams or wooden supports.

The situation changed rapidly. Shortly after their installation, the temporary structures fell into disuse and were removed. This was followed by bouts of heavy plundering that, taken together, compromised the functionality of the entire building. The building material (slabs, bricks, columns, roof tiles, timber, etc.) was removed from the site and transferred elsewhere, probably for reuse. This series of spoliations was intensive but probably not systematic and was facilitated by the building being left in a state of momentary abandonment and perhaps even freely accessible from the outside. Having lost its domestic function, the house thus became a sort of quarry for the reclamation of building material and a suitable place for the lighting of occasional fires. In all likelihood, these events occurred a few years after the capitulation of 452. Moreover, the decay of the building does not appear to be due to a single devastating event, such as an arson attack or a simultaneous demolition, but rather to a series of episodes that occurred, in a non-systematic manner, over a period of time. In this specific case, we are therefore left with the impression that this critical situation occurred not so much as a direct result of the Huns, but rather because of the very unstable conditions pertaining after Attila's sack.

At a still later date, non-occasional frequentation of the surviving structures resumed. Initially, the front sector of the building was affected by repeated dumping of rubbish (meal remains, coals, fragments of ceramic, glass and iron artefacts, as well as building debris), which led to the formation of a small tip. This was followed by the laying of a new clay floor, which restored a modicum of decorum and usability to the front sector of the building, in which the forge was reactivated and ironworking activities resumed. Soon, however, the custom of discarding refuse in the front area of the building resumed: it was in this new dump that a purse containing about 560 coins was inadvertently lost (Figure 7.2). This exceptional numismatic find makes it possible to precisely date the

Figure 7.2 Aquileia, National Archaeological Museum. The Late Antique hoard of around 560 coins found in Titus Macer's House (J. Bonetto).

event between 460 and 475, offering a previously unpublished record of everyday life in Aquileia in the decades immediately following Attila's siege. The fact that the building was in some way redeveloped, restoring the production activities that had been abruptly interrupted in the middle of the century, suggests that the legitimate owners had finally returned to the city, retaking control of it.

From the fall of the Western Roman Empire to the end of the Gothic War

Twenty-five years after surviving the Hunnic sack of 452, Aquileia had to face the consequences of the fall of the Western Roman Empire (476), an epochal event that coincided with the deposition of the Emperor Romulus Augustulus by Odoacer, leader of the *Heruli*. The end of imperial power had an extraordinarily important impact, with all the consequences that followed.[13]

In Aquileia, the effects of this crisis, with all its political-administrative implications, are well illustrated by the abandonment of the forum and its buildings, which fell into a state of pitiful ruin over the course of the fifth century. The void left by the abandonment of the institutions was filled, at least in part, by the bishop's authority. Continuing a process that had been underway for some time, city life was concentrated in the south-eastern sector of the city, the site of the episcopal complex and the nearby marketplaces, whose system of river landing places remained in use until the first decades of the sixth century. Up to that time discrete trade networks survived, ensuring a certain economic well-being for those inhabitants who had remained in the city or had returned once the repercussions of the Hunnic invasion had faded. Others, however, fearing the frequent invasions, found refuge on the islands of the nearby lagoon, contributing to the formation of the Grado *castrum*.

From an archaeological point of view, there is an almost total absence of material evidence in Aquileia in Odoacer's time (476–93), while there is somewhat more substantial documentation for the period of the subsequent Gothic Kingdom of Italy (493–535), also known as the Ostrogothic Kingdom, when Aquileia and the whole of the *Venetia* finally began to benefit from the relative stability and a long period of peace (at least by the standards of those years). Although reduced in size compared to its glorious past and marginalized with respect to the new geopolitical dynamics, Aquileia maintained a role of some importance in its territorial context. Significant in this sense is the material evidence, dating back to the Ostrogothic Age, connected with Germanic culture, among which we must mention some significant grave goods, belonging to high-ranking individuals who probably resided in the city.[14]

Several elegant residences, inhabited by high-ranking individuals, remained in use within the walls. One such was probably the wealthy owner who commissioned the extensive restoration of the well-known 'Mosaic of the Good Shepherd in the singular garment' inside his home between the fifth and sixth centuries. Of course, there was no lack of more, very simple, humble houses, often built in the spaces of pre-existing domestic structures, as in the case of the nearby Titus Macer's House (from the second half of the fifth century), or built within large public buildings that had fallen into disuse, such as the forum basilica (between the fifth and the first half of the sixth century), the amphitheatre (from the mid-fifth century) and the Great Baths (from the sixth century). From an urban planning point of view, the coexistence of such different housing solutions, sometimes even within the same neighbourhood, was very much part of the broader phenomenon of the disintegration of the city space. Vast run-down areas alternated with the remains of old buildings, now often converted to other functions, while new constructions were much rarer. At the dawn of the Middle Ages, Aquileia was therefore a city in an advanced phase of transformation compared to the previous Roman urban layout, not least due to the abandonment of the sewage system and street paving.

After forty years of relative peace, the Eastern Emperor Justinian decided to put his long-held plan to reconquer Italy into action, sparking the Gothic War (535–53), a conflict in which Aquileia was only marginally involved. By the end of the war, which concluded with a Byzantine victory, the urban area of Aquileia had significantly shrunk. A new, imposing defensive wall with a broken-line pattern (known as M4; Figure 1, n. 27)[15] was constructed immediately south of the forum area. The segmented design of these walls, characterized by a series of triangular bastions and a rectilinear outer wall, served a specific military purpose: this design was particularly useful for breaking the momentum of enemy assaults, ensuring effective control of siege operations and providing advanced artillery positions. Beyond its defensive aspects, the consequences for urban life were significant. The city's space was now reduced to the southern portion of the Late Antique city, centred on the episcopal complex, while the entire central–northern sector, including the circus and the forum area, was left in a state of abandonment.

CHAPTER 8
CHRISTIAN AQUILEIA: THE EPISCOPAL COMPLEX AND THE PATRIARCHATE*

The origins of Christianity in Aquileia

Traditional sources state that Christianity arrived early in Aquileia thanks to the preaching of St Mark the Evangelist, appointed by St Peter the Apostle, the first bishop of Rome and the first pontiff of the Catholic Church. It was long believed that, after landing on the shores of the nearby lagoon of Grado (near today's Pineta di San Marco locality), Mark founded the first Christian community in Aquileia. In that context the brilliant figure of Hermagoras (or Hermacoras)[1] would emerge, who was consecrated bishop of Aquileia directly by Peter, in the presence of Mark himself. Hermagoras then chose Fortunatus as deacon, who faithfully assisted his bishop until his martyrdom. The sequence of events related to the so-called Marcian Legend and the lives of Saints Hermagoras and Fortunatus is illustrated in the cycle of twelfth-century frescoes in the crypt of the basilica. However, it should be noted that in the written sources, the first reference to Mark's Aquileian mission, culminating in the episcopal appointment of Hermagoras, cannot be dated earlier than the eighth century.

The proposed events that took place in the first century clearly lack historical connections. In fact, mapping the panorama of early Aquileian Christianity is a complex undertaking.[2] In the current state of studies, apart from the possible Aquileian origin of Pope St Pius I (140–55), the first records of the spread of Christianity in Aquileia seem to date back to the third century. The figure of Hermagoras, whose martyrdom is supposed to date back to the period of the Emperor Decius' (249–51) anti-Christian persecutions, is more likely to be traced to this century. He is said to have contributed to the stable organization of the Church in Aquileia through the establishment of the diocese, which he later led as the first bishop.

The historical reconstruction described above was evidently done *a posteriori*, to vindicate or reinforce the presumed apostolic origins of the patriarchal see (through the evangelist Mark). Certainly, the close connection between Hermagoras and Mark also suggests other points of interest. Mark is said to have conducted his evangelizing work not only in Aquileia but also in Alexandria, of which he is said to have become the first bishop. It is likely that the alleged relationship between Mark and Hermagoras alludes to the strong Eastern and, particularly, Alexandrian influences exerted on the early Church of Aquileia. Conversely, from a Western perspective, the fact that Mark was a disciple of Peter would be a reminder of how the churches founded by Mark were originally dependent on the Church of Rome.

Another factor in the establishment of Christianity in Aquileia, as elsewhere, was the testimony of faith and the moral legacy of the martyrs.[3] After Hermagoras and Fortunatus, we have information about other Aquileian martyrs from the second half of the third century, perhaps under the Emperor Numerian (283–4). Although historical connections are again rather uncertain, these martyrs include Saint Hilary, traditionally considered the second bishop of Aquileia, and his deacon Saint Tatian.[4] There seems to be more certainty, however, about the seven saints who were martyred in Aquileia and nearby San Canzian d'Isonzo during the great persecution of the Emperor Diocletian, between 303 and 305: the two brothers Felix and Fortunatus; the Aquileian bishop Chrysogonus;[5] and the three Cantiani siblings – Cantius, Cantianus and their sister Cantianilla[6] – with their tutor Protus. In Salona, Dalmatia, St Anastasius, known as 'the Washerman', of Aquileian origin, was also martyred.

All these events were taking place at a time when Aquileia had taken on the role of capital of *Venetia et Histria*, heir to the Augustan *decima regio* and transformed into a province through Diocletian's territorial and administrative reorganization. By the dawn of the fourth century, the Upper Adriatic city had become a real metropolis of the Roman Empire and was constantly growing in importance. In it, thousands of residents with different languages, cultures and religions coexisted without any particular conflict. However, the political authorities attempted – without any real success – to repress freedom of worship, sowing terror among those who professed the Christian faith. We also need to consider that, in contemporary Aquileia, Christianity had already spread not only among the people but also among its leaders, if it is true that the bishop Chrysogonus had been a high Roman dignitary (though there is some uncertainty about his identification). These may have been exemplary, not systematic, condemnations. However, the anachronism inherent in these actions was all too evident.

Bishop Theodore and the building of the episcopal complex

The time was ripe for a drastic change of course. The epochal turning point was not long in coming and it affected everyone in the empire. In 313, two years after the Emperor Galerius had sanctioned the end of the persecution of Christians, the emperors Constantine and Licinius signed the agreement that went down in history as the Edict of Milan or Edict of Tolerance. With Constantine and Licinius' act, freedom of worship was granted to the faithful of all religions, including Christianity.[7]

The Aquileian Christians, of course, also benefited from this change. As soon as they were allowed, they publicly showed that they belonged to an already solid and well-organized ecclesiastical community by speedily building a substantial episcopal complex (Figure 0.1, n. 23).[8] As we will learn, it consisted of two parallel halls for worship, a third transverse hall, a baptistery and other rooms with different functions. The building was constructed next to the new *horrea* in the south-eastern sector of the city, in a rather out-of-the-way urban block that had been recently enclosed within the Late Antique city walls. Its construction required the acquisition and demolition of a number of pre-existing buildings and at the same time partially exploited their walls.

The initiator and main author of this building project was Bishop Theodore,[9] who headed the diocese of Aquileia in the second decade of the fourth century. He was the first bishop from Aquileia for whom we have a secure historical record, having participated in the Council of Arles in 314 together with his deacon, Agathon. The dedicatory inscription in the mosaic of the cycle of Jonah that paves the chancel of the south hall commemorates his involvement: 'O blessed Theodore, with the help of almighty God and the flock entrusted to you from heaven, you have happily completed all these works and solemnly dedicated them' (Figure 8.1). A second mosaic inscription in the north hall also commemorates Theodore.

As the inscription suggests, there is no shepherd without his flock. The entire community of the faithful, who actively collaborated with their bishop, played a crucial role in the building venture. Theodore, in particular, relied on the financial support of some wealthy Christian Aquileians, who are depicted in the male and female busts in the

Figure 8.1 Aquileia, Christian basilica. Bishop Theodore's dedicatory inscription in the floor mosaic of the cycle of Jonah (© M. Vecchi, Società di Conservazione della Basilica di Aquileia).

floor mosaic of the southern hall. These images, along with the epigraphic text and the monumentality of the new episcopal complex, highlighted the official role the Church had undertaken in contemporary society, in alignment with imperial power. A new chapter had begun in the history of Rome and, in its own small way, in Aquileia.

In the case of Aquileia's episcopal complex, it is not possible to establish whether Emperor Constantine was directly involved. However, we do know that having overcome their initial hostility, the emperor granted the Aquileians significant advantages, which were also reflected in the urban and monumental development of the Upper Adriatic city. It is also known that the emperor was in contact with Bishop Theodore, since he invited the latter to attend the above-mentioned Council of Arles in 314. But we should also take into account another element. In the southern hall, within the mosaic clypeus enclosing Theodore's dedicatory inscription, the epigraphic text is surmounted by a conspicuous Christological monogram (*Chrismon*). This symbolized the name and figure of Christ, but also corresponded to the celestial sign that a few years earlier, in 312, had led Constantine to victory in the Battle of the Milvian Bridge against his rival Maxentius. In other words, the symbol would have recalled the famous motto '*In hoc signo vinces*', referring as much to Constantine's temporal power as to the spiritual power of the Church. And the two powers were destined to work closely together, with their roles intimately intertwined.

The earliest version of the episcopal complex, dating back to the time of Theodore, had a compact plan, arranged in a north–south direction, with access from the road flanking it on the eastern side (Figure 8.2). The two main buildings of this complex are undoubtedly the two rectangular basilica halls (37.40 × 17.25 metres on the north side; 37.40 × 20.40 metres on the south side), without apses, which were arranged parallel to each other in an east–west direction. Inside, the space extends without interruption, apart from six large intermediate pillars used to support the ceiling beams. The architecture is very simple and modular. Some scholars believe that different liturgical functions took place in the two halls; others think that one of the two was intended for liturgical functions and the other for the instruction of catechumens – that is, still unbaptized adults. Despite various theories, the reason for having two side-by-side basilicas has not yet been clearly determined, despite being a model well known in the Late Antique world. Moreover, at Aquileia there was also a third hall, similar to the previous ones but smaller (28.80 × 13.70 metres) and paved in *cocciopesto*, placed at right angles to the others on the west side of the building complex, with access only from the northern hall. The intermediate space between these three buildings, arranged in a U-shape, was occupied by the baptistery and other rooms with an uncertain function, but perhaps at least partly linked to the episcopal residence.

The two basilica halls had mosaic floors that extended over the whole surface: the one in the southern hall, inside the current basilica, is almost completely preserved, whilst the one in the northern hall is severely damaged due to the superimposition of Poppo's bell tower. Both had frescoed walls and ceilings decorated with vivid colour contrasts which had a strong visual impact. On the walls these frescoes alternated with imitation marble panels, but on some walls of the south hall there were also pleasant views of

Figure 8.2 Aquileia. Virtual reconstruction of the episcopal complex with the two parallel basilica halls, built by Bishop Theodore (© Altair4 Multimedia).

lush gardens. The ceilings were painted in a coffered style. Recent speculation about an integrated interpretation of the pictorial and mosaic decoration have produced interesting insights.[10] The layout of the extensive floor coverings of the two halls reflects on the ground the spatial organization of the ceilings above. The arrangement of the large transverse mosaic panels, separated by wide bands of plant motifs, is better understood in this way; the layout in the panels appears further divided in the southern hall. In both buildings, the chancel space at the back of the hall, intended for the clergy and originally separated by special transennae, is clearly emphasized; a similar separation was also present at the back of the smaller central hall.

Various geometric patterns containing a rich selection of figurative subjects are developed within this compositional scheme. These appear to be fully consistent with the Aquileian figurative repertoire of the time, here evidently expressed from a Christian perspective, as is the case for the paradisiacal allusion suggested by the 'garden paintings' on the walls.[11] As already noted, the mosaic flooring of the southern hall, covering an area of 760 square metres, is exceptionally well preserved (Figure 8.3). It mainly features numerous representations of animals and birds (also very frequent in the northern hall), as well as personifications of the seasons and various figures of worshippers; taken together, these images evoke peace and prosperity. There are also several portraits, including those of the meritorious financiers of the work; the evangelical figure of the Good Shepherd; the fight between the cockerel and the tortoise (a scene also repeated in the north hall), alluding to the clash between the light of truth and the darkness of evil;

Figure 8.3 Aquileia, Christian basilica. The interior of the basilica with the extraordinary mosaic floor dating from the second decade of the fourth century (© M. Vecchi, Società di Conservazione della Basilica di Aquileia).

and the so-called winged 'Christian Victory', bearing a palm and a laurel wreath. Finally, the entire chancel space is occupied by the extraordinary depiction of a sea of fish, which forms the backdrop to the clypeus with the dedication to Theodore and three scenes from the Jonah cycle:[12] Jonah, thrown into the sea from a boat, is swallowed by a whale; Jonah is thrown back onto a beach after spending three days and three nights in the belly of the sea monster; Jonah rests under a pergola. The prominent position reserved for these three biblical episodes, inspired by the Old Testament Book of Jonah, serves their symbolic interpretation as a herald of Christ's Resurrection. This was an 'open book', narrated in images, which lent themselves to different levels of interpretation, as can be seen in the numerous interpretations advocated by modern scholars.

The Arian threat

In the central decades of the fourth century the dynamic Aquileian Church was growing rapidly.[13] Christianity was spreading through the city's social fabric, and while there was perhaps some resistance among the ruling class, it was generally gaining widespread acceptance among the people. Yet, despite the favourable circumstances, in that same period the Church was forced to face the frustrating effects of theological disputes concerning Arianism,[14] a doctrine which denied the divine nature of Christ and which had already been condemned as heretical at the Council of Nicaea in 325 (convened and presided over by Constantine himself, confirming the incipient Caesaropapism). This conflict was particularly felt in Aquileia, to the point that – around 340 – an attempted occupation of the episcopal see triggered serious unrest. This was one of the difficulties faced by Bishop Fortunatianus (*c.* 342–70),[15] who was also forced to suffer interference by the pro-Arian Emperor Constantius II (337–61), which intensified after the death of his brother Constans in 350. Moreover, Fortunatianus also had to deal with the rise and fall of the usurper Magnentius (who between 350 and 352 made Aquileia his headquarters) and the siege launched between 361 and 362 by Julian the Apostate's army.

Some scholars attribute the early replacement of the northern Theodorian hall to Fortunatianus. This new and larger basilica (not preserved) was intended to accommodate the growing number of Aquileian worshippers. Evidence of this comes from the testimony of Athanasius of Alexandria, who in 345 celebrated Easter in Aquileia with Fortunatianus himself, in the presence of Emperor Constans, in an as yet incomplete basilica.

The northern post-Theodorian basilica was much larger than its predecessor (73 × 31 metres) and reproduced its non-apsed rectangular plan. Divided into three naves by two rows of fourteen columns, it was the same as the original hall on the north and west sides, whilst it extended it further eastward and southward. This meant sacrificing the intermediate Theodorian hall, but at the same time obtaining a new baptismal space. Significantly, the entrance to the basilica was moved to the western side, to face the town, rather than being on the east, facing the walls and river. The interior was paved in mosaic, with the chancel at the back, preceded by a central aisle that allowed the clergy to pass among the faithful. The new floor plan overlaid, and thereby preserved, the original Theodorian one. A large quadriporticus was built in front of the building, with a central uncovered area, corresponding to the space of today's Piazza Capitolo. Further north were the rooms of the Episcope.

The Council of Aquileia of 381 and the figure of Chromatius

However, the work on extending Aquileia's episcopal complex was still not finished. The most accredited current hypothesis is that the southern post-Theodorian basilica dates back to Bishop Chromatius (388–408). Constructed parallel to the newly built northern basilica, it also overlies the previous hall, which had been demolished because it had become too small for the needs of Aquileia's Christians. Fortunately, the extraordinary mosaic floor and the lower portion of the painted Theodorian phase walls were buried and remained so until their modern rediscovery. The new building was slightly smaller (67 × 29 metres) than the northern post-Theodorian basilica but, like it, had a non-apsidal rectangular floor plan with access from the west. It was paved in mosaic and divided internally into three naves marked by two rows of fourteen columns.

A long narthex connected the fronts of the two post-Theodorian basilicas, which were aligned with each other. Towards the south this narthex terminated in a small apse, whose floor mosaic depicted a peacock among vine shoots. Probably, in the Chromatian period, another building complex centred on the new baptistery was also built to the west of the narthex and parallel with the southern basilica. This was preceded by an atrium (later partly occupied by the Church of the Pagans in the ninth century) and was flanked by two long rooms with mosaics, known as the *Nordhalle* and *Südhalle*.[16] In this phase, apart from the various building transformations that took place in the following centuries, the layout and size of the southern basilica and the baptistery in front of it would have been quite similar to the present ones.

The enlargement of the episcopal complex responded 'in real time' to the needs of the clergy and the growing number of the faithful who were embracing the Christian faith. If the size of the two basilicas and the surrounding buildings gives a clear picture of the importance that the Aquileian episcopal power had then acquired, equally emblematic is the fact that the new 'Christian quarter' had by then taken on a central role in the city, radically overturning the sense of marginality (urbanistic and perhaps, at least in part, social) that had characterized its birth in Theodore's time. Soon afterwards, a vast cemetery area also began to develop around the episcopal complex.

The extraordinary flourishing of the Church in Aquileia in the second half of the fourth century[17] was mainly due to the influential personalities of the bishops Valerian (368–88)[18] and Chromatius (388–408),[19] both of whom were recognized as saints after their deaths. Thanks to their staunch and declared hostility towards the Arian heresy, the Church of Aquileia achieved a leading role in the discussion of sensitive dogmatic controversies during this period, which put it in close contact with other important episcopal sees in the ancient world. This eminent role reached its peak with the Council of Aquileia in 381,[20] convened to condemn Arianism and its last supporters. The Council was held in the city at the above-mentioned episcopal complex and presided over by Valerian, under the distinguished leadership of Ambrose, Bishop of Milan. In the same year, the First Council of Constantinople reaffirmed the validity of Nicene orthodoxy in Trinitarian matters, as professed in the Nicaean Creed (the version of the 'Creed' most normally recited during church services).

Only a year earlier, through the Edict of Thessalonica in 380, the Emperor Theodosius (379–95), together with Gratian and Valentinian II, had proclaimed Christianity the state religion of the Roman Empire. Christianity was now fully established.

Although political upheavals and military instability remained virtually the order of the day, by the end of the fourth century Aquileia was finally enjoying a newfound climate of social peace and the benefits of the good relationship established with Theodosius and his court. And, from a religious and cultural point of view, it could boast not only the stable presence of Chromatius, but also the intermittent one of Rufinus of Concordia,[21] both of whom were learned theologians and acute exegetes, numbered among the Fathers of the Church. In short, this was the Aquileia remembered by the poet Ausonius as the ninth city of the empire:[22] populous, prosperous and well defended. But another momentous event now lay on the horizon: in 395, on the death of Theodosius, the Roman Empire was destined to be split between West and East.

The suburban basilicas

In 402, Emperor Honorius (395–423), who succeeded his father Theodosius in the western part of the empire, moved the imperial court from Milan to Ravenna, thereby altering the geopolitical balance that had been established in northern Italy after the Diocletian reform. In 408 (the same year as Chromatius' death) the Visigoths under Alaric descended into Italy for the second time, menacing, but not attacking, Aquileia. They continued their advance as far as Rome, resulting in the dramatic sack of 410. Rome's political and military decline was as evident as it was unstoppable. Aquileia itself must have suffered in those years from a climate of deep disquiet, accentuated, in this case, by a lack of confidence due to the loss of prestige compared to the splendour of the previous century.

We can assume that, in these dark times, Aquileia's large Christian community sought comfort in its faith by going to the basilicas of the episcopal complex as well as other newly constructed buildings of worship.[23] We know little about those in the city itself. In contrast, we have far greater archaeological knowledge of the suburban basilicas, which were built outside the Late Roman city walls, generally in the vicinity of earlier pagan necropolises. They are the *Basilica di Monastero*, in the north-eastern suburbs; the *Basilica di San Giovanni in Foro*, in the south-western suburbs; the *Basilica di San Felice*, in the south-eastern suburbs; and the *Basilica di Fondo Tullio* in the Beligna locality, in the southern suburb about 2 kilometres south of the town. We know little about when they were first built, but there is no shortage of evidence that they seem to date back to the late fourth century. Although these buildings no longer exist, we can describe each one briefly.

To the north-east of the town, in the Monastero suburb between the *Natiso cum Turro* and one of its tributaries, stood a suburban basilica (Figure 0.1, n. 26) that, over the centuries, underwent a series of intriguing architectural and functional transformations.[24] As early as the ninth century a Benedictine women's monastery was first built on the remains of the basilica. Following the suppression of the monastery in 1782, the walls of the church were exploited to make a rustic building for crushing grapes. Finally, in the last century, the Aquileia Early Christian Museum was created inside the latter. The original structures were investigated several times between the nineteenth and twentieth centuries. Preceded by a frontal narthex, the basilica was initially conceived as a single nave, a very elongated rectangular hall (48.25 × 16.85 metres), crossed longitudinally by a central aisle that led to the chancel delimited by a transenna and finished at the back by an apsidal wall; from here there was access to a room behind the apse or to three side rooms. The mosaic floor of the hall and side rooms, divided into panels with geometric decorations, remains in a good state of preservation and the numerous inscriptions in Latin and Greek in it commemorate the sponsors of the mosaics themselves. According to some scholars, the building dates to the late fourth or early fifth century and later underwent some floor renovations. Others, however, believe that it was built around the mid-fifth century. The division of the hall into three naves is more recent (eighth–ninth centuries).

At the current stage of studies, most of the basilicas seem to be in the southern suburban sector. To the south-west stood the *Basilica di San Giovanni in Foro* (Figure 0.1, n. 24), later part of the medieval-era settlement and finally demolished in 1852. Its ancient origin was only recognized in 1970, thanks to the identification of the narthex and the discovery of a Christian cemetery in use between the late fourth and fifth centuries. The plan of the building still remains rather uncertain. It is believed that the church held some relics of St John the Evangelist, brought to Aquileia in the late fourth century. Indeed, Chromatius' focus on the veneration of and prestigious role of saints' relics is well known, and this was very much in line with a popular trend of the Church of that time.

To the south-east stood the *Basilica di San Felice* (Figure 0.1, n. 25), built opposite a bend in the *Natiso cum Turro*. It was a three-nave basilica (31 × 21 metres) divided by two rows of eight columns, decorated with a mosaic floor with inscriptions bearing the names of the mosaics' sponsors. The basilica probably dates to the fifth century and is believed to have been built on the site of an earlier martyrial memorial to the saints Felix and Fortunatus, erected on the site of their burial in a cemetery just outside the city. In turn, the evidence of a cult of the two martyrs soon became a focus for new Christian graves, collected in a vast cemetery. Enclosed within the medieval walls, the building gradually fell into disrepair and was finally demolished in 1774.

Outside the city, towards Grado, was the *Basilica di Fondo Tullio*, excavated at various times in the nineteenth and twentieth centuries. It stood near a vast Roman necropolis in the Beligna locality, a suburb whose name still retains the memory of the pagan deity Belenus, to whom the Aquileians had been particularly devoted. Sadly now lost, this building was comparable in size and in the ornamentation of its floor mosaics to the two post-Theodorian basilicas located in the city centre. It was in fact a magnificent three-aisled basilica (53.5 × 25 metres), divided by two rows of nine columns or pilasters, completed at the back by a transept and a large apsidal sector provided with a curved corridor (22.20 × 11.40 metres). The hall, crossed in the centre by an aisle similar to that of the northern post-Theodorian basilica, had a mosaic floor, of which extensive portions of panels with geometric decorations have been found; it was financed by some generous benefactors, whose names are feature in the mosaics themselves. The floor mosaic of the curved corridor is particularly well preserved. Interrupted in the centre and slightly lower than the rest of the basilica space (creating a sort of crypt), it is adorned with vine shoots, with leaves and bunches of grapes growing out of angular acanthus bushes. Between the vine shoots are twelve lambs (perhaps symbolic of the Apostles) and numerous birds, including a peacock (symbol of immortality) and a cockerel (symbol of rebirth). The mosaic is on display at the Early Christian Museum in Aquileia. According to some scholars, the basilica was the *Basilica dei Santi Apostoli*, noted in the sources as being built in Aquileia by Chromatius at the end of the fourth century. Others, however, lean towards a later date, or, more likely – based on the structural and mosaic evidence – different construction phases. From the fourth century a large Christian cemetery also developed around the basilica, from which we have numerous funerary inscriptions. In the medieval period the Benedictine monastery of *San Martino alla Beligna* was built nearby.

The Aquileian Church from the sack of Attila to the Gothic War

In 452, Aquileia was besieged and devastated by Attila's Huns. Fortunately, they only stayed for a short time. Although the city had been in crisis for some time, this event marked a particularly symbolic break in its long history. The fall of this stronghold, once thought to be impregnable, signalled the decline of imperial power. Just three years later, in 455, Rome itself suffered a ruinous sacking by Gaiseric's Vandals. The Western Roman Empire, now nearly at its end, would finally collapse in 476.

After having suffered the devastating raid by the Huns and losing its political-military anchors, Aquileia was now experiencing an extremely difficult time. Yet, despite everything, the city had not been abandoned, and trade was still active, but symptoms of a marked social and urban transformation were starting to appear. The episcopal complex itself suffered severe blows, and it seems that the final disappearance of the post-Theodorian northern basilica, devastated by fire, can be placed in this phase. In such a climate of uncertainty and to deal with the frequent invasions, the Aquileians began to seek refuge on the islands of the nearby lagoon as early as the fifth century, contributing to the formation of the Grado *castrum*. Conditions for greater stability were probably recreated with the establishment of the Gothic Kingdom of Italy in 493, but this favourable situation was soon interrupted by the outbreak of the Gothic War (535–53). At the end of the conflict and with the temporary Byzantine reconquest,[25] Aquileia's urban area contracted drastically within a new defence line (Figure 0.1, n. 27). At this point the centre of the city corresponded to the area around the episcopal complex with its surviving basilica and all other forms of civic administration were dissolved, leaving the bishop as the undisputed ruler.

The establishment of the Lombard Duchy and the birth of the Patriarchate of Aquileia

The situation in the city deteriorated dramatically with the arrival of the Lombards in 568, another epochal event that brought about the formation of new geopolitical balances not only in the *Venetiae* but also in much of the Italian peninsula.[26] At that point Aquileia fell within the boundaries of the newly established Lombard Duchy of Friuli, with Cividale (the ancient *Forum Iulii*) as its capital. As it witnessed the loss of what little remained of its political role, the city was embroiled in a complex new theological dispute. This was the 'Three Chapters Controversy',[27] which, among other consequences, led to the schism between the Church of Aquileia and the Church of Rome for almost a century and a half (557–698). This schism was brought about by the refusal of several

Western Churches to accept the papal endorsement of a decision made by the Second Council of Constantinople in 553, at Emperor Justinian's behest. This was an *a posteriori* condemnation of the writings of three theologians (known as the 'Three Chapters'). Although their positions on Christological matters had been considered orthodox at the Council of Chalcedon in 451, a century later the same writings were accused of Nestorianism, since they tended to separate the two natures (human and divine) of Christ, and were therefore declared heretical.

During these turbulent years the Christian community of Aquileia was led by Bishop Paulinus I (557–69),[28] who has gone down in history for making two long-lasting decisions. The first, connected with the ongoing schism, was to proclaim himself Patriarch (or, according to others, to continue to improperly boast of a title already in use), claiming for the Church of Aquileia a role comparable to that of the great metropolitan sees.[29] The second decision was prompted by the Lombard invasion, which caused him to take refuge in nearby Grado, taking with him the treasure of the Aquileian Church, including religious books and the relics of the saints. His successors remained there and despite retaining the title of Patriarch did not return to Aquileia. Grado, significantly referred to as *Nova Aquileia*, achieved its maximum splendour in this short period of time. In particular, Bishop Helias (571–87)[30] is credited with the completion and consecration in 579 of the cathedral dedicated to St Euphemia (martyr of Chalcedon, a city in Asia Minor where the Council of 451 had been held). In the same year the basilica hosted a synod that reaffirmed the schismatic position of the Aquileian bishop and those of the suffragan dioceses. In all likelihood, this was the period when the tradition of the Marcian evangelization of Aquileia took hold, in order to legitimize the patriarchal title of the city's bishop.

In 606, during the Three Chapters Controversy, two parallel patriarchal lines emerged. The patriarchs of Aquileia were closer to the Lombards, rooted in the mainland, and steadfast in their positions. Meanwhile, the patriarchs in Grado were supported by the Byzantines and leaned towards maritime *Venetia*. Under pressure from the exarch of Ravenna, they returned to communion with the Church of Rome. Despite their proximity, Aquileia and Grado were worlds apart. When the Three Chapters Controversy was finally resolved in 698, the two patriarchs remained rigidly separated, each with papal recognition of their distinct sees.

After 606, the Patriarch of Aquileia moved to mainland Lombard territory, eventually settling in Cormons, a fortified settlement, where the patriarchal see remained for over a century. This move brought them closer to Cividale, the centre of ducal power. Finally, Patriarch Callistus (726–56)[31] managed to settle in Cividale in 737, establishing a close relationship between the religious and civil institutions. This period marked a time of particular splendour for Cividale, which, like Aquileia, is recognized as a UNESCO site.

Aquileia in the Holy Roman Empire and Poppo's basilica

The Frankish victory over the Lombards in 774 soon led to the establishment of the March of Friuli, which also included Aquileia. A few years later, the appointment of King

Charlemagne's trusted man Paulinus II (787–802)[32] as patriarch brought about many benefits for both the political authority of the Franks and the ecclesiastical community of Aquileia. A churchman, celebrated theologian and man of letters, Paulinus was recognized as a saint after his death in Cividale.

Among Aquileia's ninth-century patriarchs we should mention Maxentius (811–37),[33] who – with the emperor's blessing – brought the seat of the patriarchate permanently back to Aquileia and carried out a radical renovation of the southern basilica (Figure 0.1, n. 23),[34] which had long been decaying. The work mainly concerned the eastern sector of the building. Here, he added a large apse onto the back wall, two apsidal side chapels with a transept and a spacious crypt below the chancel, whose floor level was specially raised. In this way, the Maxentian basilica acquired for the first time the Latin cross plan that it still retains today. In front of the entrance to the basilica, between it and the Chromatian Baptistery, was built the Church of the Pagans, originally intended for the catechesis of unbaptized pilgrims. Aquileia once again boasted a prominent patriarchal complex.

Even more impressive was the reconstruction of the basilica by Patriarch Poppo (1019–42).[35] Poppo belonged to the aristocratic Bavarian family of the Ottocari and was very close to the emperors Henry II, Conrad II the Salian and Henry III, whom he actively supported politically and militarily, obtaining in return a sort of de facto investiture as imperial vicar. Poppo was determined to re-establish the importance of the Patriarchate of Aquileia, even at the cost of promoting violent actions, as in the case of the 1024 attack on its bitter rival Grado, during which atrocities were committed, including the devastation and looting of treasures and relics from churches.

As for the basilica, while retaining the Maxentian plan, Poppo had the building completely renovated, reusing ancient columns to raise the entire structure. The back wall of the main apse was entirely frescoed with a majestic celebratory scene. In the centre of the apsidal semi-dome, within a mandorla surrounded by the symbols of the Evangelists, is depicted the enthroned Madonna with the Blessing Child; on the right are Prince Henry III, St Hermagoras, Emperor Conrad II, St Fortunatus, St Euphemia and the imperial consort Gisella; on the left are St Mark, Emperor Henry II, St Hilary, Poppo himself with a model of the basilica, and St Tatian. The figures of the saints are larger than those of the members of the imperial family and the patron. In the tambour below is a procession of martyrs from the local tradition: Chrysogonus, Protus, Largius, Felix, Fortunatus, Dionysius, Primigenius and Anastasia. Further below runs a long dedicatory inscription in honour of the Mother of God and the martyred saints Hermagoras and Fortunatus. Images and text trace the history of the Church of Aquileia and project it into the radiant Popponian present, legitimizing both the role of the Patriarch and that of the emperor.

Poppo was also responsible for the construction of the imposing bell tower (73 metres), which was unfortunately placed on top of the floor mosaics of the northern basilica (which no longer existed), and for the construction of the new patriarchal palace (90 × 66 metres), which exploited – by adapting them – the wall structures of the Late Roman *horrea* (Figure 0.1, n. 21). The renovated basilica of Aquileia, solemnly consecrated in 1031, represented to all intents and purposes the grandiose culmination of Poppo's political and religious programme. Architecturally, it has remained largely unaltered to the present day

Figure 8.4 Aquileia. Piazza Capitolo and the Christian basilica; in front of the bell tower, on a column, is the bronze copy of the Lupa Capitolina erected in 1919 (© G. Baronchelli).

(Figure 8.4), despite the fourteenth-century restoration carried out by Patriarch Marquard of Randeck (1365–81),[36] made necessary by the devastating 1348 earthquake.

After the great Poppo phase, in addition to the restoration, numerous other alterations were made inside the basilica. Among these should be mentioned the eleventh-century installation of a marble replica of the Holy Sepulchre of Jerusalem in the left aisle, and the extraordinary cycle of frescoes that entirely covered the walls and ceiling of the crypt, probably commissioned by Patriarch Ulrich of Treffen (1161–82).[37] The pictorial cycle includes the following images: the twelve Apostles and the same number of saints in the corbels of the vaults; six bishops in the corbels of the semicircle; the *Dormitio Virginis*, the Crucifixion, the Deposition from the Cross and the Lamentation over the Dead Christ in the wall lunettes; twenty-two episodes from the lives of Saints Hermagoras and Fortunatus in the vault (mentioned at the beginning of this chapter); the Madonna and Child, Christ between two Archangels, and Saint Hermagoras between Saint Fortunatus and Saint Syrus in the three panels of the ceiling of the nave; and at the base, in the socle, a false veil with various scenes.

The ecclesiastical principality and the end of the Patriarchate

Since the time of Charlemagne and Paulinus II, the Patriarchate of Aquileia had shared many of its strategic interests with the imperial court, sometimes even fulfilling military tasks (e.g. at the time of the devastating Hungarian incursions, between the end of the ninth and the first half of the tenth centuries). This connection had gradually intensified until, in Poppo's time, it took on very clear proportions. Formal recognition of the temporal power of the Patriarchate of Aquileia came in 1077, when Emperor Henry IV granted Patriarch Sigehard of Sighardinger (1068–77)[38] a feudal investiture over the County of Friuli. In this way an ecclesiastical principality was born within the Holy Roman Empire, with the characteristics of a true patriarchal state.

The territory of this principality, which from the thirteenth century was also called *Patria del Friuli*, covered Friuli itself and parts of some neighbouring regions. The boundaries of the patriarchal state, however, did not always coincide with those of the very large ecclesiastical province, which was also subject to various changes over time. Traditionally, the latter included the territory under the direct jurisdiction of the metropolitan see of Aquileia and that belonging to the ancient suffragan dioceses of Como, Mantua, Trento, Verona, Vicenza, Padua, Treviso, Feltre, Belluno, Ceneda (Vittorio Veneto), Concordia, Trieste, Koper, Novigrad, Poreč, Pula and Pićan.

In the first half of the thirteenth century, Patriarch Berthold of Andechs-Meran (1218–51)[39] moved his residence to Udine, a city towards which Friuli's political and cultural centre of gravity was shifting. The patriarchal state exercised its political autonomy for another two centuries, until 1420, when its territory was conquered by the Venetian Republic. The latter then took over the temporal power of the territories of the *Patria del Friuli*, while the Patriarchate of Aquileia maintained its spiritual role, both as a diocese and as an ecclesiastical province.

For some time, however, the territory of Aquileia had been suffering from a continuous, inexorable decline, partly due to the spread of malaria and widespread poverty that had led to the relentless depopulation of the countryside and the urban area. This decline was accentuated with the defeat inflicted on the Venetian Republic by the armies of the League of Cambrai (Battle of Agnadello, 1509). The *Serenissima* was then replaced by the Habsburgs, and Aquileia was gradually reduced to the size of a modest village. In 1751, an agreement between the Austrian and Venetian governments led to Pope Benedict XIV's suppression of the Patriarchate of Aquileia and its dismemberment into two new ecclesiastical districts. Part of the territory thus went to the newly-formed archdiocese of Gorizia in the person of Karl Michael von Attems, who, in addition to the title of archbishop, could boast that of prince of the Holy Roman Empire. The other part was given to the Republic of Venice and the archdiocese of Udine, established in the same year and assigned to Archbishop Daniele Dolfin,[40] who, at least formally, retained the title of 'Patriarch' already conferred on him in 1734. But with his death (1762), even this prestigious title disappeared. This was the epilogue to the thousand-year history of the Aquileian patriarchate.

CHAPTER 9
THE REDISCOVERY OF THE ANCIENT CITY BETWEEN THE EIGHTEENTH AND TWENTIETH CENTURIES

A landscape of decay: ruins, desolation and looting

Over the centuries, Aquileia's ancient buildings, dating back to Roman times, fell into disrepair and became quarries for building materials. This process continued throughout the Middle Ages and into the following centuries.

The climate of total and desolating destruction into which the vestiges of the ancient Roman city fell can be fully felt in the carmen attributed to Paulinus II, Patriarch of Aquileia (787–802), entitled *Versus de destructione Aquilegiae numquam restaurandae*. Although highly rhetorical and overly emphatic, this poetic composition describes Aquileia as the shadow of the illustrious city it had once been. Now depopulated, it appeared reduced to a collection of decaying, and now irretrievable, ruins set in a vast agricultural landscape. Notwithstanding the poetic tones of Paulinus' lament, and despite the fact that he was referring to the time of the city's destruction by Attila's Huns (mid-fifth century), it is quite plausible that the reality described by the Aquileian saint is the one that he could actually see three centuries later (eighth century), in the midst of the early Middle Ages.

From Paulinus' description, two interesting observations of a historical-archaeological nature emerge. The first was that, by then, Aquileia had become strongly ruralized, a common situation for long-standing settlements, and which in other north Italian cities had started much earlier. Paraphrasing a common saying, we might say 'where now is countryside, once was all town'. The second observation is that the remains of ancient buildings and even necropolises were clearly systematically plundered for building material and valuable marble, which were then sold and reused.

The monumental and repeatedly renovated Christian Episcopal complex, around the basilica, was an obvious exception to this scenario. On several occasions, it took advantage of the availability of building material (column bases, columns, capitals, architectural elements, variously sized blocks and different stone materials, inscriptions, etc.) from the ancient monuments of Aquileia.

The dispersal of building and epigraphic materials from Aquileia was truly significant and widespread.[1] The remains of the Roman city were seen as a kind of quarry of processed stones, ready to be reused in the city's new building sites (civil and, above all, ecclesiastical) or to be transported to other localities for the same purpose.

Furthermore, it should be kept in mind that not all stone material was reused in the form of building blocks. Many stones and especially many ancient marbles, including fragments of statues and inscriptions, were irretrievably lost by being burnt in special lime kilns. There is archaeological and literary evidence of these from throughout the Middle Ages, as found in a collection of documents called *Necrologium Aquileiense*,[2] which attests to the presence in Aquileia of as many as fourteen different lime producers active between the thirteenth and fourteenth centuries.

All this inevitably led to the gradual disappearance of much of the ancient evidence. However, it was Aquileia's reputation as a privileged place for the extraction of building materials that helped ensure that the memory of the Roman city was not lost. This situation remained unchanged until the end of the Middle Ages. In Marin Sanudo's 1483 *Itinerario per la terraferma veneziana* (Itinerary for the Venetian mainland), Aquileia is described as 'once a very powerful and great city, now almost abandoned',[3] with scattered ruins emerging from the rural landscape.

For centuries, the Aquileian countryside was the object of chance finds, which remained largely ignored. However, it should not be forgotten that, at least from the fifteenth century onwards, excavations in Aquileia were aimed not only at the clearing of farmland and the recovery of building material, but also at the discovery of precious objects destined for antiquarian collections[4] promoted by the humanists of the time, who included Patriarch Lodovico Trevisan (1439–65).[5] As far as the following century is concerned, excavations were commissioned in 1548 by the noble Savorgnan family, in the Beligna locality, with the aim of gifting some finds to Patriarch Giovanni Grimani.[6] But there were many other occasions when reliefs, inscriptions or other artefacts from Aquileia, often of significant historical value or great artistic value, went to enrich Venetian collections or those of other Venetian cities.

Gian Domenico Bertoli (1676–1763) and the birth of Aquileian archaeology

It was not until the eighteenth century that attitudes towards Aquileian archaeological evidence began to change.[7] Indeed, this was a rather happy period for antiquarianism in the whole of Friuli. The remains of the past started to become the object of historical interest and there was deep admiration for the glorious Roman city. The ancient remains were no longer considered cumbersome piles of rubble scattered across the countryside, to be plundered, dispersed and never more reunited.

An innovative figure in this new scenario was canon Gian Domenico Bertoli (Mereto di Tomba, 1676–Aquileia, 1763),[8] unanimously considered to be the 'father of Aquileian archaeology'. He was moved by the desire to preserve the archaeological heritage of the Friulian town and put a stop to its continuous pillaging. Passionate about history, Roman antiquities and especially Latin epigraphy, Bertoli personally directed a number of archaeological excavations between 1720 and 1726 and, thanks to his incessant work as a collector, was able to recover (and save) a large number of inscriptions, sculptures, coins, gems and other artefacts that he assembled in his home in Aquileia, today the headquarters of the National Association for Aquileia. An erudite scholar, in correspondence with illustrious personalities such as Scipione Maffei, Apostolo Zeno and Giusto Fontanini,[9] Bertoli was also the author of the three-volumed *Le antichità d'Aquileja profane e sacre*, the first volume of which was published in Venice in 1739. Over time, his important epigraphic collection underwent several changes of ownership by noble families. Purchased in 1783 by Count Antonio Cassis Faraone, it then passed to Baron Eugen Ritter von Záhony in 1866 and finally arrived in the *lapidarium* of the State Museum, established in 1882.

Although Bertoli's work was a decisive innovation compared to the past, it did not have much of an immediate impact. This setback was due not only to a certain intellectual backwardness among contemporary antiquarians, but also to the attitude of the Austrian authorities, who at the time were more intent on carrying out the substantial land reclamation works initiated in 1763 by Maria Theresa of Austria, with the associated plundering of ancient remains, than on promoting new archaeological research and providing for the recovery and conservation of the finds that were continually being made.

However, something was about to change.[10] After two brief periods of French occupation, Aquileia was caught up in the Napoleonic interlude of the Kingdom of Italy between 1807 and 1814. During this period, the painter Leopoldo Zuccolo (Udine, 1761–1833)[11] was commissioned to carry out some public excavations in various parts of the city. Zuccolo himself, together with the war commissioner Étienne-Marie Siauve,[12] was involved in the foundation of Aquileia's first public museum, the Eugenian Museum[13] (named after the Viceroy of Italy, Eugène de Beauharnais), housed in the Baptistery and the Church of the Pagans. The Eugenian Museum was opened to the public in 1807 but soon closed in 1813.

Figure 9.1 Aquileia. The external walls of Moschettini's stable (© Archives of Museo Archeologico Nazionale di Aquileia).

Closely linked to the Austrian administration was the nobleman, wealthy landowner and civil servant Girolamo de' Moschettini (Aquileia, 1755–1832),[14] who was a very active collector between the second half of the eighteenth and the first decades of the nineteenth century. He supervised the protection of Aquileian antiquities and, thanks to funding from the Austrian authorities, directed research excavations at various sites in Aquileia between 1815 and 1832.[15] Having taken possession of them in a manner that was considered improper, Moschettini decorated the outer walls of a stable he owned with sculptures and inscriptions (Figure 9.1), effectively preventing them from being sent to Vienna, unlike other less fortunate finds. Once the unique layout of Moschettini's stable had been dismantled, the inscriptions fixed to the walls also found their final resting place in the Museum of Aquileia's *lapidarium*.

Enrico Maionica (1853–1916) and the founding of the Archaeological Museum of Aquileia

Despite the changes taking place in the perception of archaeology, mining operations by diggers and quarrymen were still carried out in Aquileia, partly due to a rather permissive Austrian law, introduced in 1846, which had effectively given them free range. However, research became better organized and archaeological evidence better protected in 1850, thanks to the establishment of the Kaiserlich-Königliche Central-Commission zur Erforschung und Erhaltung der Baudenkmale (Imperial-Royal Central Commission for the Study and Conservation of Monuments).[16] Aquileia certainly benefited from this decisive change, which brought about greater protection of new finds, the undertaking of new excavations, the publication of research results, the production of topographical-archaeological maps and the planning of future activities.

It was in this climate that the Eugenian Museum temporarily reopened in 1858; then the Museo Patrio della Città, founded in 1873 in the old Town Hall was briefly opened by the Town Council, and, finally the Imperial-Regio Museo dello Stato in Aquileja (also known as the Caesareum Museum Aquileiense)[17] was inaugurated in 1882, housed in the centrally located Villa Cassis Faraone, where the National Archaeological Museum of Aquileia still exists today. The new museum, which could avail of the former municipal museum's collections, was of central importance in contemporary cultural policy and, at the same time, a useful instrument to bring the central power closer to the peoples of different nationalities that coexisted within the Austro-Hungarian Empire. In this specific case it was an obvious act of recognition and appreciation of the Roman origins of Aquileia and its territory. It is therefore not surprising that the founding of the museum was due to the direct initiative of Emperor Franz Joseph and that the inauguration was solemnly held in the presence of Archduke Charles Ludwig.

The first director of the museum was Enrico Maionica (Trieste, 1853–1916)[18] (Figure 9.2), an antiquities scholar educated at the University of Vienna, who was able both to progressively bring the contents of important private collections (such as the Bertoli-

Figure 9.2 Aquileia. Enrico Maionica, on the right, at the entrance to the Imperial-Regio Museo dello Stato (© Archives of Museo Archeologico Nazionale di Aquileia).

Cassis-Ritter, Monari, Moschettini, Gregorutti and others) into the museum collections, and also to reach agreements with private individuals for the acquisition of new finds, thus avoiding their dispersal. The return to Aquileia of some previously scattered monuments is also significant.

However, it must also be remembered that, in the period in question, some collections of Aquileian artefacts unfortunately went in other directions. This happened, for example, with the Aquileian antiquities from the collection of Vincenzo Zandonati,[19] sold to the Trieste Museum after 1870, and with the archaeological collection of Francesco di Toppo,[20] donated to the Udine Museum in 1883. In addition, some particularly valuable artefacts were transferred to Vienna,[21] and only a few have returned.

In any case, in just a few years Maionica was able to expand the museum collections with important new acquisitions; he also arranged for new exhibition rooms, built a new *lapidarium* and reorganized the garden. From 1887 onwards, he also initiated excavations in the city and necropolises, supervised or conducted directly by the Museum of Aquileia, sometimes undertaken in agreement with the municipality, whilst at the same time discouraging extemporary excavations by private individuals. His work over the years was assiduous and very productive. The publication of his *Fundkarte von Aquileja*,[22] a map of Aquileia's discoveries printed in 1893, was fundamental, systematically recording and mapping the archaeological discoveries that had taken place up to that time. Two museum guides published in 1884[23] and 1910[24] are also Maionica's work. In short, according to historian Aristide Calderini, Maionica's period of influence could rightly be called 'the golden age of Aquileian archaeology'.[25]

Another significant milestone in the cultural rebirth of Aquileia was the establishment in 1906 of the Society for the Preservation of the Basilica of Aquileia, on the initiative of the archbishop of Gorizia, Francesco Borgia Sedej. Only a few years later, between 1909 and 1915, the world-famous mosaic floor of the southern Theodorian hall, the largest in the Roman West, was fully uncovered. This led to a momentary conflict between the museum run by Maionica, a government official more interested in the promotion of Roman antiquities, and the new cultural centre in Aquileia which, gravitating towards the basilica and the ecclesiastical authority, was more focused on the promotion of Christian antiquities.

Maionica remained in office as director of the museum until 1914.

Aquileia 'the second Rome': the First World War and annexation to the Kingdom of Italy

During the First World War, the long-held dream of the irredentists for Aquileia finally came true. Their goal was to annex to the Kingdom of Italy those territories and cities of the Three Venetias still under Austro-Hungarian rule. This would complete the unification of the new national state, established in 1861 under the Savoy crown. Aquileia, located just across the border, directly felt the impact of the war, which brought immense loss of life to both sides. On 24 May 1915, the very day Italy entered the war, the town was occupied by the Bersaglieri and temporarily became part of the Kingdom of Italy. However, it briefly returned to Austro-Hungarian control in 1917 after the Battle of Caporetto (now Kobarid, Slovenia) and only finally became part of Italian territory in 1918, at the end of the conflict.[26]

Aquileia's fate was to be that of a border town. The strategic position of the ancient colony came fully back into focus in those years, taking on a highly symbolic meaning in political terms. Considered as a 'second Rome', many saw Aquileia as a bulwark of Romanity and Italianness, against the oppression and barbarism that – in their view – characterized the Germanic world. This concept referred to a deep-rooted idea, dating at least to the time of the Siege of Aquileia in 238, during which the Upper Adriatic city was able to resist and emerge victorious from the siege of Maximinus Thrax, confirming itself as an impregnable stronghold in defence of Rome and the whole of Italy, whose natural and insuperable limit was historically identified in the Alps.[27] But even before the episode of Maximinus, a similar concept had been clearly expressed in a passage by Strabo,[28] according to which Aquileia was a garrison founded by the Romans against the barbarians of the hinterland.

But let us return to the events in Aquileia during the First World War. In 1914, Mihovil Abramić (Pola 1884–Split 1962)[29] was appointed director of the museum. He was another antiquarian educated at the University of Vienna, who had already joined Enrico Maionica (who was nearing retirement) the previous year. In 1915, Don Celso Costantini

(Castions di Zoppola 1876–Rome 1958)[30] took over as regent pastor and conservator of the basilica. In the first role he replaced Monsignor Giovanni Meizlik, who was forcibly removed because he was considered an Austrian sympathizer; in the second role he replaced the previous conservator Anton Gnirs (Žatec 1873–Loket 1933).[31] The appointment was made on the recommendation of the intellectual Ugo Ojetti, then an army lieutenant tasked with overseeing artistic heritage conservation in war zones. Indeed, it was between 1915 and 1917 that archaeological activities resumed apace in Aquileia, as the Kingdom of Italy desired to reassert the Italian character of those lands through the promotion of the Roman era remains, in contrast to the alleged disinterest shown by the Austrian authorities. In the same years, the cemetery for those Italians who had been killed in the First World War (known as the Cemetery of Heroes) was built behind the basilica, which soon led to the transfer of the civic cemetery to an area far from the town where the Late Roman circus had once stood.

The small Friulian town thus found itself at the centre of national debate and military propaganda, receiving wide publicity through the media of the time. An exceptional promoter of the incorporation of Aquileia into the Kingdom of Italy was the famous poet Gabriele d'Annunzio, an extravagant patriot, whose literary output and daring exploits enjoyed wide acclaim in the culture and society of the time. D'Annunzio himself is credited, among other things, with a dedication to Aquileia written on an inscription that was placed in the Cemetery of Heroes in 1915, destroyed by the Austrians after the Battle of Caporetto and finally restored in 1918.

In 1919, the direction of the museum was assigned to the Celso Costantini, who was soon entrusted with a growing number of demanding ecclesiastical appointments (which in time would lead to him becoming a cardinal). In those years the Friulian town, with its thousand-year history, its museum and monuments, its Christian basilica with its recently uncovered marvellous mosaics, its glorious fame perpetuated over the centuries, became the natural setting for nationalistic and political celebrations. Firstly, in 1919, the 2,100th anniversary of the Latin colony's foundation was celebrated. On that occasion, Rome presented Aquileia with a bronze copy of the *Lupa Capitolina*, which was erected on an ancient column in Piazza Capitolo, opposite the basilica's bell tower. The monument enshrined the inseparable bond between the capital and its colony, whose centuries-old prerogatives and loyalty were reaffirmed. The She-Wolf erected next to the basilica is still one of the most iconic images of Aquileia's monumental landscape today (Figure 8.4).

But the most significant event occurred a couple of years later. In 1921, the interior of the basilica was the site of a heart-rending ceremony that touched national sentiments to the core. Maria Maddalena Bergamas, the mother of a missing Italian soldier who had fallen at the front, was entrusted with the painful task of choosing one of eleven unidentified Italian bodies from eleven battlefields to be sent to Rome and buried in the tomb of the Unknown Soldier in the Vittoriano monumental complex. There, at the centre of the Altar of the Fatherland, would rest the nameless soldier, in perpetual memory of all the soldiers who died to give Italy its longed-for borders. The remains of the ten other unknown, unselected soldiers were buried in a monumental tomb in the centre of Aquileia's Cemetery of Heroes, significantly facing the Karst mountains, where so much blood had been shed in the name of the Fatherland. Next to the ten unknown soldiers who remained in Aquileia, Bergamas herself was later buried, representing all the Italian mothers who had seen their sons die in the war.

Giovanni Battista Brusin (1883–1976)

The year 1922 was a seminal one in Italy's recent history. On 28 October 1922, the March on Rome marked Fascism's rise to power, symbolically marking the progressive establishment of Benito Mussolini's totalitarian regime. That same year saw a change at the top of the Royal Archaeological Museum of Aquileia with the appointment of Giovanni Battista Brusin (Aquileia, 1883–1976)[32] as director. He had gained Costantini's respect and trust through working alongside him for the previous two years. In the same year, Brusin also was elected mayor of Aquileia.

An antiquarian and epigrapher with a *Mitteleuropean* outlook, having also trained at Austrian universities, Brusin was a leading figure in Aquileian archaeology in the first half of the twentieth century. He was director of the Aquileia Museum for thirty years, until 1952. In 1936, he was also called to direct the Superintendency of Antiquities and Art of Friuli, Venezia Giulia and Istria (based in Trieste) and then the Superintendency of Antiquities of the Three Venetias (based in Padua); in this case, too, he held the post until 1952. Of his prolific scholarly production, largely focused on Roman and Christian Aquileia, of central importance were the volume *Gli scavi di Aquileia*,[33] published in 1934, and the monumental epigraphic collection entitled *Inscriptiones Aquileiae*, published posthumously in three volumes between 1991 and 1993.

During the thirty years that Brusin was director of the museum, the cultural life of Aquileia was energized by many initiatives. Among the various bodies active during this period, mention must be made of the National Association for Aquileia, founded in 1928 and still active today. The aim of this organization was and still is to promote research and disseminate Aquileia's historical, archaeological and artistic heritage. Among the founders were Brusin himself and the historian Aristide Calderini,[34] author of the volume *Aquileia romana. Ricerche di storia e di epigrafia*.[35] In 1930 the National Association began publishing the scientific journal *Aquileia Nostra*, still published annually and distributed nationally and internationally across the various countries of the Upper Adriatic region. In addition to these extensive publishing and dissemination activities (including the bulletin *Aquileia Chiama* and various monographs), in its first decades of life the National Association also carried out an effective archaeological survey. Needless to say, this helped provide financial and operational support for the research directed by Brusin, who over time undertook challenging excavations such as those of the forum, the river port, the necropolis and the Late Roman walls and markets, as well as various residential areas and some early Christian buildings.

But his commitment to Aquileia did not end there. Brusin had in fact developed a personal and modern sensitivity for the dissemination of research results. As he wrote a few years later, 'Digging means preserving and enhancing what the subsoil brings to light, since we dig for people and the new generations.'[36] This is how he became concerned with publishing popular texts,[37] updating the archaeological map of the Roman city (the version engraved on the plaque displayed to the public at the beginning of Via Patriarca Poppone, which leads to Piazza Capitolo and the basilica, dates back to 1953), opening the recently investigated archaeological areas to the public and carrying out major restoration work and improvements.

In this context, we should also note the opening of the so-called Via Sacra (also known as *Viale degli Scavi*) in 1934, and the anastylosis of the eastern colonnade of the forum, carried out in 1936. The former is a pleasant archaeological promenade in the shade of cypress trees (Figure 5.2), carved out of the ancient bed of the *Natiso cum Turro*, which leads from the Cemetery of Heroes to the Monastero area, bordering the remains of the river port on the eastern side of the city walls. The second is a symbolic vision of the Roman city, now fully integrated into the urban landscape (Figure 5.1). The excavation of the forum continued over the years by gradually freeing the archaeological area from the overlying dwellings; unfortunately, moving the road that still crosses the square and concealing part of its surface was not considered.

These two archaeological sites provided the ideal backdrop for the celebration of the Augustan Bimillenary in 1937[38] and for the visit of the Duce in 1938, who walked along the Via Sacra accompanied by Brusin himself (Figure 9.3). Compared to the period of

Figure 9.3 Aquileia. Benito Mussolini visiting the Via Sacra accompanied by Giovanni Battista Brusin in 1938 (© Archives of Museo Archeologico Nazionale di Aquileia).

transition to the Kingdom of Italy, characterized by the promotion of nationalism and strong irredentist feelings, during the twenty-year Fascist period the historical role of Aquileia was further emphasized by the regime.[39] Fascist propaganda in fact drew on the myth of Romanity with imagery steeped in references to the civilizing role and triumphant destiny of the 'eternal city', ancient Rome; a destiny that would fully once again befall Italy under Mussolini. Given the positions he held, Brusin was not immune from fostering relations with the fascist regime, but he was apparently able to maintain a certain detachment from the most negative aspects of the then prevailing ideology. The dramatic period of the German occupation between 1943 and 1945 must have been extremely difficult, when Friuli became part of the *Operationszone Adriatisches Küstenland*.

The end of the Second World War in 1945 brought about the restoration of democracy and predated the birth of the Italian Republic by one year. In the immediate postwar period, Brusin's career did not suffer any setbacks. In addition to holding the posts of Director of the Aquileia Museum and Superintendent of Antiquities of the Three Venetias, from 1946 to 1953 he also taught *Archeologia delle Venezie* at the *Scuola di perfezionamento storico-filologica* in the University of Padua. Later, from 1956 to 1963, he was president of the *Deputazione di Storia Patria per il Friuli* and in 1965 became a member of the *Accademia dei Lincei*. Throughout his life, Brusin devoted himself passionately to the study and social and cultural growth of his native Aquileia.

Luisa Bertacchi (1924–2011)

In 1952 the Brusin era ended with his retirement. After a period of closure in order to carry out essential renovation and refurbishment, the National Archaeological Museum of Aquileia was reopened in 1954 under the direction of the archaeologist Valnea Scrinari (Trieste, 1922–2010). Scrinari was director of the museum until 1959, when the archaeologist Luisa Bertacchi (Formia 1924–Aquileia 2011)[40] took over. Her work for Aquileia was indefatigable, strenuously protecting archaeological evidence after the Second World War in a period of strong economic and demographic growth. This was an era of dynamic urban development which, in the case of Aquileia, had to be combined with an equally firm and responsible effort to protect the archaeological sites. It must be remembered that at that time preventive archaeology was not yet explicitly provided for in Italian legislation, and that – in everyday practice – it was rarely considered in urban planning.

Even at the risk of being unpopular with those who did not share her objectives, Bertacchi succeeded in guiding the development of modern Aquileia in a manner as compatible as possible with the requirements to protect the archaeological remains. This was not an easy undertaking, both for the reasons mentioned above and because the ancient Roman city was much larger than that of the modern town (something that was already quite exceptional, at least in northern Italy). Thus, compulsory purchase of several pieces of private land were necessary (e.g. the large area of the Great Baths and the *Fondo Comelli*). At the same time the wise decision was made to plan a vast new urban district to the south, outside the ancient city walls. In addition, between the late 1960s and early 1970s, the town was given a modern sewerage system, which offered the opportunity to conduct extensive archaeological excavations. In this way, the remains of several ancient structures came to light, including the forum's civic basilica, a section of the so-called Decumanus of Aratria Galla, a monumental porticus and a portion of the Byzantine walls.

Bertacchi was undoubtedly gifted with practical sense and great organizational and management skills. Director of the museum until 1989 (for thirty years, like Brusin), she was also active within the National Association for Aquileia.[41] This period included the opening of the Early Christian Museum of Aquileia, in 1961, housed in an old farm building built over the remains of the Christian Basilica of Monastero. The museum was made possible thanks to generous funding by the 'captain of industry' Franco Marinotti (Vittorio Veneto 1891–Milan 1966),[42] then president of the National Association.

Lastly, Bertacchi was responsible for various publications of the excavations and monuments of Aquileia, conducted with a modern approach to the subject. In particular, her *New Archaeological Map of Aquileia*,[43] published in 2003, was essential reading. It is a tool that is still very useful today, both for the purposes of conservation and research, bringing together the results of decades-long work conducted in the field and employing – for that time – advanced surveying and mapping techniques.

The archaeology of Aquileia between the present and the future

The rest is recent history.[44] In addition to the daily and admirable commitment of the Superintendency of Archaeology, Fine Arts and Landscape of Friuli Venezia Giulia; the extraordinary tourist and cultural appeal of the Christian basilica and the National Archaeological Museum, now splendidly restored; and the traditional role played by the National Association for Aquileia, two important factors have recently helped in the development of the Upper Adriatic town, which in 1998 received prestigious recognition as a UNESCO site.

The first factor is the direct involvement of a number of Italian universities, from as early as the 1980s. This has led to a rapid and noticeable increase in our knowledge of many archaeological contexts in Aquileia, namely the area east of the forum, the two insulae of the northern quarters and the House of the Dancing Putti (University of Trieste); the Great Baths (University of Udine); the eastern bank of the river port and the suburbs (University of Venice); the *domus* of the *Fondo CAL* and *Fondo Beneficio Rizzi* (Sapienza University of Rome); the amphitheatre and the Late Roman walls and markets (University of Verona); and the *insula* of the Wounded Beasts, Titus Macer's House, the republican walls and the theatre (University of Padua). The contribution of important foreign institutions, such as the École Française de Rome, the Österreichisches Archäologisches Institut and Macquarie University (Sydney), as well as that of many professional archaeologists and independent scholars or those belonging to other institutions, has also been important. The results of the research have been published in monographic editions of the excavations and in other scientific publications. These include the aforementioned journal *Aquileia Nostra*. International Journal of Ancient Studies on Northern Adriatic Regions and the *Atti delle Settimane di Studi Aquileiesi*, published in the series *Antichità Altoadriatiche* founded by Mario Mirabella Roberti.

The second factor in the town's development is the establishment of the Fondazione Aquileia,[45] created in 2008 under an innovative Italian law concerning Cultural Heritage. This body is responsible for preparing strategic plans, managing archaeological areas and promoting cultural tourism. The Ministry of Culture, the Friuli Venezia Giulia Region, the Municipality of Aquileia, the Province of Udine and the Archdiocese of Gorizia are all involved in the Fondazione Aquileia. Since its inception, the organization has brought about a noticeable change in the cultural landscape of Aquileia. It has financed research by universities and other institutions, promoted extensive conservation and development at archaeological sites and organized popular cultural initiatives. Currently, the Fondazione manages a large part of the ancient city and is working on creating a unified tour of the archaeological areas, museum buildings and the Christian basilica. This tour will wind through the town centre and some untouched, picturesque areas of the Friulian countryside, helping advance this ambitious project to create the largest archaeological park in northern Italy.

APPENDIX: THE ARCHAEOLOGICAL AREAS AND MUSEUMS OF AQUILEIA

The remains of the ancient city are still visible in many archaeological sites scattered throughout the modern town of Aquileia.[1]

The Roman forum

Aquileia's forum (Figures 0.1, n. 4; 5.1; 5.4) is the best-preserved monumental structure of the ancient city.[2] Today it is crossed by the modern road leading to Grado. On either side of the road are the remains of what was once the city's most important square. In it, the political, administrative and economic life of the city took place.

As early as the final stages of the second century BCE, citizens gathered here for all public activities. The square gradually took on a monumental appearance and an elongated rectangular plan. The forum was situated in the centre of the urban space to facilitate access for all inhabitants; moreover, some of the most important roads leading to the city gates and port converged here.

From the first half of the first century CE, the square was gradually surrounded by columned porticoes, some of which can still be seen after G. B. Brusin's 1930s reconstruction. The columns, restored with modern bricks, are surmounted by mid-Imperial Age capitals. Above the columns and lintel of the portico is a balustrade made up of blocks with stone slabs in the spaces between them. Significant reliefs (putti or eagles) can be seen on the slabs. The blocks were carved with reliefs depicting the heads of Jupiter Ammon and Medusa, symbolically representing the eastern and western halves of the empire and demonstrating Rome's great dominion.

The forum had an overall length of 141 metres and was about 55 metres wide. The open space was paved with limestone slabs from the nearby Karst hills. Behind the arcades were shops selling a variety of goods.

The basilica (Figure 0.1, n. 16), built between the end of the first century BCE and the beginning of the first century CE occupied the entire southern side of the forum. This 90 × 29-metre complex had an administrative function. In particular civil and criminal justice was administered here. It was in direct communication with the forum on one side and with the main road running south of it on the other. The basilica was completely renovated in the second century CE and two apses were added along its short side. It completely lost its function in the sixth century CE when it was partially demolished to make way for the building of a defence wall, totally changing the layout of the city and its public spaces.

At present, archaeological research has not yet been able to explain the layout of the northern side of the square. However, along this side there must have been the *Comitium* (Figure 0.1, n. 6), a particularly important building, with a circular interior shape where popular assemblies were held in the Republican Age.

The open space of the forum was occupied by numerous celebratory and votive monuments. As a public space par excellence, the forum was the place where the most famous citizens and magistrates had statues erected of them. Not many years ago, an important inscription was found in the western part of the forum, celebrating Titus Annius Luscus (Figure 3.2), one of the magistrates responsible for the second inauguration of the colony in 169 BCE. The inscription, engraved on the base of the statue (now lost), recalls the tasks entrusted to the magistrate: drafting laws for the colony's administration, new appointments to the local senate, and the building of a temple whose precise location is unknown but must have overlooked the square.

The river port

As already noted, the river port (Figures 0.1, n. 14; 5.2) was Aquileia's most important infrastructure.[3] Celebrated in the sources, the port allowed the city to connect directly to the sea and thus establish a commercial link with all other Mediterranean regions and cities.

The buildings of the port were uncovered as early as the nineteenth century, but it was only with G. B. Brusin's excavations in the 1920s and 1930s that their characteristics and functions were clearly recognized. Further excavations were carried out in the 1980s and 1990s by the French School in Rome and Trieste University.

This complex is unique in the whole north of Italy, with comparisons only found in central Italy. Thanks to the impressive excavations by G. B. Brusin, a large area is visible and many of the buildings are uncovered which, despite the overlapping of several building phases, allows us to understand its architectural layout. It has crucial historical importance for the public understanding of the ancient city, especially that of the important commercial role played by Aquileia, whose far-flung commercial activities were carried out thanks to the port facilities.

Most of the buildings were constructed at the beginning of the first century CE after the demolition of residential areas and other older buildings. Structures extend over more than 400 metres in width along the western bank of today's Natissa river – once a great waterway, up to 50 metres wide (*Natiso cum Turro*), which flowed past Aquileia's walls connecting it to the sea and international trade. It comprises a long quay made of vertical limestone slabs and rectangular blocks, which formed the upper loading and unloading platform and was equipped with two sets of mooring rings placed at different heights. Less than two metres from the quay ran a pavement, which could be used for the loading and unloading of goods from smaller vessels.

Behind the quay were warehouses and rooms for commercial use, between which at least three communication passages (ramps or steps) connected the urban road system and the quay. The warehouses extended the entire length of the port – about 300 metres – and were about 13 metres wide.

Looking at the quay today you can also see the remains of massive walls built above what used to be the loading and unloading area. This is the line of the new fortifications built in the fourth century CE which brought the port's functionality to an end. We know from literary sources that at this time (361 CE) the course of the river had to be diverted and drained. From this time on, the river port began to lose its importance for the city.

A promenade was built in the 1930s between the ancient river port and the course of the present-day Natissa river, from which you can see the remains. This pedestrian walkway was named 'Via Sacra' in the Fascist era and connected the Roman antiquities with Christian memories and the First World War cemetery behind the basilica.

Titus Macer's House

The *domus di Titus Macer* (Titus Macer's House) (Figures 0.1, n. 7; 6.1; 10.1), which can be visited at the Fondi Cossar, is one of the most important remains of Roman Aquileia. It is a large private residence that existed without interruption for almost 600 years and was opened to the public in 2020 after a long restoration project and the covering of the remains.[4]

Excavations in this area began as early as the nineteenth century by Austrian archaeologists. During these excavations, the famous Rape of Europa mosaic, the

Figure 10.1 Aquileia. The reconstruction of Titus Macer's House in the Cossar funds (J. Bonetto).

beautiful floor with vine shoots, the 'unswept floor', now on display in the National Archaeological Museum, and the Good Shepherd mosaic, temporarily placed in Palazzo Meizlik, were recovered. But it was not until the 1950s that archaeological research unearthed remains of great monumental significance. This entire area of the city was distinguished by a number of rich private *domus*, inhabited during the Roman Imperial Age and furnished with all sorts of refined decoration (mosaics and wall frescoes). However, research in the last century was not able to bring these large houses to light in their entirety. Only a few portions remained visible, and these were difficult for the public to fully comprehend.

In 2009 the Fondazione Aquileia started a new research project which it entrusted to the University of Padua. After several excavation operations, one of the *domus* was brought to light in its entirety. It sits between two of the town's road axes. The discovery of a weight with an inscription bearing a Latin name led to the *domus* being given the name 'Titus Macer's House', although it is not certain whether this person was really this house's owner.

The *domus* is one of the largest known houses not only in Aquileia but also in northern Italy and has few equals even in the rest of Europe. It is, however, the only one in Aquileia whose full extent is known, measuring approximately 1,260 square metres.

The careful research carried out by archaeologists has allowed us to identify the different phases of this house. The first, rather narrow part, was built at the start of the first century BCE. It is the westernmost part of the large *domus* that can be seen today, built around an open porticoed space called the atrium and featuring four columns. Around the atrium are spaces for the owner (*tablinum*) and for relaxing (*cubicula*). This layout derives from second- and first-century BCE houses common in central and southern Italy, and with many examples in Pompeii. The *domus* 'ad atrio' of the Fondi Cossar is the only example of its kind in Aquileia and is one of the few examples of this specific type in northern Italy. It is likely that this first house was designed by architects who came to Aquileia from central Italy, perhaps following the movement that led to the foundation of the colony. This first 'atrium house' was soberly decorated with black-and-white mosaics and occupied about half the block. The adjacent streets were surfaced with gravel and sand.

The house was expanded over time. In particular, at the beginning of the first century CE the house came to occupy the whole space between the two city streets. Next to the diminished 'atrium house', the new part of the house was organized around a large open courtyard, decorated with a pool and fountain. Aligned alongside the garden was a large reception hall of about 90 square metres. Decorated with an enormous mosaic, this room was used by the owners for prestigious events. Around the courtyard ran a long four-armed corridor whose floor was made of black-and-white mosaics and had several rooms with different functions opening onto it. To the north was the kitchen, equipped with a work surface for cooking food and a room for resting, while to the south were other spaces used as a living room by the owner and his guests. Prominent among these was the *triclinium*, so called because of the three beds that lined the walls used for eating and resting.

As had been the case with the 'atrium house', the large first-century CE house was separated from the streets by a row of shops and a portico. The shops sold various foodstuffs, which certainly included meat and fish. One of the shops must also have sold bread, as excavations have discovered an oven that was almost certainly a bread oven; this bread was then sold to people passing along the street and under the portico. The entrance to the house was through the series of shops.

The house was again modified in the Late Imperial Roman Age (fourth century CE). The most obvious sign of the owner's wealth at this stage is the large mosaic known as the 'fishing' mosaic that decorated the reception room in front of the garden. The history of the house is a good reflection of the history of the city, which reached perhaps unprecedented heights of wealth during the fourth century CE.

But the history of Titus Macer's House also tells us how the city was losing its vitality in the following centuries. From the end of the fourth century and into the fifth, the house was gradually transformed: some rooms were subdivided, while others lost their function as living spaces and housed workshops. The house and its inhabitants also had to endure the turbulent times of Attila's siege (452 CE) and its aftermath. In the wake of the siege, people living in the *domus*, perhaps now in ruins, lost a treasure of 560 coins, never to be recovered by the owner and only found in 2010 by archaeologists. By the sixth century CE, the *domus* was either abandoned altogether or used as a shelter and refuge for those who still lived in the city.

Many finds come from the area of the *domus*, although not all of them belong to the people who lived there. Among the most valuable is a beautiful gold and glass paste ring, dating to the second and third centuries CE. Thousands of fragments of ceramic containers (bowls, plates, amphorae jugs frying pans), which were used for everyday storage and food consumption, have also been found. Excavations have also discovered 1,200 coins from all living levels of the house as well as in the preparation layers. They are an important testimony to the circulation of money in Aquileia for all periods from the second century BCE to the sixth century CE.

The *domus* and episcopal palace

The archaeological area of the *domus* and episcopal palace occupies an area north of the basilica square and was an important part of the original early Christian complex (Figure 0.1, n. 23).[5] Furthermore, the area gives us a better understanding of the dense succession of buildings and phases of life that characterized the entire urban space of Aquileia.

This area has been recently restored and opened to the public. Finds have been made in this part of the town since the 1950s, when the Venetian Antiquities Superintendency under Luisa Bertacchi discovered rooms of what was believed to be a section of the fifth-century episcopal palace. Following new investigations and the exceptional discoveries made between 2009 and 2010, it was decided to turn it into a museum.

In this way the remains from different periods are visible today. The oldest concern the growth of the city, which in the first century BCE occupied areas outside the original city walls. Starting from the earliest layers, we have the remains of several Early Imperial *domus*, characterized by their very well-preserved frescoed walls, at times over one metre high. Above these, a large apsidal hall sitting directly on top of the first *domus* may have been part of the bishop's residence. This hall extends for over 100 metres and repeats architectural models found throughout Aquileia and built during the fourth century. Many private residences were equipped with apses to close off the reception halls.

In this case the apse was about 5 metres wide and slightly higher than the hall it stood in front of. The frescoes, discovered during excavation, are particularly valuable. They covered the walls and ceiling of the apse with motifs of vine shoots, bunches of grapes and birds. The mosaic floor comprised a curtain-like pattern of tesserae in subtle colours. The floor of the hall, on the other hand, was divided into three fields by elegant strips of plants with a box in the centre, of which only a part of the frame is preserved. The geometric patterns were juxtaposed with figurative motifs similar to those decorating the neighbouring basilica halls. They show fish, octopus, shells and birds, as well as bunches of grapes, flowering tendrils, baskets and bowls of fruit that gave an idea of the community's wealth and prosperity. As with the earliest basilicas, the apsidal hall can be dated to after the Edict of Constantine in 313 CE.

In a higher layer are the mosaic and wall remains of the fifth-century episcopal palace, which was located immediately behind the large complex of churches found underneath the nearby Piazza Capitolo and the medieval basilica.

The episcopal palace consisted of a long hall that was a central part of the state residence of the bishop of Aquileia, who during the fourth century became one of the most prominent figures not only in Aquileia itself but also across much larger territories stretching from the Adriatic to the transalpine regions.

The mosaic of the fifth-century building consists of two spaces separated by a band of yellow tiles. To the north is a motif of small concentric squares around a black button made of terracotta tiles. The elongated space, on the other hand, is decorated with a grid-like composition decorated with lozenges and squares, also used in other Christian contexts in Aquileia.

The Christian basilica

The Christian religious complex of Piazza Capitolo is outstanding and one of the Western world's most important historical monuments. It is unique in northern Italy in terms of its historical importance, rarity and the size of the archaeological and architectural remains (Figures 0.1, n. 23; 8.2–8.4).[6]

Known for centuries, the complex has received special attention and investigation since the end of the nineteenth century, with excavations conducted at the time of Austrian rule by Count Karl von Lanckoroński, who in 1893 uncovered part of the extremely rich mosaic carpets, which were fully revealed in 1909.

Located just outside the south-eastern corner of the oldest city wall, the first church building can be dated to the time of Bishop Theodore (308–19 CE) (Figure 8.1) and is one of the earliest Christian buildings already active in the second decade of the fourth century. This first church even predates many similar religious buildings erected later in Rome and is distinguished by its totally original architectural design.

It is also a fascinating record of the economic, social and religious strength of the Aquileian community in the first half of the fourth century and provides a valuable stratigraphic and structural palimpsest of the transition from the Roman to the Christian city.

The new Christian religion's first public church comprised three halls within one of the city-blocks that extended outside the city walls. The church overlaid some earlier *domus*, completely changing their layout. The two parallel halls had dimensions of 37 × 17–20 metres and were decorated with some extraordinarily well conserved mosaic carpets covering an area of approximately 1,300 square metres; these mosaics have now been uncovered and are visible from the walkways that lead visitors through the later basilica.

The iconographic opulence of the mosaics and the remains of the wall frescoes have sparked lively debate among scholars about their interpretation and are a uniquely valuable part of Christian heritage in the Mediterranean.

It may be that by the middle of the fourth century the north hall had already been replaced by an enormous basilica (73 × 31 metres) divided into three naves by fourteen columns and with a four-sided portico to the west (found in the 1970 excavations). The entrance to the church must have opened onto this large porticoed space. In the same period, in the second half of the fourth century, the second basilica was also built, which overlaid the first southern hall of Theodore's time; this new hall (67 × 29 metres) consisted of three naves with a narthex and a vestibule which housed the large hexagonal baptistery, which can still be seen and visited today.

In the eleventh century, at the behest of the Patriarch Poppo, the northern church was demolished and the bell tower built atop it (in 1031), whilst in the same period the southern church underwent major remodelling with the addition of the apse, the expansion of the transept and the transformation of the crypt. After the 1348 earthquake the roof was restored in Gothic style.

The Late Roman markets

After the mid-fourth century CE the river port along the eastern side of the city lost its importance. The course of the river had partly dried up and the main trading area of the city moved south of the Christian basilicas of Piazza Capitolo near *Fondo Pasqualis*.[7] This area contains the city's southern markets (Figures 0.1, n. 19; 7.1), which had already been investigated during the past century and have been studied by the University of Verona for several years.

Today, three large paved areas are visible in this area, which must have been three squares where trading took place. The squares were surrounded by porticoes that allowed stalls to be placed with goods on display and also provided shelter from bad weather and the sun for those who frequented the area.

The first of the squares, to the east, also had a water well and a drainage system. The central square had arcades with shops behind them. It is likely that various foodstuffs, including cereals, were traded here, evidenced by the discovery of a series of amphorae inside one of the shops in the central square that contained half-burnt grains of wheat.

The third square (to the west) had a similar layout to the others (open space and arcades) and has yielded an exceptional find: a gold Solidus of Emperor Leo I (457–74 CE). As has been rightly suggested, this find and others made at the Fondi Cossar prove that Attila's siege of 452 CE did not mean the end of the city's life. Even after this event, trading locations and private houses experienced the circulation of merchants and wealthy people.

Furthermore, recent investigations by the University of Verona have demonstrated that the area was still used in the early Middle Ages. On the pavement of the third square, in fact, a strange construction was built using a wooden palisade that may have belonged to a village that we know nothing about.

It should also be noted that the three squares were closely connected to a large warehouse, built around a big central courtyard and located between the squares and the Christian basilicas.

The area of the Late Antique market also preserves the remains of the city's imperial Roman fortifications. During the fourth century CE a new defensive wall was built around this area and followed the Natissa river. Excavations by G. B. Brusin in the last century and recent investigations were able to uncover all of this new wall. It was constructed using a lot of second-hand material and was reinforced by at least one tower that is no longer visible. The wall is about three metres thick.

In a second phase, a new wall was built running parallel to the previous one. It was probably a reinforcement of the mid-fifth-century defences. Recent excavations have shown that there was a system of passageways that allowed the wall to be crossed, enabling goods to be transferred from the boats docked along the river to the market squares.

The *domus* of the *CAL* area

The area of the *CAL* and *Beneficio Rizzi* estates (Figure 0.1, n. 8) is located along the modern main road that crosses modern Aquileia in the southern sector of ancient Aquileia (via Giulia Augusta, S.S. 352).[8] This area is just outside the oldest ring of Roman fortifications.

This space was investigated several times during past century and the whole area has been extensively remanaged with newer buildings constructed on top of the ancient ones. The area of the *CAL* and *Beneficio Rizzi* estates is one of the largest in Aquileia where it is possible to see how the dwellings were laid out. In particular, the area features a variety of residential buildings typical of northern Italy throughout the Imperial Age (first–fourth centuries CE).

One such is a highly prestigious *domus*, centred on porticoed courtyards laid out as gardens, around which large reception rooms, family apartments and small, private thermal baths were arranged. Almost all the spaces are decorated with elaborate mosaic carpets.

There are two areas, separated by embankments, containing at least six private residences which had a long use. The profound transformations that they underwent over time has made the understanding of the history of these houses very complex.

A group of houses on the eastern side (the House of the Colonnaded Courtyard, the House of Dionysus with Satyrs and Silenes and the House of the Small Baths) has a large absidal room to the north, now protected by a modern structure and which was preceded by a colonnaded courtyard. This space was long considered an area dedicated to Christian worship due to the presence of a 'Good Shepherd' mosaic dating to the early stages of Christianity (fourth century). This 'Good Shepherd' mosaic is one of the most famous in Aquileia and depicts a figure at the centre of a circle formed by geometric motifs and surrounded by fish, dolphins, peacocks, ducks and male and female busts. This series of motifs is typical of fourth-century CE decorations, which can be found in other mosaic floors in the city. More recently, however, studies suggest that it was a reception hall where the owner welcomed his most important guests and could display his personal prestige and wealth.

In the westernmost area you can see another important residence (the House of the Black and White Mosaics). This is organized around a peristyle and consisted of several rooms that appear to be part of a house enlargement dating from between the first century BCE and the first century CE.

The Decumanus of Aratria Galla

As mentioned in the chapter on Aquileia's foundation, the urban spaces in the city were soon divided in a regular pattern. This created numerous city-blocks, delimited by a chessboard pattern of urban streets. At first (during the second century BCE) the streets had a base of gravel and sand for water drainage. Later, the city made important changes to the road system and gradually built stone-paved urban roads (trachyte from the Euganean Hills near Padua or Aurisina limestone from the Karst) and a system of canals for water drainage under the roadway. Not many of these streets are preserved and visible today because most of these infrastructures were demolished in order to reuse the bricks of the sewer conduits and the paving stones.

In the central area of the city, immediately south of the forum, a section of one of these city streets, known as the 'Decumanus of Aratria Galla', is preserved (Figure 0.1, n. 11). This is a very wide street, approximately 5.8 metres in width, the same as almost all streets in imperial Aquileia. Its particular name derives from that of an Aquileian citizen who donated a lot of money to give this street its final layout.

It is clear, then, that even private individuals could contribute with their own finances to improve the urban road system, and at the same time remind their fellow citizens of the generosity of their gesture. In fact, two inscriptions have been found that mention the paving of this road thanks to Aratria Galla's euergetism. Her donation was made as part of her will. The pair of inscriptions, one found to the west of the forum (in 1970) and the other near the Monastero site (in 1887), date to the transition phase between the first century BCE and the first century CE.

The road is visible today and much of it can be visited. It played a particularly important role in antiquity as it connected the western quarters near the Roman theatre with the Roman forum and the river port, thereby linking three major urban hubs.

The south-western burial grounds

The south-western burial ground ('Sepolcreto'; Figures 0.1, n. 15; 6.3) is part of the only necropolis visible and visitable today in Aquileia.[9] It lies to the west of the town and in ancient times flanked a minor road heading south-west. This arrangement is very characteristic of all cities in the ancient world. Since Greek times, in fact, cemeteries were located outside the city itself and lined the main roads in order to be seen and admired by travellers.

The visible part of the south-western necropolis was excavated between 1939 and 1941 by G. B. Brusin, who immediately noted its excellent state of preservation. For this reason, the necropolis was restored and parts of it reconstructed. Recently, this section of the necropolis was again restored and made publicly accessible.

What makes this archaeological area particularly valuable is its uniqueness in the archaeological landscape of Aquileia. In fact, it is the only remaining visible cemetery of all those the city had established along its extra-urban roads. This part of the ancient city thus offers an excellent example of what the areas that lined all the roads leading to the city must have looked like in the Roman Imperial Age.

As of today, five variously-sized burial enclosures, united by the same back wall, are visible. Inside are incineration and inhumation burials that can be dated between the end of the first and the third century CE. In one case the burial area continued to be used into the fourth century and even beyond. The names of some families who used these small spaces to lay their deceased loved ones are known. These include the Statii, Iulii, Trebii and Cestii families, as well as others whose names have not been passed on. Later burials (fourth and fifth centuries CE) also used sarcophagi to lay and preserve the deceased. These sarcophagi have recently been placed on pillars to show the exact level at which they were found.

The National Archaeological Museum

The National Archaeological Museum of Aquileia (Figure 10.2) was opened on 3 August 1882 and since then has been the most important venue for exhibiting the Roman city's antiques (Figure 9.2). The museum, housed in the nineteenth-century villa that once belonged to the Cassis Faraone family, immediately became the first point of reference for all activity related to research, conservation and promotion of the city and surrounding area's archaeological heritage.[10]

Figure 10.2 Aquileia. Interior rooms of the National Archaeological Museum after the recent renovation (© A. Chemollo).

The museum was founded at the behest of the Emperor Franz Joseph and the Austro-Hungarian government, which governed a large part of Friuli Venezia Giulia until the First World War. In fact, the Act of Foundation reveals that the Archduke Charles Ludwig was present at its opening. The first director of the museum was Enrico Maionica, a Triestine who trained at the University of Vienna. Thanks to his work, the new museum housed material from the municipal collection and the most important private collections, such as those of the Monari and Ritter von Záhony families.

A few years after it opened, a *lapidarium* was added to the villa and museum. This was comprised of a series of external porticoes which gradually expanded over time to house the ever-increasing number of finds from the city excavations and which could not be part of the existing exhibition.

For a long time the museum was organized along antiquarian lines, with the exhibits arranged typologically. Although the museum was completely reorganized in 1954 it is only recently (between 2016 and 2021) that the museum underwent a radical overhaul to increase accessibility and improve the narration of the cultural heritage. The new layout highlights the importance of Aquileia's vast archaeological collection, with the materials presented as part of their original context so as to engage the visitor and give them a clearer understanding of the ancient Roman metropolis as they pass through the museum.

The new layout is arranged on three floors of the historic building as well as the *lapidarium*, where large fragments of the ancient city's architecture, funerary monuments, mosaics and hundreds of inscriptions have been collected.

The entrance to the ground floor of villa Cassis houses an illustration of the city and the territory's history and an extraordinary relief depicting the ploughing of the *sulcus primigenius* (Figure 3.3), the furrow/ditch that surrounded the city at the time of its foundation and marking the line of the future walls. Alongside this is the inscription commemorating one of the magistrates who participated in the city's foundation. Then we have an account of the excavations that rediscovered the city and the history of the Aquileian collections and the museum itself. Further on, the visitor can admire the remains of the public monuments and many finds from the cemetery areas, including monuments commemorating important deceased persons and various portrait statues (Figure 6.5).

The first floor contains the extraordinary remains of some of Aquileia's private residences. Their richness is underlined by the mosaic floors (Figure 6.2) with geometric patterns and polychrome figured motifs that adorned the large reception halls.

The museum's collection also includes many furnishings that help to reconstruct the interior appearance of Aquileia's *domus*, including remnants of furniture and their decorations, obtained from embossed metal sheets or full-length figurines in bronze, bone and ivory.

Furthermore, the first floor also contains the extremely rich series of materials that tell of Aquileia's vast commercial outreach and its multicultural character, due to the city's strategic position, connecting it with continental Europe and the entire Mediterranean.

Aquileia's role as a mediator hosting men and goods from all over the ancient world was reinforced when, during the reign of Diocletian (284–305 CE), the city became the seat of the governor of *Venetia et Histria*. At that point it became the headquarters of the terrestrial and naval military command and was thus the point of reference for all goods related to the management of the armies active on the eastern front: footwear, helmets, vestments, weapons and ammunition, chariot and horse accessories and much more. The Aquileia necropolises also provide information about this military presence from very different areas.

The cultural diversity of the peoples present in Imperial Aquileia is reflected in the multiplicity of cults present and documented by the many museum exhibits: the gods of the traditional pantheon, who came in the wake of the first settlers, were joined by Isis and Serapis (from Egypt), Cybele, Attis and Artemis Ephesia (from Asia) and the Iunones from Gaul.

On the second floor of the museum, precious artefacts are displayed that document the exceptional levels of expertise that art and craftsmanship had reached in Aquileia. This is proven by the different classes of materials for which the city is famous, such as gems, glasses (Figure 6.6), jewellery and worked amber.

The picture is completed by the extraordinary collection of coins, which are the clearest reflection of the commercial role that the city played from the very beginning of its life until the last days of its existence before its progressive decline in importance from the early Middle Ages onwards (Figure 7.2).

Outside Villa Cassis Faraone, visitors can stroll along the galleries displaying architectural fragments (columns, entablatures, capitals), the remains of mosaic floors and parts of the funerary and honorary monuments (Figure 6.4) that have been recovered from the late nineteenth century to the present day in different parts of the city. Although fragmentary, they clearly show us the grandeur of Aquileia's architecture.

Of equal, if not greater, importance is the exceptional collection of inscriptions illustrating the monuments, society, daily life, professions and intercultural relations of one of the greatest cities of the ancient world. Also recently opened to the public are the storerooms, which house mosaics, inscriptions, fragments of sculptures and glass, and ceramic and metal objects, as well as the naval section, where it is possible to admire a Roman-era ship found near the ancient city.

The Early Christian Museum

The Early Christian Museum of Aquileia (Figure 10.3) is located in the north-eastern suburb of the modern town, in an area known as Monastero (Monastery).[11] The area is so named because it was the site of a monastic building founded in the ninth century as a female coenoby of the order of St Benedict and endowed by donations made by Patriarch Poppo in 1036.

Figure 10.3 Aquileia. The Early Christian Museum in the Monastero neighbourhood (J. Bonetto).

The closure of the monastery (in 1782) led, after various vicissitudes, to the acquisition of the building by private individuals who used it to house the archaeological remains found in the surrounding areas.

In 1852, the building was bought by Baron Eugen Ritter von Záhony, and the church belonging to the former monastery was converted into a wine-making facility. Finally, in 1961, because of the discovery of mosaic floors, it was turned into a museum.

Subsequent investigations have shown that the monastery church, now transformed into a museum, had reused a space that had been a Christian basilica from the end of the fourth century.

As mentioned, the museum occupies part of the original rectangular church (approximately 58 × 19 metres), with a single nave and polygonal apse. Originally, a portico with three entrance doors had stood in front of the façade.

The floor pattern is made up of geometric mosaics (without figurative motifs) with a double series of six panels, separated in the centre by a long strip. Latin and Greek inscriptions can be seen on various parts of the floor, commemorating the worshippers who visited the sacred place and contributed donations for parts of the floor. This first church underwent modifications after Attila's invasion and again in the ninth century, but little evidence remains of these phases.

On the first floor there are remains of another Christian basilica with three naves, found to the south of Aquileia (Beligna – *Fondo Tullio* locality, along the road to Grado) in 1894. On display are some mosaics with inscriptions and vine shoot motifs from acanthus bushes that decorated the floor of the nave and apse. Among the clusters of flowers are twelve lambs and birds, among which a peacock with splendid plumage stands out.

According to a recent interpretation, the twelve lambs could represent the twelve Apostles and refer to Christ's words about the Good Shepherd, while the peacock could be a symbol of immortality. Also in the case of the basilica of Beligna, there are floor inscriptions commemorating generous worshippers, including a certain Parecorius Apollinaris, a public administrator, who makes reference to a donation he made to the basilica.

On the second floor can be found a rich collection (about 130) of Christian funerary inscriptions.[12] This is the second largest collection after that of Rome and are very important for reconstructing the history of Christian Aquileia and the society of the time. The texts commemorate the deceased and their relatives and allow us to reconstruct in detail not only the lives of these believers, but also the language they spoke. They are dated between the fourth and fifth centuries.

NOTES

Chapter 1

1. Maselli Scotti (2004).
2. Maselli Scotti, Sernandi, Degrassi, Pugliese, Tiussi and Mandruzzato (1996).
3. Maselli Scotti, Paronuzzi and Pugliese (1999).
4. Carre, Marocco and Maselli Scotti (2003); Arnaud-Fassetta, Carre, Marocco, Maselli Scotti, Pugliese, Zaccaria, Bandelli, Bresson, Manzoni, Montenegro, Morhange, Pipan, Prizzon and Siché (2003).
5. Fontana (2006); Fontana, Mozzi and Marchetti (2014).
6. Amorosi, Fontana, Antonioli, Primon and Bondesan (2008).
7. Fontana, Mozzi and Bondesan (2008).
8. Marocco (2009).
9. Marocco (1989); Fontana, Vinci, Tasca, Mozzi, Vacchi, Bivi, Salvador, Rossato, Antonioli, Asioli, Bresolin, Di Mario and Hajdas (2017); Fontana, Vinci, Tasca, Mozzi, Vacchi, Bivi, Salvador, Rossato, Antonioli, Asioli, Bresolin, Di Mario and Hajdas (2018).
10. Carre, Marocco, Maselli Scotti and Pugliese (2003); Carre (2004); Polisca and Nicosia (2024).
11. Jordanes, *Getica* 42.21; Paulus Diaconus, *Historia Romana* 14.8-10.
12. Plinius the Elder, *Natural History* 3.18.126.
13. Maggi and Oriolo (1999).
14. Groh (2011).
15. Maggi and Oriolo (1999).
16. Buora and Prenc (2000); Carre (2004) and other works quoted in chapter 4.
17. Vitruvius, *De architectura* 1.4.11.
18. Marocco (1991); Fontana, Vinci, Tasca, Mozzi, Vacchi, Bivi, Salvador, Rossato, Antonioli, Asioli, Bresolin, Di Mario and Hajdas (2018).
19. Rosada (1984).
20. Carre and Maselli Scotti (2001).
21. Bonetto (2007).
22. Strabo, *Geography* 5.1.8.
23. Polybius, *Histories* 2, 14.7–15.7; 16.6–17.12.
24. Polybius, *Histories* 3.34.2; 3.44.8; 3.48.11.
25. Cato, *Origines* fr. 43.
26. Strabo, *Geography* 5.1.12.
27. Livy, 5.33.
28. Vergil, *Georgics* 2.195-202.

29. Pliny the Elder, *Natural History* 14.16, 39; 17.20, 201; 18.101, 127, 141, 205; 19.9, 16.
30. Pliny the Younger, *Letters* 4.6.
31. Tacitus, *Histories* 2.17.
32. Cicero, *Philippicae* 3.13.3.
33. Maselli Scotti (2004).
34. Maselli Scotti, Sernandi, Degrassi, Pugliese, Tiussi and Mandruzzato (1996); Maselli Scotti (2004).
35. Marchesini, Marvelli and Rizzoli (2024).
36. Marchesini, Marvelli and Rizzoli (2024), 64–5, 74–5.
37. Marchesini, Marvelli and Rizzoli (2024), 65–6, 74–5.
38. Marchesini, Marvelli and Rizzoli (2024), 66–8, 74–5.

Chapter 2

1. Càssola Guida (1989); Vitri (2004).
2. All information about this site can be found in Gnesotto (1981); Borgna, Corazza, Fontana and Fozzati (2018).
3. The early connection between Aquileia and the ambra trade (clearly evident in Roman Age) is discussed in Maselli Scotti (1996).
4. Maselli Scotti (2004); Maselli Scotti (2009).
5. Maselli Scotti, Sernandi, Degrassi, Pugliese, Tiussi and Mandruzzato (1996); Maselli Scotti (2009).
6. For wooden construction methods in pre-Roman times, see the first volume of Previato and Bonetto (2023).
7. For an overview of human figurine bronzes in protohistoric times, see Càssola Guida (1989).
8. The study of botanical remains (pollen and seeds) was presented by Castiglioni, Motella and Rottoli (1996); Maselli Scotti and Rottoli (2007).
9. Archaeozoological findings have been discussed by Petrucci (2004).
10. Maselli Scotti (2004); Maselli Scotti (2009), 5.
11. Maselli Scotti (2009), 6–7.
12. Silius Italicus, *Punica* 8.604.
13. Maselli Scotti (2004); Maselli Scotti (2009), 5–6.

Chapter 3

1. An excellent overview of the colony's earliest history is provided by Chiabà (2009), 7–12. Also fundamental are Bandelli (2003) and Zaccaria (2003a).
2. Livy, 39.55.5-6; 40.34.2-3.
3. Regarding the provenance of the settlers, see Chiabà (2003).
4. Livy, 39.22.6-7; 45.6-7; 54.2-12; 54.13–55.4-6.

5. Livy, 39.22.6-7; 39.45.6-7; 39.54.2-13; 39.55.1-6.

6. Livy, 39.55.4.

7. Bandelli (2003); Chiabà (2003).

8. On the administration of the city, see Chiabà (2009), 12–13.

9. Chiabà (2009), 13–14.

10. Livy, 39.55.6 (183 BCE); 40.34.3 (181 BCE).

11. Livy, 39.54.13.

12. Livy, 40.53.5-6.

13. Livy, 41.5.9.

14. Livy, 41.10.10-11.

15. Livy, 43.1.5-6.

16. Chiabà (2009), 10–12.

17. Livy, 43.17.1.

18. Zaccaria (2003a); Zaccaria (2014).

19. Maselli Scotti, Mandruzzato and Tiussi (2009).

20. For a general overview of the urban layout of Aquileia according to the more recent archaeological finds, see Basso, Bonetto, Cottica, Dilaria, Fontana, Ghiotto, Rubinich, Tiussi and Ventura (2024).

21. All information on Aquileia's defensive system during the Roman Republic and Empire can be found in Bonetto (2004) and Bonetto (2009).

22. Bonetto (2004), 156–8.

23. For the reconstruction of the building process of the walls, see Bonetto and Previato (2018).

24. Bonetto (2004), 158–61.

25. The excavation along the western side of the wall is presented in Bonetto, Ghiotto and Previato (2019–20).

26. A general overview of the building techniques used in Roman Aquileia is provided by Previato (2015).

27. The recent discoveries in the Fondi Cossar area are presented in detail by Bonetto (2024a).

28. Vitruvius, *De architectura* 2.3.3.

29. The Greek contribution to the construction of the republican wall is discussed in Bonetto (2020).

30. Bonetto, Artioli, Secco and Addis (2016). See also Dilaria (2024), 105–10, for the very special mortar in the foundation of the wall.

31. Bonetto and Previato (2013a).

32. Bonetto (2004), 162; Bonetto (2023).

33. Philo, ed. Garlan, A3.

34. Vitruvius, *De architectura* 1.5.5.

35. For a general overview of the gates of the republican wall, see Bonetto (2004), 163–7.

36. Bonetto (2023).

37. Bonetto and Previato (2018).

38. On the chronology of the city walls, see Bonetto (2004), 167–71.

39. Bonetto (2020).
40. Bonetto and Previato (2013b). For this and others building techniques, see Previato, Dilaria, Canciani and Piazza (2024).
41. See Bonetto, Ghiotto and Previato (2019–20) for the use of this technique in the western sector of the city wall.
42. Maselli Scotti, Mandruzzato and Tiussi (2009).
43. Many important contributions have been made to the debate about the division of urban space in Aquileia. See the following, which summarize the current state of the play on this subject: Muzzioli (2004); Tiussi (2006); Tiussi (2009b); Ghiotto (2013); Previato, Ghiotto and Dilaria (2023).
44. Bonetto (2024b), 170–7.
45. The excavation of two segments of the roads was carried out in the Fondi Cossar area: Bonetto (2024b), 160–70.
46. Bonetto, Previato, Maritan and Mazzoli (2014).
47. Furlan (2024), 288–328.
48. Basso, Bonetto, Cottica, Dilaria, Fontana, Ghiotto, Rubinich, Tiussi and Ventura (2024).
49. Bonetto (2024b), 176–7.
50. Bonetto and Previato (2013a).
51. Maselli Scotti, Mandruzzato and Tiussi (2009); Tiussi (2011).
52. The distribution and trade system for goods is discussed by Tiussi (2004).
53. For this topic (republican religious buildings and cults), see Fontana (1997); Känel (2005); Tiussi (2009a).
54. Zaccaria (2014).
55. Känel (2005).

Chapter 4

1. Bandelli (2003).
2. Horvat and Mušič (2007).
3. The marshy nature of certain areas to the west of the city is discussed by Bertacchi (1988).
4. Vitruvius, *De architectura* 1.4.11.
5. This infrastructure was studied by many scholars, such as Vale (1950); Brusin (1939); Bertacchi (1979); Marchiori (1982); Bertacchi (1983); Buora and Prenc (2000); Auriemma, Degrassi, Gaddi and Maggi (2016); Maggi, Maselli Scotti, Mattioli Pesavento and Zulini (2017); and Bonetto, Furlan, Ghiotto and Missaglia (2020).
6. Groh (2011).
7. Bertacchi (1979); Bertacchi (1983). See also Bertacchi (1990).
8. Bertacchi (1990); Bertacchi (2003).
9. Brusin (1939); Galliazzo (1994).
10. A summary on the topic of chronology can be found in Bonetto, Furlan, Ghiotto and Missaglia (2020), 181, 195–8.

11. The most recent studies are Bianchetti (2004); Muzzioli (2004); Muzzioli (2005); Prenc (2000); Prenc (2002); Maggi and Oriolo (2009), 156–8.

12. Details in Prenc (2000).

13. Muzzioli (2005), 12–16.

14. For a general overview of the villas scattered in the territory of the city, see Busana (2009).

15. Horvat and Mušič (2007).

16. The topic of the small settlements is discussed by Maggi and Zaccaria (1994, 1999); Buora (1999); Maggi (2003).

17. Maggi (1992).

18. Livy, 41.1.2; 41.2.1.

19. Tassaux (1984); Verzár-Bass (1984).

20. The evolution of villas in the Imperial and Late Antique periods is discussed by Brogiolo (1996) and Magrini (1997).

21. Brogiolo (1996); Valenti (2005).

22. The Roman cemeteries in the countryside are presented in Adam, Balista, Càssola Guida, Moretti and Vitri (1983–4), Buora (1993), Buora (1996) and De Cecco (2002).

23. A general overview of the Roman road system around Aquileia is provided by Blason Scarel (2000) and Maggi and Oriolo (2009).

24. The Via Annia was deeply studied a few years ago during a research project: see Veronese (2009), Rosada, Frassine and Ghiotto (2010) and Veronese (2011).

25. Uggeri (2012).

26. Busana (2004).

27. Busana (2004).

28. Complete information about the Via Postumia is condensed in two miscellaneous works: Sena Chiesa and Arslan (1998); Sena Chiesa and Lavizzari Pedrazzini (1998).

29. Tacitus, *Historiae* 2–3.

30. Buora (1996).

31. Bonetto (2023).

32. Bonetto (2007).

33. These roads are discussed by Blason Scarel (2000).

34. *CIL* V, 7989 = *ILS*, 487; *CIL* V, 7990.

35. Strabo, *Geography* 4.6.10.

36. Tacitus, *Annales* 1.

37. Herodian, *History of the Roman Empire* 8.

38. Pesavento Mattioli and Basso (2004).

Chapter 5

1. Regarding Aquileia in the Imperial Age, see Bandelli (2000); Cuscito (2003a); Cuscito and Verzár-Bass (2004, 2007); Ghedini, Bueno and Novello (2009); Fozzati (2010); Previato

(2015); Barca (2022). Recent archaeological data can be found in Basso, Bonetto, Cottica, Dilaria, Fontana, Ghiotto, Rubinich, Tiussi and Ventura (2024).

2. Chiabà (2009), 17.

3. Verzár (2015).

4. Maselli Scotti and Rubinich (2009), 96–8; Tiussi (2009b), 68–9; Tiussi (2011), 171–6.

5. Regarding the Roman aqueduct of Aquileia, see Tiussi (2018).

6. Tiussi (2004), 282.

7. Zaccaria (2003b).

8. *CIL* V, 2157.

9. *Inscr. Aq.*, 842, 3495.

10. Casari (2004), 45–77.

11. Mian (2004), 444–70.

12. Zaccaria and Pesavento Mattioli (2009).

13. Strabo, *Geography* 5.1.8.

14. Tiussi (2004), 283–8; Maselli Scotti and Rubinich (2009), 103–6; Tiussi (2009b), 71–2; Basso, Bonetto, Cottica, Dilaria, Fontana, Ghiotto, Rubinich, Tiussi and Ventura (2024), 60–2.

15. Tiussi (2009b), 66–8.

16. Tiussi (2009b), 69–70.

17. Ghiotto and Furlan (2025).

18. Basso (2018).

19. Martial, *Epigrams* 4.25.

20. *CIL* V, 854 = *Inscr. Aq.*, 437.

21. Tiussi (2009b), 73–5.

22. Chiabà (2009), 20. Regarding Aquileia in the Antonine period, see Tiussi (2022).

23. Maselli Scotti (2009), 98–9; Tiussi (2009b), 75.

24. Casari (2004), 68–73, 77.

25. Tiussi (2011), 176–8.

26. Ghiotto and Furlan (2005), 30–1.

27. *IG* XIV, 2342 = *Inscr. Aq.*, 710 = Lettich (2003), 295.

28. Chiabà (2009), 20–1.

29. Herodian, *History of the Roman Empire* 8.2-6.

30. Bonetto (2004), 175–8; Bonetto (2009), 87.

31. *Inscr. Aq.*, 266 = Lettich (2003), 10.

32. Cigaina (2020).

33. Tiussi (2009b), 76–7.

34. Chiabà (2009), 21–2; Marano (2009), 23–4.

35. Ponzellini (2009); Stella (2019), 161, 174.

36. Regarding Aquileia in the Tetrarchic and Constantinian eras and in the fourth century, see Haug (2003), 86–106, 325–67, Taf. 2, 44–55; Sotinel (2005), 7–64; Tiussi (2009b), 77–81; Tiussi, Villa and Novello (2013); Cuscito (2014); Tiussi and Villa (2017).

37. Bonetto (2004), 178–89; Bonetto (2009), 87–9; Tiussi and Villa (2017), 110–17.

38. *Inscr. Aq.*, 446–447.
39. Tiussi (2009b), 79–80; Tiussi and Villa (2017), 105–38.
40. Maselli Scotti and Rubinich (2009), 108–10; Rubinich (2012–13).
41. Rubinich, Bonetto, Cadario, Dilaria and Martinelli (2024).
42. Lettich (2003), 196 = Witschel (2012–13), 1.
43. Witschel (2012–13), 2.
44. Maselli Scotti and Rubinich (2009), 101–3; Tiussi and Villa (2017), 117–24.
45. Groh (2011), 155–77.
46. *Panegyrici Latini* 7 [VI].6.2.
47. Mian (2012–13); Tiussi and Villa (2017), 125–35.
48. Mian (2004), 470–94; Sperti (2004); Sperti (2012–13), 255–62.
49. *CIL* V, 8269 = *Inscr. Aq.*, 448 = Lettich (2003), 76 = Witschel (2012–13), 3.
50. Tiussi and Villa (2017), 136–8.
51. Maselli Scotti and Rubinich (2009), 99–100; Tiussi (2009b), 79; Zaccaria (2000).
52. *Inscr. Aq.*, 501; AE 1996, 686; AE 1999, 697.
53. Tiussi (2004), 300–1.
54. Tiussi (2004), 298–9; Tiussi and Villa (2017), 101–2.
55. Tiussi (2004), 297–8; Basso (2021); Basso (2024), 222–6.
56. Tiussi (2004), 293–7.
57. *Expositio totius mundi et gentium* LVI.
58. Marano (2009), 24–6.
59. Ammianus Marcellinus, *Res gestae* 21.11-12.
60. Bonetto (2004), 189–91; Bonetto (2009), 89–90.
61. Regarding Aquileia in the Theodosian Age, see Bratož (2003), 479–503.
62. Ausonius, *Ordo urbium nobilium* 9.
63. *Inscr. Aq.*, 450.
64. Zaccaria (2017).
65. Borsato (2021).
66. Tiussi (2009b), 80–1.
67. Sotinel (2005), 178.

Chapter 6

1. Verzár-Bass and Mian (2001); Verzár-Bass and Mian (2003); Ghedini and Novello (2009); Novello (2009); Dupré and Novello (2012); Bonetto and Salvadori (2012).
2. Bonetto, Furlan and Previato (2024); Ghiotto and Madrigali (2024).
3. Salvadori, Mantovani and Scalco (2020).
4. Fontana (2012–13).
5. Furlan (2024).

6. Ghiotto (2013).

7. Previato, Ghiotto and Dilaria (2023), 147–54.

8. Previato (2024).

9. Ghiotto (2024), 120–65.

10. Novello (2012–13); some papers in Tiussi, Villa and Novello (2013).

11. Several papers in Bonetto and Salvadori (2012).

12. Ghedini, Bueno, Novello and Rinaldi (2017).

13. Clementi, Rinaldi, Novello and Bueno (2009), 245–52; Ghedini, Bueno, Novello and Rinaldi (2017), 547–9.

14. Oriolo and Salvadori (2001, 2009); Oriolo (2019); Didonè (2020), 41–78. Some papers in Oriolo and Verzár (2012).

15. Maggi and Oriolo (2009), 165–70; Maggi and Oriolo (2012–13). On Late Antique developments, see Magrini (2004).

16. Busana (2009), 179–82; Maggi and Oriolo (2012).

17. Ciliberto (2016).

18. Rebaudo, Savioli and Braidotti (2012).

19. Regarding Aquileian necropolises and funerary monuments, see Reusser (1987); Bertacchi (1997); Maselli Scotti (1997); Verzár-Bass and Oriolo (1998, 1999); Hope (2001); Giovannini (2009, 2012–13, 2015).

20. Zaccaria (2005).

21. Brusin (1941); Tiussi and Ventura (2025).

22. Ciliberto (2015).

23. *Il Mausoleo Candia* (2010).

24. Recent works on Aquileian sculpture include Maselli Scotti (2002); Maselli Scotti, Giovannini and Ventura (2003); Rebaudo (2007b); Verzár, Mian, Casari and Ciliberto (2009); Ciliberto (2011); Ciliberto (2012); Casari (2012–13); Cigaina (2012–13); Cigaina (2015); Ventura and Giovannini (2015); Cadario (2017); Sperti (2017); Verzár and Cigaina (2017). In general, regarding the artistic culture of Aquileia, see Cuscito and Verzár-Bass (2005); Cuscito (2006); Tiussi, Villa and Novello (2013); Novello, Plattner and Tiussi (2019); Ciliberto (2020).

25. Santa Maria Scrinari (1972).

26. Fontana (1997), 27–51; Känel (2005).

27. Renesto (2023).

28. Mian (2004), 426–43.

29. Different interpretations are found in Di Filippo Balestrazzi (2005), 94–106; Verzár (2016).

30. Sena Chiesa and Gagetti (2009b).

31. Sena Chiesa (1966); Ciliberto and Giovannini (2008); Sena Chiesa and Gagetti (2009a); Sena Chiesa and Gagetti (2009b), 255–9.

32. Calvi (2005); Sena Chiesa and Gagetti (2009b), 264–8.

33. Calvi (1968); Mandruzzato and Marcante (2005, 2007); Mandruzzato (2008); Mandruzzato (2012–13).

34. Sena Chiesa and Gagetti (2009b), 259–64.

Chapter 7

1. Regarding Aquileia in the first half of the fifth century, see Bratož (2003), 503–12; Sotinel (2005), 233–41; Marano (2009), 26–8.

2. Ponzellini (2009), 289; Stella (2019), 126.

3. Bonetto (2009), 90–1.

4. Basso, Dobreva and Laserra (2022); Basso (2024), 218–22.

5. Ghiotto (2024), 165–263.

6. Blason Scarel (1994); Bratož (2003), 512–17; Sotinel (2005), 241–4; Roberto (2016).

7. Procopius, *De bellis* 3.4.

8. Janniard (2006).

9. Sotinel (2005), 244.

10. Villa (2004); Marano (2012); Villa (2012). See also recent archaeological data in Buora, Magnani and Villa (2021).

11. Nicetas, *Epistulae* CLIX.

12. Ghiotto (2024), 195–263.

13. Regarding Aquileia in the period from Attila's siege to the end of the Gothic War, see Bratož (2003), 517–20; Sotinel (2005), 244–8; Marano (2009), 28–32.

14. Villa (2004), 617–25.

15. Villa (2004), 606–14; Bonetto (2009), 92.

Chapter 8

*   The dates given next to the names of the patriarchs mentioned here refer to the period of their patriarchate, and not to their biographical dates; the same applies to pontiffs and emperors. Due to gaps in the sources, these dates have often been handed down with various uncertainties. In these cases, in order not to overburden the text, we have opted for the best-documented or most recurrent dates in the bibliography, reporting them without question marks or alternative indications. The kind reader will forgive any inaccuracies.

1. https://www.dizionariobiograficodeifriulani.it/ermagora-e-fortunato. Other excellent biographical records on the figures mentioned in this and the next chapter can be found at https://www.dizionariobiograficodeifriulani.it; a printed version is available in Scalon, Griggio, Rozzo and Bergamini (2006–11).

2. Bratož (1999); Cuscito (2003b), 425–47.

3. Cuscito (1992).

4. https://www.dizionariobiograficodeifriulani.it/ilario-e-taziano.

5. https://www.dizionariobiograficodeifriulani.it/crisogono-san.

6. https://www.dizionariobiograficodeifriulani.it/canziani; Toplikar and Tavano (2005).

7. Regarding the Aquileian Church from the Roman Age to Lombard Duchy, see Cuscito (1987); Bandelli (2000); Cuscito (2003b); Sotinel (2005).

8. Regarding the Aquileian basilica and the episcopal complex, see von Lanckoroński (1906); Cuscito and Lehmann (2010); Villa (2012–13); Zanetto (2017), 11–43; Ulmer (2022). See also several papers in Cuscito (2006).

9. https://www.dizionariobiograficodeifriulani.it/teodoro; Tiussi, Villa and Novello (2013).

10. Novello, Salvadori, Tiussi and Villa (2013).

11. Salvadori and Pavan (2012–13).

12. *La storia di Giona* (2019).

13. Cuscito (2003b), 447–64.

14. Cuscito (1987), 27–46; Sotinel (2005), 111–45.

15. https://www.dizionariobiograficodeifriulani.it/fortunaziano.

16. Fozzati (2015).

17. Sotinel (2005), 171–232.

18. https://www.dizionariobiograficodeifriulani.it/valeriano.

19. https://www.dizionariobiograficodeifriulani.it/cromazio-san; Cuscito (1987), 77–86; Piussi (2008); Beatrice and Peršič (2011); McEachnie (2017).

20. *Atti del Colloquio* (1981); Cuscito (1987), 47–75; Sotinel (2005), 145–69.

21. https://www.dizionariobiograficodeifriulani.it/rufino-di-concordia.

22. Ausonius, *Ordo urbium nobilium* 9.

23. Cuscito (2004); Cantino Wataghin (2006); Cuscito (2009).

24. Buora and Casadio (2018).

25. Bratož (2003), 520–1; Sotinel (2005), 295–305; Marano (2009), 32–3.

26. Sotinel (2005), 338–70.

27. Cuscito (1987), 95–133; Cuscito (2003b), 466–9; Sotinel (2005), 306–38.

28. https://www.dizionariobiograficodeifriulani.it/paolo-i.

29. Useful and accurate information on the history of the Patriarchate of Aquileia can be found at https://www.librideipatriarchi.it/en; see also *Aquileia e il suo Patriarcato* (2000); Cammarosano (2000); Murat and Vedovetto (2021).

30. https://www.dizionariobiograficodeifriulani.it/elia.

31. https://www.dizionariobiograficodeifriulani.it/callisto.

32. https://www.dizionariobiograficodeifriulani.it/paolino.

33. https://www.dizionariobiograficodeifriulani.it/massenzio.

34. Cozzi (2010).

35. https://www.dizionariobiograficodeifriulani.it/ottocari-degli-poppone; Blason Scarel (1997).

36. https://www.dizionariobiograficodeifriulani.it/randeck-di-marquardo.

37. https://www.dizionariobiograficodeifriulani.it/treffen-di-ulrico.

38. https://www.dizionariobiograficodeifriulani.it/sighardinger-di-sigeardo.

39. https://www.dizionariobiograficodeifriulani.it/andechs-merania-di-bertoldo.

40. https://www.dizionariobiograficodeifriulani.it/dolfin-daniele.

Chapter 9

1. Regarding architectural elements, see Pensabene (2006, 2010, 2012); and for inscriptions, see Zaccaria (1984, 2012).
2. Scalon (1982).
3. Brown (1847), 143.
4. Regarding the collections of Aquileian antiquities, see Favaretto (2009).
5. https://www.dizionariobiograficodeifriulani.it/trevisan-ludovico.
6. https://www.dizionariobiograficodeifriulani.it/grimani-giovanni.
7. Regarding the birth of the Aquileian antiquarian and archaeological research, see *Gli scavi di Aquileia* (1993); Buora, Marcone (2007); Giovannini and Maselli Scotti (2009).
8. https://www.dizionariobiograficodeifriulani.it/bertoli-gian-domenico.
9. Feruglio and Vidon (2024).
10. Regarding Aquileian epigraphy in the first half of nineteenth century, see Rebaudo (2007a).
11. https://www.dizionariobiograficodeifriulani.it/zuccolo-leopoldo.
12. https://www.dizionariobiograficodeifriulani.it/siauve-etienne-marie.
13. Giovannini (2004).
14. https://www.dizionariobiograficodeifriulani.it/moschettini-de-girolamo; Mainardis (2023).
15. Rebaudo and Didonè (2019–20, 2022, 2023).
16. Buora and Pollack (2010).
17. Giovannini (2013).
18. https://www.dizionariobiograficodeifriulani.it/maionica-majonica-enrico-heinrich.
19. https://www.dizionariobiograficodeifriulani.it/zandonati-vincenzo.
20. https://www.dizionariobiograficodeifriulani.it/toppo-di-francesco. Part of the collection of Francesco di Toppo is in Buttrio at Villa Florio: Verzár-Bass (2007).
21. Novello, Plattner and Tiussi (2019).
22. Buora, Tesei (2000).
23. Maionica (1884).
24. Maionica (1910).
25. Calderini (1930), LXII.
26. Regarding Aquileia during the first decades of twentieth century, see Milocco (2010).
27. Livy, 39.54.12.
28. Strabo, *Geography* 5.1.8.
29. https://www.dizionariobiograficodeifriulani.it/abramić-mihovil; Milocco (1999).
30. https://www.dizionariobiograficodeifriulani.it/costantini-celso-benigno-luigi.
31. Buora (2021).
32. https://www.dizionariobiograficodeifriulani.it/brusin-giovanni-battista; *Atti della Giornata di Studio* (1990); Cigaina (2018); Buora (2024).
33. Brusin (1934).
34. https://www.dizionariobiograficodeifriulani.it/calderini-aristide; Perelli Cippo (2010).

35. Calderini (1930).

36. Brusin (1941), 52.

37. For example, Brusin (1929), reprinted several times; Brusin and Zovatto (1957).

38. Privitera (2015).

39. Bandelli (2010).

40. On the figure and the scientific legacy of L. Bertacchi, see *Aquileia Nostra LXXXV* (2014).

41. Tiussi (2010).

42. https://www.dizionariobiograficodeifriulani.it/marinotti-francesco-franco; Tiussi (2001).

43. Bertacchi (2003).

44. Fozzati and Benedetti (2011); Cuscito (2020).

45. https://www.fondazioneaquileia.it/en.

Appendix

1. A general guide to the ancient and the modern town of Aquileia is Commessatti (2023). Regarding archaeological sites of Aquileia, see https://aquileia.arte.it/art-guide/aquileia; https://www.discoveraquileia.com/en; https://www.fondazioneaquileia.it/en/must-see. General overviews are also presented in Ghedini, Bueno and Novello (2009); Basso, Bonetto, Cottica, Dilaria, Fontana, Ghiotto, Rubinich, Tiussi and Ventura (2024). Bertacchi (2003) published a map of ancient Aquileia.

2. Maselli Scotti and Rubinich (2009), 93–100; Tiussi (2009b), 64–9; Tiussi (2011); Commessatti (2023), 189–91.

3. The city's port is visible and open to visitors. The various excavation projects are presented in Bertacchi (1990); Carre, Maselli Scotti (2001); Maselli Scotti and Rubinich (2009), 103–6; Basso, Bonetto, Cottica, Dilaria, Fontana, Ghiotto, Rubinich, Tiussi and Ventura (2024); Commessatti (2023), 191–4.

4. Bonetto, Furlan and Previato (2024); Ghiotto and Madrigali (2024); Commessatti (2023), 178–80.

5. Commessatti (2023), 177–8.

6. Brusin, Zovatto (1957); Cuscito (2004); Cuscito (2006); Cuscito and Lehmann (2010); Novello, Salvadori, Tiussi and Villa (2013); Fozzati (2015); Ulmer (2022); Commessatti (2023), 130–65.

7. Maselli Scotti and Rubinich (2009), 107–8; Basso (2021); Commessatti (2023), 170–3.

8. Ghedini and Novello (2009); Novello (2012–13); Commessatti (2023), 183–4.

9. Brusin (1941); Giovannini (2009), 183; Commessatti (2023), 125–30; Tiussi and Ventura (2025).

10. Ventura (2013); Novello, Braidotti, de Franzoni (2018); Commessatti (2023), 99–122; https://museoarcheologicoaquileia.beniculturali.it.

11. Buora, Casadio (2018); Commessatti (2023), 198–204; https://museoarcheologicoaquileia.beniculturali.it.

12. Vergone (2007).

BIBLIOGRAPHY

Adam, A., C. Balista, P. Càssola Guida, M. Moretti and S. Vitri (1983–4), 'Pozzuolo del Friuli: scavi 1981–1983', *Atti dei Civici Musei di Storia ed Arte di Trieste* 14: 127–214.

Amorosi, A., A. Fontana, F. Antonioli, S. Primon and A. Bondesan (2008), 'Post-LGM sedimentation and Holocene shoreline evolution in the NW Adriatical coastal area', *GeoActa* 7: 41–67.

Aquileia e il suo Patriarcato (2000), *Atti del Convegno internazionale (Udine, 21–23 ottobre 1999)*, Udine.

Arnaud-Fassetta, G., M. B. Carre, R. Marocco, F. Maselli Scotti, N. Pugliese, C. Zaccaria, A. Bandelli, V. Bresson, G. Manzoni, M. E. Montenegro, C. Morhange, M. Pipan, A. Prizzon and I. Siché (2003), 'The site of Aquileia (northeastern Italy): example of fluvial geoarchaeology in a Mediterranean costal plain', *Géomorphologie: relief, processus, environment* 4: 223–41.

Atti del Colloquio internazionale sul Concilio di Aquileia del 381 (Aquileia, 6–7 maggio 1981) (1981), *Antichità Altoadriatiche* XXI, Udine.

Atti della Giornata di Studio in onore di G. B. Brusin (Aquileia, 20 dicembre 1987) (1990), Udine.

Auriemma, R., V. Degrassi, D. Gaddi and P. Maggi (2016), 'Canale Anfora: uno spaccato sulle importazioni di alimenti ad Aquileia tra I e III secolo d.C.', in G. Cuscito (ed.), *L'alimentazione nell'antichità, Antichità Altoadriatiche*, LXXXIV, 379–403, Trieste.

Bandelli, G. (2003), 'Aquileia colonia Latina *dal senatus consultum del 183 a.C. al* supplementum *del 169 a.C.*', in G. Cuscito (ed.), *Aquileia dalle origini alla costituzione del Ducato longobardo. Storia, amministrazione, società, Antichità Altoadriatiche*, LIV, 49–78, Trieste.

Bandelli, G. (2010), 'Aquileia romana e archeologia fascista. 25 aprile 1928–21 settembre 1938', *Aquileia Nostra* LXXXI: 81–116.

Bandelli, G. (ed.) (2000), *Aquileia romana e cristiana fra II e V secolo, Antichità Altoadriatiche*, XLVII, Trieste.

Barca, N. (2022), *Roman Aquileia: The Impenetrable City-Fortress, a Sentry of the Alps*, Oxford and Philadelphia.

Basso, P. (2018), *L'anfiteatro di Aquileia. Ricerche d'archivio e nuove indagini di scavo*, Quingentole (Mantua).

Basso, P. (2021), 'Aquileia's market spaces', in F. Vermeulen and A. Zuiderhoek (eds), *Space, Movement and the Economy in Roman Cities in Italy and Beyond*, 180–200, London and New York.

Basso, P. (2024), 'New archaeological perspective on Late Antique Aquileia', in A. Launaro (ed.), *Roman Urbanism in Italy: Recent Discoveries and New Directions*, 213–34, Oxford and Philadelphia.

Basso, P., J. Bonetto, D. Cottica, S. Dilaria, F. Fontana, A. R. Ghiotto, M. Rubinich, C. Tiussi and P. Ventura (2024), 'Aquileia and its urban development in the light of recent and ongoing research', in J. Horvat, S. Groh, K. Strobel and M. Belak (eds), *Roman Urban Landscape: Towns and Minor Settlements from Aquileia to the Danube*, 53–76, Ljubljana.

Basso, P., D. Dobreva and S. Laserra (2022), 'Aquileia: le mura tardoantiche nel settore meridionale della città fra indagini d'archivio e dati di scavo', *Atlante Tematico di Topografia Antica* 32: 87–112.

Beatrice, P. F. and A. Peršič (eds) (2011), *Chromatius of Aquileia and his Age, Proceedings of the International Study Congress (Aquileia, 22–24 May 2008)*, Turnhout.

Bibliography

Bertacchi, L. (1979), 'Presenze archeologiche romane nell'area meridionale del territorio di Aquileia', in *Il territorio di Aquileia nell'antichità, Antichità Altoadriatiche*, XV, 259–89, Udine.

Bertacchi, L. (1983), 'Il Canale Anfora', *Aquileia Chiama* XXX: 3–5.

Bertacchi, L. (1988), 'Aquileia. Marignane Basse', *Aquileia Nostra* LIX: 371.

Bertacchi, L. (1990), 'Il sistema portuale della metropoli aquileiese', in *Aquileia e l'arco adriatico, Antichità Altoadriatiche*, XXXVI, 227–53, Udine.

Bertacchi, L. (1997), 'I monumenti sepolcrali lungo le strade di Aquileia', in M. Mirabella Roberti (ed.), *Monumenti sepolcrali romani in Aquileia e nella Cisalpina, Antichità Altoadriatiche*, XLIII, 149–67, Trieste.

Bertacchi, L. (2003), *Nuova pianta archeologica di Aquileia*, Udine.

Bianchetti, A. (2004), 'La centuriazione', in A. Bianchetti (ed.), *Terra di castellieri. Archeologia e territorio nel Medio Friuli*, 103–40, Tolmezzo (Udine).

Blason Scarel, S. (ed.) (1994), *Attila. Flagellum Dei?, Atti del Convegno internazionale di Studi storici (Aquileia, settembre 1990)*, Rome.

Blason Scarel, S. (ed.) (1997), *Poppone. L'età d'oro del Patriarcato di Aquileia, Catalogo della Mostra (Aquileia, 1996–1997)*, Rome.

Blason Scarel, S. (ed.) (2000), *Cammina, cammina . . . dalla via dell'ambra alla via della fede*, Marano Lagunare (Udine).

Bonetto, J. (2004), 'Difendere Aquileia, città di frontiera', in G. Cuscito and M. Verzár-Bass (eds), *Aquileia dalle origini alla costituzione del Ducato longobardo. Topografia, urbanistica, edilizia pubblica, Antichità Altoadriatiche*, LIX, 151–96, Trieste.

Bonetto, J. (2007), 'Animali, mercato e territorio in Aquileia romana', in G. Cuscito and C. Zaccaria (eds), *Aquileia dalle origini alla costituzione del ducato longobardo. Territorio, economia e società, Antichità Altoadriatiche*, LXV, 687–730, Trieste.

Bonetto, J. (2009), 'Le mura', in F. Ghedini, M. Bueno and M. Novello (eds), *Moenibus et portu celeberrima. Aquileia: storia di una città*, 83–92, Rome.

Bonetto, J. (2020), 'Costruttori e costruzioni greche nella Cisalpina di età ellenistica: il caso di Aquileia', in A. Coppola (ed.), *Atti del Convegno internazionale 'I Greci in Occidente. Aggiornamenti, revisioni, nuove prospettive' (Padova, 17–18 ottobre 2019), Hesperìa. Studi sulla Grecità di Occidente* 37: 225–42.

Bonetto, J. (2023), 'Entrando ad Aquileia: la porta settentrionale e l'architettura ellenistica nella Cisalpina repubblicana', *Atlante Tematico di Topografia Antica* 33: 259–83.

Bonetto, J. (2024a), 'Le mura (area I)', in J. Bonetto, G. Furlan and C. Previato, *Aquileia. Fondi Cossar*, 2.1, *La domus di Tito Macro e le mura. L'età repubblicana e imperiale*, 87–155, Rome.

Bonetto, J. (2024b), 'Le strade, lo smaltimento delle acque, i portici in età repubblicana', in J. Bonetto, G. Furlan and C. Previato, *Aquileia. Fondi Cossar*, 2.1, *La domus di Tito Macro e le mura. L'età repubblicana e imperiale*, 159–77, Rome.

Bonetto, J., G. Artioli, M. Secco and A. Addis (2016), 'L'uso delle polveri pozzolaniche nei grandi cantieri della Gallia Cisalpina in età romana repubblicana: i casi di Aquileia e Ravenna', in J. De Laine, S. Camporeale and A. Pizzo (eds), *Proceedings of the 5th International Workshop on the Archaeology of Roman Construction (Oxford, April 11–12, 2015), Anejos de Archivo Español de Arqueología*, 77, 29–44, Mérida.

Bonetto, J., G. Furlan, A. R. Ghiotto and I. Missaglia (2020), 'Il Canale Anfora e il centro urbano di Aquileia: osservazioni cronologiche alla luce di nuovi dati', *Journal of Ancient Topography* XXX: 175–202.

Bonetto, J., G. Furlan and C. Previato (2024), *Aquileia. Fondi Cossar*, 2.1, *La domus di Tito Macro e le mura. L'età repubblicana e imperiale*, Rome.

Bonetto, J., A. R. Ghiotto and C. Previato (2019–20), 'Le mura repubblicane di Aquileia: nuove indagini archeologiche lungo il lato occidentale della cinta urbica', *Aquileia Nostra* XC–XCI: 35–47.

Bonetto, J. and C. Previato (2013a), 'Trasformazioni del territorio e trasformazioni della città: le cave di pietra per Aquileia', in G. Cuscito (ed.), *Le modificazioni del paesaggio nell'Altoadriatico tra pre-protostoria ed altomedioevo*, *Atti del Convegno (Aquileia, 10–12 maggio 2012)*, Antichità Altoadriatiche, XLIII, 141–62, Trieste.

Bonetto, J. and C. Previato (2013b), 'Tecniche costruttive e contesto ambientale. Le sottofondazioni a sedimenti nella Cisalpina e nel Mediterraneo', in G. Cuscito (ed.), *Le modificazioni del paesaggio nell'Altoadriatico tra pre-protostoria ed altomedioevo*, *Atti del Convegno (Aquileia, 10–12 maggio 2012)*, Antichità Altoadriatiche, XLIII, 231–64, Trieste.

Bonetto, J. and C. Previato (2018), 'The construction process of the republican city walls of Aquileia (North-Eastern Italy): a case study of quantitative analysis on ancient buildings', in A. Brysbaert, V. Klinkenberg, A. Gutiérrez Garcia-M. and I. Vikatou (eds), *Constructing Monuments, Perceiving Monumentality and the Economics of Building: Theoretical and Methodological Approaches to the Built Environment*, 309–30, Leiden.

Bonetto, J., C. Previato, L. Maritan and C. Mazzoli (2014), 'Aquileia e le cave delle regioni alto-adriatiche: il caso della trachite euganea', in J. Bonetto, S. Camporeale and A. Pizzo (eds), *Le cave nel mondo antico: sistemi di sfruttamento e processi produttivi*, *Atti del Convegno internazionale (Padova, 22–24 novembre 2012)*, 149–66, Madrid and Mérida.

Bonetto, J. and M. Salvadori (eds) (2012), *L'architettura privata ad Aquileia in età romana*, *Atti del Convegno (Padova, 21–22 febbraio 2011)*, Padova.

Borgna, E., S. Corazza, A. Fontana and L. Fozzati (2018), 'Prima di Aquileia: l'insediamento di Canale Anfora', in E. Borgna, P. Càssola Guida and S. Corazza (eds), *Preistoria e Protostoria del Caput Adriae*, *Atti della XLIX Riunione Scientifica dell'Istituto italiano di Preistoria e Protostoria (Udine-Pordenone, 2014)*, 193–208, Firenze.

Borsato, A. (2021), 'Il riuso artigianale dei vani sostruttivi del teatro romano di Aquileia', in M. Buora, S. Magnani and L. Villa (eds), *Italia Settentrionale e regioni dell'arco alpino tra V e VI secolo*, *Atti del Convegno (15–17 aprile 2021)*, 393–409, Trieste.

Bratož, R. (1999), *Il Cristianesimo aquileiese prima di Costantino fra Aquileia e Poetovio*, Udine and Gorizia.

Bratož, R. (2003), 'Aquileia tra Teodosio e i Longobardi (379–568)', in G. Cuscito (ed.), *Aquileia dalle origini alla costituzione del Ducato longobardo. Storia, amministrazione, società*, Antichità Altoadriatiche, LIV, 477–527, Trieste.

Brogiolo, G. P. (ed.) (1996), *La fine delle ville romane: trasformazioni nelle campagne tra tarda antichità e alto Medioevo. Atti del 1° Convegno archeologico del Garda (Gardone Riviera, 14 ottobre 1995)*, Mantova.

Brown, R. (1847), *Itinerario di Marin Sanuto per la terraferma veneziana nell'anno MCCCCLXXXIII*, Padova.

Brusin, G. (1929), *Aquileia. Guida storica e artistica*, Udine.

Brusin, G. (1934), *Gli scavi di Aquileia. Un quadriennio di attività dell'Associazione Nazionale per Aquileia (1929–1932)*, Udine.

Brusin, G. (1939), 'Scavi dell'Associazione dal dicembre 1938 al luglio 1939', *Aquileia Nostra* X: 65–76.

Brusin, G. (1941), *Nuovi monumenti sepolcrali di Aquileia*, Venice.

Brusin, G. and P. L. Zovatto (1957), *Monumenti paleocristiani di Aquileia e di Grado*, Udine.

Buora, M. (1993), *Castions di Strada. Necropoli del periodo tardo-antico*, Quaderni Friulani di Archeologia 3: 63–73.

Buora, M. (1996), *I soldati di Magnenzio: scavi nella necropoli romana di Iutizzo Codroipo*, Trieste.

Buora, M. (1999), 'Insediamenti sparsi nell'agro di Aquileia: il caso di Codroipo', in S. Santoro Bianchi (ed.), *Studio e conservazione degli insediamenti minori romani in area alpina*, *Atti dell'incontro di Studi (Forgaria del Friuli, 20 settembre 1997)*, 49–61, Bologna.

Bibliography

Buora, M. (2021), 'Il boemo Anton Gnirs e altri archeologi mitteleuropei ad Aquileia a ridosso della Prima Guerra Mondiale', in J. Dudáš, M. Gay-Šmondrková and L. Vančo (eds), *Liberté et Patrie. Mélanges offerts à Jozef M. Rydlo, membre de l'Institut slovaque*, 125–37, Bratislava.

Buora, M. (ed.) (2024), *Giovanni Brusin. Scritti su quotidiani ('Corriere della Sera', 'Il Piccolo', 'Messaggero Veneto'). 1927–1974*, Trieste.

Buora, M. and P. Casadio (2018), *Monastero di Aquileia*, Trieste.

Buora, M. and M. Pollak (2010), 'La Zentralkommission e l'inizio della tutela archeologica ad Aquileia', *Aquileia Nostra* LXXXI: 365–410.

Buora, M., S. Magnani and L. Villa (eds) (2021), *Italia Settentrionale e regioni dell'arco alpino tra V e VI secolo, Atti del Convegno (15–17 aprile 2021)*, Trieste.

Buora, M. and A. Marcone (eds) (2007), *La ricerca antiquaria nell'Italia nordorientale. Dalla Repubblica Veneta all'Unità, Antichità Altoadriatiche*, LXIV, Trieste.

Buora, M. and F. Prenc (eds) (2000), *Canale Anfora. Realtà e prospettive tra storia, archeologia e ambiente, Atti del Convegno (Aquileia–Terzo di Aquileia, 29 aprile 2000)*, Trieste.

Buora, M. and F. Tesei (eds) (2000), *Introduzione e commento alla Fundkarte von Aquileia di H. Maionica*, Trieste.

Busana, M. S. (2009), 'Le ville', in F. Ghedini, M. Bueno and M. Novello (eds), *Moenibus et portu celeberrima. Aquileia: storia di una città*, 171–82, Rome.

Busana, M. S. (ed.) (2004), *La via Annia e le sue infrastrutture, Atti delle Giornate di Studio (Ca' Tron di Roncade, Treviso, 6–7 novembre 2003)*, Cornuda (Treviso).

Cadario, M. (2017), 'Tipi statuari in nudità armata e ricezione dei modelli ellenistici nella scultura iconica di Aquileia nel I secolo a.C.', in F. Fontana (ed.), *Aquileia e l'Oriente mediterraneo. 40 anni dopo, Antichità Altoadriatiche*, LXXXVI, 161–75, Trieste.

Calderini, A. (1930), *Aquileia romana. Ricerche di storia e di epigrafia*, Milan.

Calvi, M. C. (1968), *I vetri romani del Museo di Aquileia*, Aquileia (Udine).

Calvi, M. C. (2005), *Le ambre romane di Aquileia*, Aquileia (Udine).

Cammarosano, P. (ed.) (2000), *Il Patriarcato di Aquileia. Uno stato nell'Europa medievale*, Udine.

Cantino Wataghin, G. (2006), 'Le basiliche di Monastero e di Beligna: forme e funzioni', in G. Cuscito (ed.), *Aquileia dalle origini alla costituzione del Ducato longobardo. L'arte ad Aquileia dal sec. IV al IX, Antichità Altoadriatiche*, LXII, 303–33, Trieste.

Carre, M. B. (2004), 'Le réseau hydrographique d'Aquilée: état de la question', in G. Cuscito and M. Verzár-Bass (eds), *Aquileia dalle origini alla costituzione del ducato longobardo. Topografia, urbanistica, edilizia pubblica, Antichità Altoadriatiche*, LIX, 197–216, Trieste.

Carre, M. B., R. Marocco, F. Maselli Scotti and N. Pugliese (2003), 'Quelques données récentes sur le réseau fluvial et le paléoenvironnement d'Aquileia (Italie nord-orientale)', in J. Pasqual Berlanga and J. Pérez Ballester (eds), *Puertos fluviales antiguos: ciudad, desarollo e infraestructuras, IV Jornadas de arqueología subacuática Actas (Valencia, 28–30 de marzo de 2001)*, 299–311, Valencia.

Carre, M. B. and F. Maselli Scotti (2001), 'Il porto di Aquileia: dati antichi e ritrovamenti recenti', in C. Zaccaria (ed.), *Strutture portuali e rotte marittime nell'Adriatico di età romana, Antichità Altoadriatiche*, XLVI, 211–43, Trieste.

Casari, P. (2004), *Iuppiter Ammon e Medusa nell'Adriatico nordorientale. Simbologia imperiale nella decorazione architettonica forense*, Rome.

Casari, P. (2012–13), 'Ritratti tardoantichi ad Aquileia', *Aquileia Nostra* LXXXIII–LXXXIV: 289–98.

Càssola Guida, P. (1989), *I bronzetti friulani a figura umana, tra protostoria ed età della romanizzazione*, Rome.

Castiglioni, E., S. Motella and M. Rotoli (1996), 'Copertura forestale e agricoltura tra bronzo finale e romanizzazione nel Friuli occidentale', in *La protostoria fra Sile e Tagliamento. Antiche genti fra Veneto e Friuli, Catalogo della Mostra*, 461–8, Padova.

Chiabà, M. (2003), 'Spunti per uno studio sull'*origo* delle *gentes* di Aquileia repubblicana', in G. Cuscito (ed.), *Aquileia dalle origini alla costituzione del Ducato longobardo. Storia, amministrazione, società, Antichità Altoadriatiche*, LIV, 79–118, Trieste.

Chiabà, M. (2009), 'Dalla fondazione all'età tetrarchica', in F. Ghedini, M. Bueno and M. Novello (eds), *Moenibus et portu celeberrima. Aquileia: storia di una città*, 7–22, Rome.

Cigaina, L. (2012–13), 'Le stele aquileiesi con "stehende Soldaten" e il problema del reimpiego', *Aquileia Nostra* LXXXIII–LXXXIV: 299–316.

Cigaina, L. (2015), '"Microscultura" nelle stele sepolcrali di Aquileia romana', in B. Callegher (ed.), *Studia archaeologica Monika Verzár Bass dicata*, 21–35, Trieste.

Cigaina, L. (2018), 'Giovanni Battista Brusin und die Archäologie in Aquileia und in den "terre redente" (1919–1945)', in D. Steuernagel (ed.), *Altertumswissenschaften in Deutschland und Italien. Zeit des Umbruchs (1870–1940), Internationales Kolloquium in Regensburg, 25.–27. Juni 2015*, 143–66, Regensburg.

Cigaina, L. (2020), 'Reliefdarstellung eines Genius Militaris 238 n. Chr. in Aquileia', *Jahrbuch des Deutschen Archäologischen Instituts* 135: 281–305.

Ciliberto, F. (2011), 'Viri togati: forme di auto-rappresentazione delle élites locali ad Aquileia', in T. Nogales and I. Rodà (eds), *Roma y las provincias: modelo y difusión, Actas del XI Coloquio Internacional de Arte Romano Provincial (Mérida, 18–21 de mayo de 2009)*, 101–9, Rome.

Ciliberto, F. (2012), 'Donne nel privato, donne nel pubblico: la statuaria iconica femminile di Aquileia', *Lanx* 12: 57–79.

Ciliberto, F. (2015), 'La produzione dei sarcofagi altoadriatici: status quaestionis', in F. Rinaldi and A. Vigoni (eds), *Le necropoli della media e tarda età imperiale (III–IV secolo d.C.) a Iulia Concordia e nell'arco altoadriatico. Organizzazione spaziale, aspetti monumentali e strutture sociali, Atti del Convegno (Concordia Sagittaria, 5–6 giugno 2014)*, 379–88, Rubano (Padua).

Ciliberto, F. (2016), 'Tiberio e Aquileia. Considerazioni in margine al complesso edilizio dell'ex Fondo Tuzèt', in F. Slavazzi and C. Torre (eds), *Intorno a Tiberio. 1. Archeologia, cultura e letteratura del Principe e della sua epoca*, 82–8, Sesto Fiorentino (Firenze).

Ciliberto, F. (2020), 'La cultura artistica di Aquileia romana: status quaestionis, novità e prospettive', in G. Cuscito (ed.), *Bilanci e prospettive. Aquileia e le sue musealizzazioni, Antichità Altoadriatiche*, XCIII, 207–24, Trieste.

Ciliberto, F. and A. Giovannini (eds) (2008), *Preziosi ritorni. Gemme aquileiesi dai Musei di Vienna e Trieste, Catalogo della Mostra (Aquileia-Vicenza, 2008–2009)*, Aquileia (Udine).

Clementi, T., F. Rinaldi, M. Novello and M. Bueno (2009), 'La produzione musiva', in F. Ghedini, M. Bueno and M. Novello (eds), *Moenibus et portu celeberrima. Aquileia: storia di una città*, 231–52, Rome.

Commessatti, E. (2023), *Aquileia. Una guida*, Udine.

Cozzi, E. (2010), 'La Basilica dei Patriarchi: da Massenzio a Marquardo di Randeck', in L. Fozzati (ed.), *Aquileia. Patrimonio dell'Umanità*, 299–323, Udine.

Cuscito, G. (1987), *Fede e politica ad Aquileia. Dibattito teologico e centri di potere (secoli IV–VI)*, Udine.

Cuscito, G. (1992), *Martiri cristiani ad Aquileia e in Istria. Documenti archeologici e questioni agiografiche*, Udine.

Cuscito, G. (2003b), 'Il Cristianesimo ad Aquileia dalle origini al Ducato longobardo', in G. Cuscito (ed.), *Aquileia dalle origini alla costituzione del Ducato longobardo. Storia, amministrazione, società, Antichità Altoadriatiche*, LIV, 425–76, Trieste.

Cuscito, G. (2004), 'Lo spazio cristiano nell'urbanistica tardoantica di Aquileia', in G. Cuscito and M. Verzár-Bass (eds), *Aquileia dalle origini alla costituzione del Ducato longobardo. Topografia, urbanistica, edilizia pubblica, Antichità Altoadriatiche*, LIX, 511–59, Trieste.

Cuscito, G. (2009), 'Lo spazio cristiano', in F. Ghedini, M. Bueno and M. Novello (eds), *Moenibus et portu celeberrima. Aquileia: storia di una città*, 133–51, Rome.

Bibliography

Cuscito, G. (ed.) (2003a), *Aquileia dalle origini alla costituzione del Ducato longobardo. Storia, amministrazione, società, Antichità Altoadriatiche*, LIV, Trieste.

Cuscito, G. (ed.) (2006), *Aquileia dalle origini alla costituzione del Ducato longobardo. L'arte ad Aquileia dal sec. IV al IX, Antichità Altoadriatiche*, LXII, Trieste.

Cuscito, G. (ed.) (2014), *Costantino il Grande a 1700 anni dall' 'Editto di Milano', Antichità Altoadriatiche*, LXXVIII, Trieste.

Cuscito, G. (ed.) (2020), *Bilanci e prospettive. Aquileia e le sue musealizzazioni, Antichità Altoadriatiche*, XCIII, Trieste.

Cuscito, G. and T. Lehmann (eds) (2010), *La basilica di Aquileia. Storia, archeologia ed arte / Der Dom von Aquileia. Geschichte, Archäologie und Kunst, Antichità Altoadriatiche*, LXIX, Trieste.

Cuscito, G. and M. Verzár-Bass (eds) (2004), *Aquileia dalle origini alla costituzione del Ducato longobardo. Topografia, urbanistica, edilizia pubblica, Antichità Altoadriatiche*, LIX, Trieste.

Cuscito, G. and M. Verzár-Bass (eds) (2005), *Aquileia dalle origini alla costituzione del Ducato longobardo. La cultura artistica in età romana (II secolo a.C.–III secolo d.C.), Antichità Altoadriatiche*, LXI, Trieste.

Cuscito, G. and C. Zaccaria (eds) (2007), *Aquileia dalle origini alla costituzione del Ducato longobardo. Territorio, economia, società, Antichità Altoadriatiche*, LXV, Trieste.

De Cecco, C. (2002), 'Basaldella di Campoformido, necropoli di San Daniele', *Aquileia Nostra* LXXIII: 588–9.

Didonè, A. (2020), *Pittura romana nella* Regio X. *Contesti e sistemi decorativi*, Padova.

Di Filippo Balestrazzi, E. (2005), 'Il rilievo storico', in G. Cuscito and M. Verzár-Bass (eds), *Aquileia dalle origini alla costituzione del Ducato longobardo. La cultura artistica in età romana (II secolo a.C.–III secolo d.C.), Antichità Altoadriatiche*, LXI, 93–123, Trieste.

Dilaria, S. (2024), *Archeologia e archeometria delle miscele leganti di Aquileia romana e tardoantica (II sec. a.C.–VI sec. d.C.)*, Rome.

Dupré, P. and M. Novello (2012), 'Aquileia', in F. Ghedini and M. Annibaletto (eds), *Atria longa patescunt. Le forme dell'abitare nella Cisalpina romana, II, Schede*, 54–99, Rome.

Favaretto, I. (2009), 'Le antichità di Aquileia tra collezionismo e dispersione', in F. Ghedini, M. Bueno and M. Novello (eds), *Moenibus et portu celeberrima. Aquileia: storia di una città*, 51–8, Rome.

Feruglio, R. and A. Vidon (eds) (2024), *Il carteggio tra Giusto Fontanini e Gian Domenico Bertoli (1718–1736)*, Udine.

Fontana, A. (2006), *Evoluzione geomorfologica della bassa pianura friulana e sue relazioni con le dinamiche insediative antiche*, Udine.

Fontana, A., P. Mozzi and A. Bondesan (2008), 'Alluvial megafans in the Venetian–Friulian Plain (north-eastern Italy): evidence of sedimentary and erosive phases during Late Pleistocene and Holocene', *Quaternary International* 189: 71–90.

Fontana, A., P. Mozzi and M. Marchetti (2014), 'Alluvial fans and megafans along the southern side of the Alps', *Sedimentary Geology* 301: 150–71.

Fontana, A., G. Vinci, G. Tasca, P. Mozzi, M. Vacchi, G. Bivi, S. Salvador, S. Rossato, F. Antonioli, A. Asioli, M. Bresolin, M. Di Mario and I. Hajdas (2017), 'Lagoonal settlements and relative sea level during Bronze Age in Northern Adriatic: Geoarchaeological evidence and paleogeographic constraints', *Quaternary International* 439: 17–36.

Fontana, A., G. Vinci, G. Tasca, P. Mozzi, M. Vacchi, G. Bivi, S. Salvador, S. Rossato, F. Antonioli, A. Asioli, M. Bresolin, M. Di Mario and I. Hajdas (2018), 'Terra-Mare: Insediamenti lagunari e livello marino relativo durante l'età del Bronzo in Adriatico nord-occidentale', in A. Vigoni (ed.), *Percorsi nel passato. Miscellanea di Studi per i 35 anni del Gravo e i 25 anni della Fondazione Colluto*, 325–48, Rubano (Padua).

Fontana, F. (1997), *I culti di Aquileia repubblicana. Aspetti della politica religiosa in Gallia Cisalpina tra il III e il II secolo a.C.*, Rome.

Fontana, F. (2012–13), 'La casa "dei Putti danzanti"', *Aquileia Nostra* LXXXIII–LXXXIV: 195–204.

Fozzati, L. (ed.) (2010), *Aquileia. Patrimonio dell'Umanità*, Udine.

Fozzati, L. (ed.) (2015), *L'aula meridionale del Battistero di Aquileia. Contesto, scoperta, valorizzazione*, Milan.

Fozzati, L. and A. Benedetti (eds) (2011), *Per Aquileia. Realtà e programmazione di una grande area archeologica*, Venice.

Furlan, G. (2024), 'La domus di Tito Macro in età repubblicana e augusteo-tiberiana. Periodo II (100 a.C.–25 d.C.)', in J. Bonetto, G. Furlan and C. Previato, *Aquileia. Fondi Cossar, 2.1, La domus di Tito Macro e le mura. L'età repubblicana e imperiale*, 243–342, Rome.

Galliazzo, V. (1994), *I ponti romani*, II, *Catalogo generale*, Treviso.

Ghedini, F. and M. Novello (2009), 'L'edilizia residenziale', in F. Ghedini, M. Bueno and M. Novello (eds), *Moenibus et portu celeberrima. Aquileia: storia di una città*, 111–25, Rome.

Ghedini, F., M. Bueno and M. Novello (eds) (2009), *Moenibus et portu celeberrima. Aquileia: storia di una città*, Rome.

Ghedini, F., M. Bueno, M. Novello and F. Rinaldi (eds) (2017), *I pavimenti romani di Aquileia. Contesti, tecniche, repertorio decorativo*, I–II, Padua.

Ghiotto, A. R. (2013), 'Nuovi dati e nuove ipotesi sulla pianificazione urbana di Aquileia', *Rivista di Archeologia* XXXVII: 99–114.

Ghiotto, A. R. (2024), 'La domus di Tito Macro in età tardoantica. Periodo IV (250–550 d.C.)', in A. R. Ghiotto and E. Madrigali, *Aquileia. Fondi Cossar, 2.2, La domus di Tito Macro e le mura. L'età tardoantica e le fasi successive. L'intervento di valorizzazione*, 93–298, Rome.

Ghiotto, A. R. and G. Furlan (2025), 'Il teatro romano di Aquileia: strutture originarie e successive trasformazioni architettoniche', in J. Bonetto, A. R. Ghiotto and B. Marchet (eds), *Architetture e sistemi costruttivi dei teatri e degli anfiteatri antichi in area adriatica, Atti del Convegno internazionale (Padova, 14–15 dicembre 2023)*, 21–38, Rome.

Ghiotto, A. R. and E. Madrigali (2024), *Aquileia. Fondi Cossar, 2.2, La domus di Tito Macro e le mura. L'età tardoantica e le fasi successive. L'intervento di valorizzazione*, Rome.

Giovannini, A. (2004), 'Le istituzioni museali pubbliche di Aquileia: spunti per uno studio delle fasi storiche. I. Dal Museo Eugeniano all'I.R. Museo dello Stato e agli allestimenti di Enrico Maionica', *Aquileia Nostra* LXXV: 457–518.

Giovannini, A. (2009), 'Le necropoli', in F. Ghedini, M. Bueno and M. Novello (eds), *Moenibus et portu celeberrima. Aquileia: storia di una città*, 183–95, Rome.

Giovannini, A. (2012–13), 'Aquileia e l'archeologia funeraria tardoantica. Censimento dei dati, tracce di usi e costumi', *Aquileia Nostra* LXXXIII–LXXXIV: 217–47.

Giovannini, A. (2013), 'La storia del Museo Archeologico Nazionale di Aquileia', in P. Ventura (ed.), *Il Museo Archeologico Nazionale di Aquileia*, 14–17, Milan.

Giovannini, A. (2015), 'Aquileia, attestazioni funerarie di età augustea. Alcune osservazioni', in G. Cuscito (ed.), *Il Bimillenario augusteo, Antichità Altoadriatiche*, LXXXI, 295–325, Trieste.

Giovannini, A. and F. Maselli Scotti (2009), 'Dalle prime scoperte ai recenti scavi stratigrafici', in F. Ghedini, M. Bueno and M. Novello (eds), *Moenibus et portu celeberrima. Aquileia: storia di una città*, 37–49, Rome.

Gli scavi di Aquileia: uomini e opere (1993), *Antichità Altoadriatiche*, XL, Udine.

Gnesotto, F. (1981), 'L'insediamento preistorico di Canale Anfora (Terzo d'Aquileia). Relazione preliminare dello scavo 1980', *Aquileia Nostra* LII: 5–36.

Groh, S. (2011), 'Ricerche sull'urbanistica e le fortificazioni tardoantiche e bizantine di Aquileia. Relazione sulle prospezioni geofisiche condotte nel 2011', *Aquileia Nostra* LXXXII: 153–204.

Haug, A. (2003), *Die Stadt als Lebensraum. Eine kulturhistorische Analyse zum spätantiken Stadtleben in Norditalien*, Rahden and Westf (Germany).

Hope, V. M. (2001), *Constructing Identity: The Roman Funerary Monuments of Aquileia, Mainz and Nîmes*, BAR International Series, 960, Oxford.

Bibliography

Horvat, J. and B. Mušič (2007), 'Nauportus, a commercial settlement between the Adriatic and the Danube', in M. Chiabà, P. Maggi and C. Magrini (eds), *Le Valli del Natisone e dell'Isonzo tra Centroeuropa e Adriatico, Atti del Convegno internazionale (San Pietro al Natisone, 15–16 settembre 2006)*, 165–74, Rome.

Il Mausoleo Candia di Aquileia. Valorizzazione e restauro (2010), Trieste.

Janniard, S. (2006), 'La résistance d'Aquilée dans l'antiquité tardive, entre modèle littéraire et réalité (IIIᵉ–Vᵉ siècle)', in M. Ghilardi, C. J. Goddard and P. Porena (eds), *Les cités de l'Italie tardo-antique (IVᵉ–VIᵉ siècle). Institutions, économie, société, culture et religion, Actes du Colloque (Rome, 11–13 mars 2004)*, 75–89, Rome.

Känel, R. (2005), 'Le terrecotte architettoniche di Monastero', in G. Cuscito and M. Verzár-Bass (eds), *Aquileia dalle origini alla costituzione del Ducato longobardo. La cultura artistica in età romana (II secolo a.C.–III secolo d.C.)*, *Antichità Altoadriatiche*, LXI, 71–92, Trieste.

La storia di Giona nei mosaici della Basilica di Aquileia (2019), Torino.

Lettich, G. (2003), *Itinerari epigrafici aquileiesi. Guida alle epigrafi esposte nel Museo Archeologico Nazionale di Aquileia*, *Antichità Altoadriatiche*, L, Trieste.

Maggi, P. (1992), 'Un insediamento accentrato a Palazzolo?', in *Alla scoperta di un territorio/2. Topografia romana del Comune di Palazzolo della Stella*, 20–3, Latisana (Udine).

Maggi, P. (2003), 'Forme di insediamento aggregato non urbano nella Venetia orientale e nell'Histria in età romana', *Histria Archaeologica* 11: 229–42.

Maggi, P., F. Maselli Scotti, S. Mattioli Pesavento and E. Zulini (2017), *Materiali per Aquileia. Lo scavo di Canale Anfora (2004–2005)*, Trieste.

Maggi, P. and F. Oriolo (1999), 'Dati d'archivio e prospezione di superficie: nuove prospettive di ricerca per il territorio suburbano di Aquileia', in C. Zaccaria (ed.), *Archeologia senza scavo, Nuovi metodi di indagine per la conoscenza del territorio antico*, *Antichità Altoadriatiche*, XLV, 99–123, Trieste.

Maggi, P. and F. Oriolo (2009), 'Gli spazi esterni alla città', in F. Ghedini, M. Bueno and M. Novello (eds), *Moenibus et portu celeberrima. Aquileia: storia di una città*, 155–70, Rome.

Maggi, P. and F. Oriolo (2012), 'Luoghi e segni dell'abitare nel suburbio di Aquileia', in J. Bonetto and M. Salvadori (eds), *L'architettura privata ad Aquileia in età romana, Atti del Convegno (Padova, 21–22 febbraio 2011)*, 407–28, Padua.

Maggi, P. and F. Oriolo (2012–13), 'Il suburbio aquileiese in età tardoimperiale: spunti di riflessione', *Aquileia Nostra* LXXXIII–LXXXIV: 205–16.

Maggi, P. and C. Zaccaria (1994), 'Considerazioni sugli insediamenti minori di età romana nell'Italia settentrionale', in J.-P. Petit and M. Mangin (eds), *Les agglomérations secondaires. La Gaule Belgique, les Germanies et l'Occident romain, Actes du Colloque (Bliesbruck–Reinheim/Bitche, 21–24 octobre 1992)*, 163–80, Paris.

Maggi, P. and C. Zaccaria (1999), 'Gli studi sugli insediamenti minori alpini in Italia', in S. Santoro Bianchi (ed.), *Studio e conservazione degli insediamenti minori romani in area alpina, Atti dell'incontro di Studi (Forgaria del Friuli, 20 settembre 1997)*, 13–33, Bologna.

Magrini, C. (1997), 'Il territorio di Aquileia tra tardoantico e altomedioevo', *Archeologia Medievale* 24: 155–71.

Magrini, C. (2004), 'Archeologia del paesaggio suburbano di Aquileia tra tarda antichità e alto Medioevo', in G. Cuscito and M. Verzár-Bass (eds), *Aquileia dalle origini alla costituzione del Ducato longobardo. Topografia, urbanistica, edilizia pubblica*, *Antichità Altoadriatiche*, LIX, 651–72, Trieste.

Mainardis, F. (2023), *La 'passione predominante' di un indoctus pariter et incuriosus: Girolamo de' Moschettini (1755–1831) e l'epigrafia di Aquileia*, Trieste.

Maionica, H. (1884), *Wegweiser durch das k.k. Staatsmuseum zu Aquileja*, Aquileja.

Maionica, H. (1910), *Führer durch das k.k. Staatsmuseum in Aquileia*, Vienna.

Mandruzzato, L. (2012–13), 'La circolazione di suppellettile in vetro ad Aquileia in epoca costantiniana', *Aquileia Nostra* LXXXIII–LXXXIV: 407–13.

Mandruzzato, L. (ed.) (2008), *Vetri antichi del Museo Archeologico Nazionale di Aquileia. Ornamenti e oggettistica di età romana, vetro pre- e post-romano, Corpus delle collezioni del vetro nel Friuli Venezia Giulia, 4*, Trieste.

Mandruzzato, L. and A. Marcante (eds) (2005), *Vetri antichi del Museo Archeologico Nazionale di Aquileia. Il vasellame da mensa, Corpus delle collezioni del vetro nel Friuli Venezia Giulia, 2*, Trieste.

Mandruzzato, L. and A. Marcante (eds) (2007), *Vetri antichi del Museo Archeologico Nazionale di Aquileia. Balsamari, olle e pissidi, Corpus delle collezioni del vetro nel Friuli Venezia Giulia, 3*, Trieste.

Marano, Y. A. (2009), 'La città tardoantica', in F. Ghedini, M. Bueno and M. Novello (eds), *Moenibus et portu celeberrima. Aquileia: storia di una città*, 23–33, Rome.

Marano, Y. A. (2012), 'Urbanesimo e storia ad Aquileia tra V e VI secolo d.C.', in J. Bonetto and M. Salvadori (eds), *L'architettura privata ad Aquileia in età romana, Atti del Convegno (Padova, 21–22 febbraio 2011)*, 571–89, Padua.

Marchesini, M., S. Marvelli and E. Rizzoli (2024), 'Aspetti paesaggistici, ambientali e alimentari', in J. Bonetto, G. Furlan and C. Previato, *Aquileia. Fondi Cossar, 2.1, La domus di Tito Macro e le mura. L'età repubblicana e imperiale*, 59–83, Rome.

Marchiori, A. (1982), 'Canale Anfora (Aquileia)', *Aquileia Nostra* LIII: 312–14.

Marocco, R. (1989), 'Evoluzione quaternaria della laguna di Marano (Friuli–Venezia Giulia)', *Il Quaternario* 2: 125–37.

Marocco, R. (1991), 'Evoluzione tardopleistocenica-olocenica del delta del F. Tagliamento e delle lagune di Marano e Grado (Golfo di Trieste)', *Il Quaternario* 4: 223–32.

Marocco, R. (2009), 'Prima ricostruzione paleo-idrografica del territorio della bassa pianura friulano-isontina della laguna di Grado nell'Olocene', *Gortania* 31: 69–86.

Maselli Scotti, F. (1996), 'Presupposti per l'individuazione di Aquileia come terminale della via dell'ambra in epoca romana', in M. Buora (ed.), *Lungo la via dell'Ambra, Apporti altoadriatici alla romanizzazione del Medio Danubio (I sec. a.C.–I sec. d.C.), Atti del Convegno (Udine–Aquileia, 16–17 settembre 1994)*, 125–9, Udine.

Maselli Scotti, F. (1997), 'I monumenti sepolcrali del Museo Archeologico Nazionale di Aquileia', in M. Mirabella Roberti (ed.), *Monumenti sepolcrali romani in Aquileia e nella Cisalpina, Antichità Altoadriatiche*, XLIII, 137–48, Trieste.

Maselli Scotti, F. (2002), 'La grande statuaria in bronzo nel Museo Archeologico Nazionale di Aquileia', in G. Cuscito and M. Verzár-Bass (eds), *Bronzi di età romana in Cisalpina. Novità e riletture, Antichità Altoadriatiche*, LI, 207–25, Trieste.

Maselli Scotti, F. (2004), 'Aquileia prima di Roma. L'abitato della prima età del ferro', in G. Cuscito and M. Verzár-Bass (eds), *Aquileia dalle origini alla costituzione del Ducato longobardo. Topografia, urbanistica, edilizia pubblica, Antichità Altoadriatiche*, LIX, 19–38, Trieste.

Maselli Scotti, F. (2009), 'Le fasi preromane', in F. Ghedini, M. Bueno and M. Novello (eds), *Moenibus et portu celeberrima. Aquileia: storia di una città*, 3–6, Rome.

Maselli Scotti, F., A. Giovannini and P. Ventura (2003), 'Aquileia. A crossroad of men and ideas', in P. Noelke, F. Naumann-Steckner and B. Schneider (eds), *Romanisation und Resistenz in Plastik, Architektur und Inschriften der Provinzen des Imperium Romanum. Neue Funde und Forschungen, Akten des VII. Internationalen Colloquiums über Probleme des provinzialrömischen Kunstschaffens (Köln, 2.–6. Mai 2001)*, 651–67, Mainz am Rhein.

Maselli Scotti, F., L. Mandruzzato and C. Tiussi (2009), 'La prima fase dell'impianto coloniario di Aquileia. La situazione attuale degli studi e delle ricerche', in G. Cuscito (ed.), *Aspetti e problemi della romanizzazione. Venetia, Histria e arco alpino orientale, Antichità Altoadriatiche*, LXVIII, 235–77, Trieste.

Maselli Scotti, F., P. Paronuzzi and N. Pugliese (1999), 'Sondaggi geognostici per la prospezione geoarcheologica del territorio di Aquileia: il progetto SARA', in C. Zaccaria (ed.), *Strutture portuali e rotte marittime nell'Adriatico di età romana, Antichità Altoadriatiche*, XLVI, 79–97, Trieste.

Maselli Scotti, F. and M. Rottoli (2007), 'Indagini archeobotaniche all'ex essiccatoio nord di Aquileia. I resti vegetali protostorici e romani', in G. Cuscito and C. Zaccaria (eds), *Aquileia dalle origini alla costituzione del ducato longobardo. Territorio, economia e società Antichità Altoadriatiche*, LXV, 783–816, Udine.

Maselli Scotti, F. and M. Rubinich (2009), 'I monumenti pubblici', in F. Ghedini, M. Bueno and M. Novello (eds), *Moenibus et portu celeberrima. Aquileia: storia di una città*, 93–110, Rome.

Maselli Scotti, F., F. Sernandi, V. Degrassi, N. Pugliese, C. Tiussi and L. Mandruzzato (1996), 'Aquileia preromana', in F. Maselli Scotti, A. Pessina and S. Vitri (eds), *Prima dei Romani. Scoperte di preistoria e protostoria fra colline e mare*, 23–32, Aquileia (Udine).

McEachnie, R. (2017), *Chromatius of Aquileia and the Making of a Christian City*, London.

Mian, G. (2004), 'I programmi decorativi dell'edilizia pubblica aquileiese. Alcuni esempi', in G. Cuscito and M. Verzár-Bass (eds), *Aquileia dalle origini alla costituzione del Ducato longobardo. Topografia, urbanistica, edilizia pubblica, Antichità Altoadriatiche*, LIX, 425–509, Trieste.

Mian, G. (2012–13), 'Il palazzo imperiale tardo-antico ad Aquileia. Note sullo stato della questione', *Aquileia Nostra* LXXXIII–LXXXIV: 89–95.

Milocco, G. (1999), 'Michele Abramich tra la riconferma e l'internamento (maggio 1915–marzo 1919)', *Aquileia Nostra* LXX: 269–88.

Milocco, G. (2010), 'Aquileia nei primi trenta anni del Novecento', *Aquileia Nostra* LXXXI: 29–78.

Murat, Z. and P. Vedovetto (eds) (2021), *Il Patriarcato di Aquileia. Identità, liturgia e arte (secoli V–XV)*, Rome.

Muzzioli, M. P. (2004), 'Aspetti della pianificazione della colonia di Aquileia', in G. Cuscito and M. Verzár-Bass (eds), *Aquileia dalle origini alla costituzione del Ducato longobardo. Topografia, urbanistica, edilizia pubblica, Antichità Altoadriatiche*, LIX, 121–50, Trieste.

Muzzioli, M. P. (2005), 'La centuriazione di Aquileia. Scelte tecniche nella progettazione', *Atlante Tematico di Topografia Antica* 14: 7–35.

Novello, M. (2009), 'Edilizia abitativa ad Aquileia', in M. Annibaletto and F. Ghedini (eds), *Intra illa moenia domus ac Penates (Liv. 2, 40, 7). Il tessuto abitativo nelle città romane della Cisalpina, Atti delle Giornate di Studio (Padova, 10–11 aprile 2008)*, 95–116, Rome.

Novello, M. (2012–13), 'Abitare ad Aquileia nel IV secolo d.C.: aspetti architettonici e decorativi', *Aquileia Nostra* LXXXIII–LXXXIV: 155–70.

Novello, M., E. Braidotti and A. de Franzoni (2018), *Aquileia. Museo Archeologico Nazionale*, Olmi di San Biagio di Callalta (Treviso).

Novello, M., M. Salvadori, C. Tiussi and L. Villa (2013), 'Il primo nucleo episcopale di Aquileia: struttura e decorazione', in C. Tiussi, L. Villa and M. Novello (eds), *Costantino e Teodoro. Aquileia nel IV secolo, Catalogo della Mostra (Aquileia, 5 luglio–3 novembre 2013)*, 143–51, Milan.

Novello, M., G. Plattner and C. Tiussi (eds) (2019), *Magnifici ritorni. Tesori aquileiesi dal Kunsthistorisches Museum di Vienna, Catalogo della Mostra (Aquileia, 9 giugno–20 ottobre 2019)*, Rome.

Oriolo, F. (2019), 'Pittura e stucco ad Aquileia. Nuovi dati da vecchi rinvenimenti', in M. Salvadori, F. Fagioli and C. Sbrolli (eds), *Nuovi dati per la conoscenza della pittura antica, Atti del I Colloquio AIRPA (Aquileia, 16–17 giugno 2017)*, 19–30, Rome.

Oriolo, F. and M. Salvadori (2001), 'Decorazioni parietali private nella × Regio: i casi della villa "imperiale" di Aquileia e della Villa di Torre di Pordenone', in M. Verzár-Bass (ed.), *Abitare in Cisalpina. L'edilizia privata nelle città e nel territorio in età romana, Antichità Altoadriatiche*, XLIX, 629–51, Trieste.

Oriolo, F. and M. Salvadori (2009), 'La pittura', in F. Ghedini, M. Bueno and M. Novello (eds), *Moenibus et portu celeberrima. Aquileia: storia di una città*, 221–30, Rome.

Oriolo, F. and M. Verzár (eds) (2012), *La pittura romana nell'Italia settentrionale e nelle regioni limitrofe, Antichità Altoadriatiche*, LXXIII, Trieste.

Pensabene, P. (2006), 'Reimpiego e interventi edilizi nell'Aquileia tardoantica', in G. Cuscito (ed.), *Aquileia dalle origini alla costituzione del Ducato longobardo. L'arte ad Aquileia dal sec. IV al IX, Antichità Altoadriatiche*, LXII, 365–421, Trieste.

Pensabene, P. (2010), 'Disposizione e provenienza delle colonne di reimpiego nel complesso episcopale di Aquileia', in G. Cuscito and T. Lehmann (eds), *La basilica di Aquileia. Storia, archeologia ed arte / Der Dom von Aquileia. Geschichte, Archäologie und Kunst, Antichità Altoadriatiche*, LXIX, 551–660, Trieste.

Pensabene, P. (2012), 'Il reimpiego ad Aquileia: problematiche aperte', in G. Cuscito (ed.), *Riuso di monumenti e reimpiego di materiali antichi in età postclassica: il caso della Venetia, Antichità Altoadriatiche*, LXXIV, 85–102, Trieste.

Perelli Cippo, C. (2010), 'Aristide Calderini promotore degli studi aquileiesi', *Aquileia Nostra* LXXXI: 193–206.

Pesavento Mattioli, S. and P. Basso (eds) (2004), *Le strade dell'Italia romana*, Milan.

Petrucci, G. (2004), 'Le risorse faunistiche. Età del ferro (IX–V sec. a.C.)', in *Alimentazione ad Aquileia. Dal villaggio protostorico alla colonia. Il colore del vino nei riflessi del vetro aquileiese, Catalogo della Mostra*, S. Stefano Udinese (Udine).

Piussi, S. (2008), *Cromazio di Aquileia 388–408. Al crocevia di genti e religioni, Catalogo della Mostra (Udine, 6 novembre 2008–8 marzo 2009)*, 134–41, Cinisello Balsamo (Milan).

Polisca, F. and C. Nicosia (2024), 'Inquadramento geomorfologico di Aquileia', in J. Bonetto, G. Furlan and C. Previato, *Aquileia. Fondi Cossar, 2.1, La domus di Tito Macro e le mura. L'età repubblicana e imperiale*, 51–8, Rome.

Ponzellini, M. (2009), 'La zecca', in F. Ghedini, M. Bueno and M. Novello (eds), *Moenibus et portu celeberrima. Aquileia: storia di una città*, 289–92, Rome.

Prenc, F. (2000), 'Viabilità e centuriazione nella pianura aquileiese', in S. Blason Scarel (ed.), *Cammina, cammina . . .: dalla via dell'ambra alla via della fede*, 43–58, Marano Lagunare (Udine).

Prenc, F. (2002), *Le pianificazioni agrarie di età romana nella pianura aquileiese, Antichità Altoadriatiche*, LII, Trieste.

Previato, C. (2015), *Aquileia. Materiali, forme e sistemi costruttivi dall'età repubblicana alla tarda età imperiale*, Padua.

Previato, C. (2024), 'La domus di Tito Macro in età imperiale. Periodo III (25 d.C.–250 d.C.)', in J. Bonetto, G. Furlan and C. Previato, *Aquileia. Fondi Cossar, 2.1, La domus di Tito Macro e le mura. L'età repubblicana e imperiale*, 343–535, Rome.

Previato, C. and J. Bonetto (2023), *Terra, legno e materiali deperibili nell'architettura antica, Atti del Convegno internazionale (Padova, 3–5 giugno 2021)*, Rome.

Previato, C., S. Dilaria, V. Canciani and A. Piazza (2024), 'Materiali da costruzione, attività di cantiere e tecniche edilizie nella domus di Tito Macro e nelle strutture limitrofe', in J. Bonetto, G. Furlan and C. Previato, *Aquileia. Fondi Cossar, 2.1, La domus di Tito Macro e le mura. L'età repubblicana e imperiale*, 555–638, Rome.

Previato, C., A. R. Ghiotto and S. Dilaria (2023), 'Insulae in Northern Italy and the case study of Aquileia', in S. Straumann and P. Schwarz -A., *Insulae in Context, Proceedings of the International Conference (Basel–Augusta Raurica, 25th–28th September 2019)*, 141–58, Augst (Switzerland).

Privitera, S. (2015), 'Archeologia del passato: il Bimillenario augusteo del 1937–1938 ad Aquileia', in G. Cuscito (ed.), *Il Bimillenario augusteo, Antichità Altoadriatiche*, LXXXI, 365–71, Trieste.

Rebaudo, L. (2007a), 'L'epigrafia aquileiese nella prima metà dell'Ottocento', in A. Buonopane, M. Buora and A. Marcone (eds), *La ricerca epigrafica e antiquaria nelle Venezie dall'età napoleonica all'Unità*, 118–60, Florence.

Rebaudo, L. (2007b), 'Sul ritratto privato d'età altoimperiale ad Aquileia', *Aquileia Nostra* LXXVIII: 109–46.

Bibliography

Rebaudo, L. and A. Didonè (2019–20), 'I primi scavi ad Aquileia sotto il controllo statale austriaco (1815–1831). 1. Storia di Aquileia dal 1805 al 1830', *Aquileia Nostra* XC–XCI: 71–93.

Rebaudo, L. and A. Didonè (2022), 'I primi scavi ad Aquileia sotto il controllo statale austriaco (1815–1831). 2. Le campagne a sud e a nord-ovest della Basilica, a sud-ovest del Foro e presso la Chiesa dei Santi Felice e Fortunato', *Aquileia Nostra* XCIII: 61–84.

Rebaudo, L. and A. Didonè (2023), 'I primi scavi ad Aquileia sotto il controllo statale austriaco (1815–1831). 3. Le campagne in Piazza Capitolo, nella Braida di Moschettini e nell'area antistante alla chiesa di Sant'Antonio in via Roma e nell'adiacente proprietà Suppancig', *Aquileia Nostra* XCIV: 97–132.

Rebaudo, L., A. Savioli and E. Braidotti (2012), 'La villa delle Marignane ad Aquileia. La documentazione fotografica di scavo (1914–1970)', in J. Bonetto and M. Salvadori (eds), *L'architettura privata ad Aquileia in età romana, Atti del Convegno (Padova, 21–22 febbraio 2011)*, 443–73, Padua.

Renesto, G. (2023), 'Le terrecotte architettoniche rinvenute a ovest di Monastero ad Aquileia: rilievo e proposta di ricostruzione grafica', *Aquileia Nostra* XCIV: 19–36.

Reusser, C. (1987), 'Gräberstrassen in Aquileia', in H. von Hesberg and P. Zanker (eds), *Römische Gräberstrassen. Selbstdarstellung, Status, Standard, Kolloquium in München, 28.–30. Oktober 1985*, 239–49, Munich.

Roberto, U. (2016), 'Aquileia fracta est XV kal. Aug.: la distruzione dell'"emporio d'Italia" nel 452 d.C. e il valore politico e culturale di un sincronismo', in G. Cuscito (ed.), *L'alimentazione nell'antichità, Antichità Altoadriatiche*, LXXXIV, 367–77, Trieste.

Rosada, G. (1984), 'Funzione e funzionalità della Venetia romana: terra, mare, fiumi come risorse per un'egemonia espansionistica', in *Misurare la terra: centuriazione e coloni nel mondo romano. Il caso veneto*, 22–37, Modena.

Rosada, G., M. Frassine and A. R. Ghiotto (eds) (2010), *. . . viam Anniam influentibus palustribus aquis eververatam . . . Tradizione, mito, storia e katastrophé di una strada romana*, Treviso.

Rubinich, M. (2012–13), 'Le "Grandi Terme" costantiniane', *Aquileia Nostra* LXXXIII–LXXXIV: 97–117.

Rubinich, M., J. Bonetto, M. Cadario, S. Dilaria and N. Martinelli (2024), 'Le "Grandi Terme" di Aquileia: nuovi dati dai sondaggi geognostici sui metodi costruttivi e sulla cronologia di costruzione', *Orizzonti* XXV: 21–43.

Salvadori, M., V. Mantovani and L. Scalco (2020), *Abitare ad Aquileia in età romana: l'insula delle Bestie ferite*, Udine.

Salvadori, M. and G. M. B. Pavan (2012–13), 'Dall'hortus pictus al locus amoenus cristiano: sopravvivenza e risemantizzazione di un tema iconografico negli affreschi dell'aula sud della Basilica di Aquileia', *Aquileia Nostra* LXXXIII–LXXXIV: 345–57.

Santa Maria Scrinari, V. (1972), *Museo Archeologico di Aquileia. Catalogo delle sculture romane*, Rome.

Scalon, C. (ed.) (1982), *Necrologium Aquileiense*, Udine.

Scalon, C., C. Griggio, U. Rozzo and G. Bergamini (eds) (2006–11), *Nuovo Liruti. Dizionario biografico dei Friulani, 1–3*, Udine.

Sena Chiesa, G. (1966), *Gemme del Museo Nazionale di Aquileia, I–II*, Aquileia (Udine).

Sena Chiesa, G. and E. Gagetti (2009b), 'I materiali preziosi', in F. Ghedini, M. Bueno and M. Novello (eds), *Moenibus et portu celeberrima. Aquileia: storia di una città*, 253–72, Rome.

Sena Chiesa, G. and E. A. Arslan (eds) (1998), *Optima via, Atti del Convegno internazionale di Studi 'Postumia' (Cremona, 13–15 giugno 1996)*, Cremona.

Sena Chiesa, G. and E. Gagetti (eds) (2009a), *Aquileia e la glittica di età ellenistica e romana, Atti del Convegno internazionale (Aquileia, 19–20 giugno 2008)*, Trieste.

Sena Chiesa, G. and M. P. Lavizzari Pedrazzini (eds) (1998), *Tesori della Postumia. Archeologia e storia intorno a una grande strada romana alle radici dell'Europa*, Milan.

Sotinel, C. (2005), *Identité civique et Christianisme. Aquilée du IIIe au VIe siècle*, Rome.

Sperti, L. (2004), 'Scultura microasiatica nella Cisalpina tardoantica: i tondi aquileiesi con busti di divinità', *Eidola* 1: 151–93.

Sperti, L. (2012–13), 'La scultura mitologica', *Aquileia Nostra* LXXXIII–LXXXIV: 251–71.

Sperti, L. (ed.) (2017), *Scultura di Iulia Concordia e Aquileia*, Atti della Giornata di Studio (Udine, 12 aprile 2013), Rome.

Stella, A. (2019), *Aquileia tardoantica: moneta, storia ed economia*, Trieste.

Tassaux, F. (1984), 'Vidulis (Udine), Activités de l'École Française de Rome', *Mélanges de l'École Française de Rome. Antiquité* 97: 542–4.

Tiussi, C. (2001), 'Per una biografia di Franco Marinotti. L'interesse per le antichità romane e la formazione della collezione archeologica', *Aquileia Nostra* LXXII: 189–228.

Tiussi, C. (2004), 'Il sistema di distribuzione di Aquileia: mercati e magazzini', in G. Cuscito and M. Verzár-Bass (eds), *Aquileia dalle origini alla costituzione del Ducato longobardo. Topografia, urbanistica, edilizia pubblica*, Antichità Altoadriatiche, LIX, 257–316, Trieste.

Tiussi, C. (2006), 'Aquileia e l'assetto urbanistico delle colonie latine della Gallia Cisalpina', in F. Lenzi (ed.), *Rimini e l'Adriatico nell'età delle guerre puniche*, Atti del Convegno *(Rimini, 25–27 marzo 2004)*, 333–78, Bologna.

Tiussi, C. (2009a), 'Aquileia terminale della via Annia. Tracce di culti preromani e primi santuari della colonia', in G. Cresci Marrone and M. Tirelli (eds), *Altnoi. Il santuario altinate: strutture del sacro a confronto e i luoghi di culto lungo la via Annia*, Atti del Convegno *(Venezia, 4–6 dicembre 2006)*, 389–414, Rome.

Tiussi, C. (2009b), 'L'impianto urbano', in F. Ghedini, M. Bueno and M. Novello (eds), *Moenibus et portu celeberrima. Aquileia: storia di una città*, 61–81, Rome.

Tiussi, C. (2010), 'L'Associazione Nazionale per Aquileia nel secondo dopoguerra. Fatti e personaggi di una stagione significativa dell'archeologia aquileiese', *Aquileia Nostra* LXXXI: 241–72.

Tiussi, C. (2011), 'Il Foro di Aquileia: acquisizioni recenti e problematiche aperte', in S. Maggi (ed.), *I complessi forensi della Cisalpina romana: nuovi dati*, Atti del Convegno *(Pavia, 12–13 marzo 2009)*, 167–84, Borgo San Lorenzo (Florence).

Tiussi, C. (2018), 'L'acquedotto romano di Aquileia', in G. Cuscito (ed.), *Cura aquarum. Adduzione e distribuzione dell'acqua nell'antichità*, Antichità Altoadriatiche, LXXXVIII, 183–213, Trieste.

Tiussi, C. (2022), 'Aquileia nell'età degli Antonini', in F. Chausson, G. Cresci Marrone and B. Rossignol (eds), *Altino 169 d.C. Intorno alla morte dell'imperatore Lucio Vero*, Atti delle Giornate di Studio internazionali *(Venezia–Altino, 15–16 novembre 2019)*, 79–100, Venice.

Tiussi, C. and P. Ventura (2025), 'Il Sepolcreto di Aquileia. Le indagini archeologiche del 2015–2016 e i nuovi dati', in *Società dei vivi e comunità dei morti. Le tematiche funerarie nell'Italia settentrionale tra Protostoria e Medioevo*, Antichità Altoadriatiche, XCVI, Trieste.

Tiussi, C. and L. Villa (2017), 'Aquileia in età tetrarchica e costantiniana. Trasformazioni urbanistiche e monumentali nel settore occidentale', *Aquileia Nostra* LXXXVIII: 91–147.

Tiussi, C., L. Villa and M. Novello (eds) (2013), *Costantino e Teodoro. Aquileia nel IV secolo*, Catalogo della Mostra (Aquileia, 5 luglio–3 novembre 2013), Milan.

Toplikar, G. and S. Tavano (eds) (2005), *I santi Canziani nel XVII centenario del loro martirio / Sveti Kancijani ob 1700-letnici mučeništva*, Atti del Convegno internazionale *(Pieris, 19 ottobre 2003–San Canzian d'Isonzo, 8 maggio 2004)*, Ronchi dei Legionari (Gorizia).

Uggeri, G. (2012), 'La nuova Via Annia da Roma ad Aquileia (153 a.C.)', *Journal of Ancient Topography* XXII: 133–74.

Ulmer, C. (2022), *Der Dom von Aquileia, I–II*, Münsingen (Germany).

Vale, G. (1950), 'Girolamo Asquini e la romana Aquileia', *Aquileia Nostra* XXI: 51–8.

Valenti, M. (2005), *Dopo la fine delle ville: le campagne dal VI al IX secolo*, Atti dell'11° Seminario sul tardoantico e l'alto Medioevo (Gavi, 8–10 maggio 2004), Mantua.

Ventura, P. (ed.) (2013), *Il Museo Archeologico Nazionale di Aquileia*, Milan.

Bibliography

Ventura, P. and A. Giovannini (2015), 'Sorelle, spose, madri. Il mondo al femminile nei monumenti funerari di Aquileia', in C.-G. Alexandrescu (ed.), *Cult and Votive Monuments in the Roman Provinces, Proceedings of the 13th International Colloquium on Roman Provincial Art (Bucharest–Alba Iulia–Constanța, 27 May–3 June 2013)*, 343–58, Cluj-Napoca (Romania).

Vergone, G. (2007), *Le epigrafi lapidarie del Museo Paleocristiano di Monastero (Aquileia)*, Trieste.

Veronese, F. (ed.) (2009), *Via Annia, Adria, Padova, Altino, Concordia. Aquileia. Progetto di recupero e valorizzazione di un'antica strada romana, Atti della Giornata di Studio (Padova, 19 giugno 2008)*, Padua.

Veronese, F. (ed.) (2011), *Via Annia 2. Adria, Padova, Altino, Concordia, Aquileia. Progetto di recupero e valorizzazione di un'antica strada romana, Atti della Giornata di Studio (Padova, 17 giugno 2010)*, Padua.

Verzár-Bass, M. (1984), 'Notiziario. Vidulis', *Aquileia Nostra* LV: 270–1.

Verzár, M. (2015), 'Augusto ad Aquileia e Tergeste', *Aquileia Nostra* LXXXVI: 67–78.

Verzár, M. (2016), 'Il rilievo con scena di aratura di Aquileia riconsiderato', in S. Lusuardi Siena, C. Perassi, F. Sacchi and M. Sannazaro (eds), *Archeologia classica e post-classica tra Italia e Mediterraneo. Scritti in ricordo di Maria Pia Rossignani*, 265–74, Milan.

Verzár-Bass, M. (ed.) (2007), *Buttrio. La collezione di Francesco di Toppo a Villa Florio*, Rome.

Verzár, M. and L. Cigaina (2017), 'I ritratti funerari di Aquileia / The funerary portraits of Aquileia', in M. Novello and C. Tiussi (eds), *Volti di Palmira ad Aquileia / Portraits of Palmyra in Aquileia*, 57–66, Rome.

Verzár-Bass, M. and G. Mian (2001), 'Le domus di Aquileia', in M. Verzár-Bass (ed.), *Abitare in Cisalpina. L'edilizia privata nelle città e nel territorio in età romana, Antichità Altoadriatiche*, XLIX, 599–628, Trieste.

Verzár-Bass, M. and G. Mian (2003), 'L'assetto urbano di Aquileia', in J. Ortalli and M. Heinzelmann (eds), *Abitare in città. La Cisalpina tra Impero e Medioevo / Leben in der Stadt. Oberitalien zwischen römischer Kaiserzeit und Mittelalter, Atti del Convegno (Roma, 4–5 novembre 1999)*, 73–94, Wiesbaden.

Verzár, M., G. Mian, P. Casari and F. Ciliberto (2009), 'La scultura', in F. Ghedini, M. Bueno and M. Novello (eds), *Moenibus et portu celeberrima. Aquileia: storia di una città*, 199–220, Rome.

Verzár-Bass, M. and F. Oriolo (1998), 'Grab und Grabsitte in Aquileia', in P. Fasold, T. Fischer, H. von Hesberg and M. Witteyer (eds), *Bestattungssitte und kulturelle Identität. Grabanlagen und Grabbeigaben der frühen römischen Kaiserzeit in Italien und den Nordwest-Provinzen, Kolloquium in Xanten, 16.–18. Februar 1995*, 143–80, Cologne.

Verzár-Bass, M. and F. Oriolo (1999), 'Prime testimonianze funerarie aquileiesi: una problematica aperta', in G. Cresci Marrone and M. Tirelli (eds), *Vigilia di romanizzazione. Altino e il Veneto orientale tra II e I sec. a.C., Atti del Convegno (Venezia, 2–3 dicembre 1997)*, 259–83, Rome.

Villa, L. (2004), 'Aquileia tra Goti, Bizantini e Longobardi: spunti per un'analisi delle trasformazioni urbane nella transizione fra tarda antichità e alto Medioevo', in G. Cuscito and M. Verzár-Bass (eds), *Aquileia dalle origini alla costituzione del Ducato longobardo. Topografia, urbanistica, edilizia pubblica, Antichità Altoadriatiche*, LIX, 561–632, Trieste.

Villa, L. (2012), 'Modelli di evoluzione dell'edilizia abitativa in Aquileia tra l'antichità e il Medioevo', in J. Bonetto and M. Salvadori (eds), *L'architettura privata ad Aquileia in età romana, Atti del Convegno (Padova, 21–22 febbraio 2011)*, 591–618, Padua.

Villa, L. (2012–13), 'Il complesso episcopale teodoriano: una rilettura delle testimonianze archeologiche', *Aquileia Nostra* LXXXIII–LXXXIV: 119–54.

Vitri, S. (2004), 'Contributi alla ricostruzione della topografia di Aquileia preromana', in G. Cuscito and M. Verzár-Bass (eds), *Aquileia dalle origini alla costituzione del Ducato longobardo. Topografia, urbanistica, edilizia pubblica, Antichità Altoadriatiche*, LIX, 39–64, Trieste.

von Lanckoroński, K. (1906), *Der Dom von Aquileia. Sein Bau und seine Geschichte*, Vienna.

Witschel, C. (2012–13), 'Inschriften und Inschriftenkultur der konstantinischen Zeit in Aquileia', *Aquileia Nostra* LXXXIII–LXXXIV: 29–66.

Zaccaria, C. (1984), 'Vicende del patrimonio epigrafico aquileiese. La grande diaspora: saccheggio, collezionismo, musei', in *I musei di Aquileia. Arti applicate, ceramica, epigrafia, numismatica, Antichità Altoadriatiche*, XXIV, 117–67, Udine.

Zaccaria, C. (2000), 'Permanenza dell'ideale civico romano in epoca tardoantica: nuove evidenze da Aquileia', in G. Bandelli (ed.), *Aquileia romana e cristiana fra II e V secolo, Antichità Altoadriatiche*, XLVII, 91–113, Trieste.

Zaccaria, C. (2003a), 'Amministrazione e vita politica ad Aquileia dalle origini al III secolo d.C.', in G. Cuscito (ed.), *Aquileia dalle origini alla costituzione del Ducato longobardo. Storia, amministrazione, società, Antichità Altoadriatiche*, LIV, 293–338, Trieste.

Zaccaria, C. (2003b), 'Gli affari degli Aratrii. L'ascesa di una famiglia di imprenditori edili ad Aquileia tra I sec. a.C. e I sec. d.C.', in J.-P. Bost, J.-M. Roddaz and F. Tassaux (eds), *Itinéraire de Saintes à Dougga. Mélanges offerts à Louis Maurin*, 307–26, Bordeaux.

Zaccaria, C. (2005), 'Recinti funerari aquileiesi: il contributo dell'epigrafia', in G. Cresci Marrone and M. Tirelli (eds), '*Terminavit sepulcrum'. I recinti funerari nelle necropoli di Altino, Atti del Convegno (Venezia, 3–4 dicembre 2003)*, 195–223, Rome.

Zaccaria, C. (2012), 'Spolia epigrafici a Trieste, Aquileia e in Friuli', in G. Cuscito (ed.), *Riuso di monumenti e reimpiego di materiali antichi in età postclassica: il caso della Venetia, Antichità Altoadriatiche*, LXXIV, 33–46, Trieste.

Zaccaria, C. (2014), 'T. Annius T. f. tri(um)vir e le prime fasi della colonia latina di Aquileia. Bilancio storiografico e problemi aperti', in M. Chiabà (ed.), *Hoc quoque laboris praemium. Scritti in onore di Gino Bandelli*, 519–52, Trieste.

Zaccaria, C. (2017), 'Il consularis Venetiae et Histriae Valerius Adelfius Bassus e il rinnovamento edilizio ad Aquileia in età teodosiana', in S. Antolini, S. M. Marengo and G. Paci (eds), *Colonie e municipi nell'era digitale. Documentazione epigrafica per la conoscenza delle città antiche, Atti del Convegno (Macerata, 10–12 dicembre 2015)*, 635–53, Tivoli (Rome).

Zaccaria, C. and S. Pesavento Mattioli (2009), 'Uomini e merci', in F. Ghedini, M. Bueno and M. Novello (eds), *Moenibus et portu celeberrima. Aquileia: storia di una città*, 275–87, Rome.

Zanetto, S. (2017), *Tradizioni costruttive nell'alto e medio Adriatico (secoli VII–XI). Eredità e innovazione nell'alto Medioevo*, 11–43, Sesto Fiorentino (Florence).

INDEX

This index contains the names of people and places mentioned in the text, with the exception of Aquileia and Italy/Italia (which occur very frequently). For Aquileia, however, an analytical list of monuments and localities is provided.

Index

Index